FOUNDATIONS OF PROPERTY LAW

Graham Battersby

and

Peter Odell

Foundations of Property Law

Foreword

One can scarcely pick up a newspaper or magazine or listen to a broadcast conversation without encountering a set of questions regularly posed in interview. One so common that most of us have thought about our own answer is "Which teacher inspired you?" or "Who made the greatest difference to your education?" or the like.

Of the three Court of Appeal judges who in 2016 were graduates of the University of Sheffield, the two who were asked would, independently, give the same answer: Prof Battersby. The reaction is always surprise since in neither case did practice reflect trusts, equity, or real property. Since the unasked third not only writes and speaks of the Law Faculty in tones of admiration but also did his doctorate at Sheffield, we can confidently deduce his view.

This collection of scholarly lectures, now expanded, epitomizes why talent plus research plus communication skills plus a profound belief in the gold standard of law teaching will always triumph.

The law of property (a good proportion of which I do not understand as I should because Prof Battersby and Mr Odell did not have the chance to teach it to me) is vital to the lawyer in the twenty-first century. As well as ownership of homes, businesses, and goods, cyber activity is the imperative for a clear understanding of applicable law. To adopt the position that real property is the law of property and that other areas are nouveaux would be more than unwise. This splendid collection proves why.

Anne Rafferty.

Preface

The traditional approach to teaching Property Law in English law schools has been (and largely still is) a course on Land Law (or Real Property) and another course on Equity and Trusts. Personal Property is hardly mentioned. That tradition was challenged by Professor F. H. Lawson, who, in the late 1950s, delivered a course of lectures in Oxford entitled "The Law of Property". The lectures were converted into an acclaimed book with the same title (first published in 1958, now in its third edition by Lawson and Rudden). The book offers, in a short compass, an integrated approach to property in all its forms: for example land, money, intellectual property, negotiable instruments, chose in action, and stocks and shares.

This was an account of the modern law, quite unlike the traditional courses, which are historically contingent and lacking in organisational principles. However, Lawson did not provoke a revolution; the pedagogic tradition continued, even in his own university, Oxford.

In Sheffield, it was decided in the early 1970s to offer an optional course on Personal Property. That course was devised by the first-named writer and Alan Preston; it included substantial material on the sale of goods and other transactions. It was, we thought, an improvement on the previous curriculum, but by 1980 further thought persuaded us that a fully integrated course on Property Law should be introduced. The principal idea was to identify fundamental concepts common to different forms of property. There are several such concepts, described in the chapters of this book, which is an expanded version of the lectures delivered for two decades by the first-named writer, and subsequently, down to the present day, by the second-named writer.

That course, labelled Property 1, was compulsory for all law students in Sheffield (Law137 Property Law is now the compulsory first year module). Wisely or not, it is placed in the first year of the degree course. This book is aimed at that cohort of students. We have tried hard to present often quite sophisticated concepts in a user-friendly style, using, so far as possible, everyday language and homely examples. However, legal jargon cannot be avoided completely; students of property law need, for example, to learn about the fee simple, and reversions and remainders; hence the reference to learning a new language in chapter 1.

A major difficulty with Property 1 was that there was not a suitable textbook. Lawson and Rudden is excellent, but for the purposes of that course is too short and lacks detail. At the other extreme, R. J. Smith's "Property Law" is also excellent, but is overall too long and, in many places too complicated, for first year students. There has been a vacuum which we hope this book may fill.

Property 1 was improved over the years by contributions from the Property team, especially Bernadette Connell, Graham Ferris, Elise Histed, Peter Luxton, David Townend and Margaret Wilkie. Peter has also read and appraised the text. We thank them all for their help. We also thank Chris Sykes and everyone at North Wolds Printers Limited for all their help in seeing this book into print.

We are immensely grateful to the Rt Hon Lady Justice Anne Rafferty, DBE, for writing the foreword. She is triply qualified for this task, as Chancellor of the University of Sheffield, a Lady Justice of Appeal and one of the University's most eminent law graduates.

Celia makes many appearances in this book. She was the mother of the first-named writer; she knew about the writing project and was very supportive. So too was Rosemary Buckley, the long-term partner of the same writer. Before her premature death in June 2015 she read and commented on all the material then in draft.

This book is dedicated to the memory of Celia and Rosemary.

Graham Battersby,
Edward Bramley Professor of Law, Emeritus, University of Sheffield

Peter Odell
Senior University Teacher, University of Sheffield

Michaelmas Day, 2017

The School of Law, University of Sheffield

Contents

Chapter 1	What is Property?	1
Chapter 2	Ownership : Its regulation and its fragmentation	19
Chapter 3	Possession and Title	27
	Appendix 1: The Finding Cases	34
	Appendix 2: Treasure	43
Chapter 4	The Contribution of Equity	45
Chapter 5	Formalities for the Disposition of Property	81
Chapter 6	Protection of the Purchaser	109
Chapter 7	Co-ownership	117
Chapter 8	The Family Home	141

Table of Cases

A
Abbey National Bank plc v Stringer [2006] 2 P & CR DG15
Abbey National Building Society v Cann [1991] 1 AC 56
Abbott v Abbott [2008] 1 FLR 1451
A G Securities v Vaughan [1990] 1 AC 417
Ahmed Yar Khan v Secretary of State for India (1901) LR 28 IA 211
Allen v Roughley (1955) 94 CLR 98
Aquaculture Corpn v New Zealand Green Mussel Co Ltd [1990] 3 NZLR 299
Argyle Building Society v Hammond (1984) P & CR 148
Armory v Delamirie (1722) 1 Stra 505
Armstrong DLW GmbH v Winnington Networks Ltd [2012] EWHC 10 (Ch)
Ashburn Anstalt v Arnold [1989] Ch 1
Asher v Whitlock (1865) LR 1 QB 1
Attenborough v Solomon [1913] AC 76
Attorney General for Hong Kong v Reid [1994] 1 AC 324
Austerberry v Corporation of Oldham (1885) 27 Ch D 250

B
Bailey (A Bankrupt), Re [1977] 1 WLR 278
Baillie, Re (1886) 2 TLR 660
Bank of Ireland Home Mortgages Ltd v Bell [2001] 2 FLR 809
Banner Homes Group plc v Duff Developments Ltd [2000] Ch 372
Bannister v Bannister [1948] 2 All ER 133
Barca v Mears [2005] 2 FLR 1
Barclays Bank plc v O'Brien [1994] 1 AC 180
Barton v Morris [1985] 1 WLR 1257
Basham, Re [1986] 1 WLR 1498
Bateman's Will Trusts, Re [1970] 1 WLR 1463
Battison v Hobson [1896] 2 Ch 403
Beaumont, Re [1902] 1 Ch 886
Bedson v Bedson [1965] 2 QB 666
Beesley v Hallwood Estates Ltd [1960] 1 WLR 549
Belfast Corporation v O D Cars Ltd [1960] AC 490
Bell v Peter Browne & Co [1990] 2 QB 495
Berkeley Road (88) NW9, Re [1971] Ch 648
Bernstein v Skyviews & General Ltd. [1978] QB 479
Best v Chief Land Registrar [2015] EWCA Civ 17
Binions v Evans [1972] Ch 359
Birch v Treasury Solicitor [1951] Ch 298
Bird v Fort Frances (1949) 2 DLR 791
Blackwell v Blackwell [1929] AC 318
Boardman v Phipps [1967] 2 AC 46

Borwick, Re [1933] Ch 657
Bowden, Re [1936] Ch 71
Boyer v Warbey [1953] 1 QB 234
Bremner, Re [1999] 1 FLR 912
Bridges v Hawkesworth (1851) 15 Jur 1079
Bristol and West Building Society v Henning [1985] 1 WLR 778
Brooks' Settlement Trusts, Re [1939] 1 Ch 993
Brown v Raine (1796) 3 Ves 257
Buchanan-Wollaston's Conveyance, Re [1939] Ch 738
Burgess v Rawnsley [1975] Ch 429
Burns v Burns [1984] Ch 317
Byrne v Hoare [1965] Qd R 135

C

Cain v Moon [1896] 2 QB 283
Camden LBC v Shortlife Community Housing Ltd (1992) 90 LGR 358
Campbell v Griffin [2001] WTLR 981
Capehorn v Harris [2015] EWCA 955
Catt v Marac Australia (1986) NSWLR 659
Caunce v Caunce [1969] 1 WLR 286
Cedar Holdings Ltd v Green [1981] Ch 129
Central Newbury Car Auctions Ltd v Unity Finance Ltd [1957] 1 QB 371
Chaudhary v Yavuz [2011] EWCA Civ 1314
Childers v Childers (1857) 1 De G & J 482
Choitram (T) International SA v Pagarani [2001] 1 WLR 1
Chokar v Chokar [1984] FLR 313
Citro (A Bankrupt), Re [1991] Ch 142
City of London Building Society v Flegg [1988] AC 54
City of London Corporation v Appleyard [1963] 1 WLR 982
Claughton v Charambolous [1999] 1 FLR 740
Cleaver v Mutual Reserve Fund Life Association [1892] QB 147
ClientEarth v Secretary of State for the Environment, Food and Rural Affairs, R on the application of [2016] EWCA (Admin) 2740
Cochrane v Moore (1890) 25 QBD 57
Coco v A. N. Clark [1969] RPC 41
Cole, Re [1964] Ch 175
Combe v Combe [1951] 2 KB 215 QB 147
Commissioner of Stamp Duties (Queensland) v Livingston [1965] AC 694
Commonwealth of Australia v Verwayen (1990) 170 CLR 394
Cook, Re [1948] Ch 212
Cooke v Head [1972] 2 All ER 38
Corbett v Hill (1870) LR 9 Eq 671
Costello v Chief Constable of Derbyshire Constabulary [2001] 1 WLR 1437
Crabb v Arun District Council [1976] Ch 179
Crago v Julian [1992] 1 WLR 372
Craven's Estate, Re [1937] Ch 423

Crinion v Minister of Justice (1959) 25 Irish Jurist Reports 15
Cundy v Lindsay (1878) 3 App Cas 459
Curtis v Pulbrook [2011] EWHC 167 (Ch)

D
Dartstone Ltd v Cleveland Petroleum Co Ltd [1969] 3 All ER 668
Dehar, Re [1969] NZLR 574
De Mattos v Gibson (1859) De G & J 276
Denny, Re (1947) 177 L T 291
Dillwyn v Llewelyn (1867) 4 De GF & J 577
Dobson v North Tyneside Health Authority [1996] EWCA Civ 1301
Dodsworth v Dodsworth (1973) 228 EG 1115
Doe d Gill v Pearson (1805) 6 East 173
Doodeward v Spence [1908] HCA 45
Draper's Conveyance, Re [1969] 1 Ch 486
Duffield v Elwes (1827) 1 Bli (NS) 497
Dunbar v Plant [1998] Ch 412
Dyer v Dyer (1788) 2 Cox Eq Cas 92

E
Eastbourne Mutual Building Society Hastings Corporation [1965] 1 WLR 861
Edwards v Lloyds TSB Bank plc [2001] 2 All ER (Comm) 920
Elwes v Brigg Gas Co (1886) LR 3 Ch D 562
Equity & Law Homes Ltd v Prestidge [1992] 1 WLR 137
Errington v Errington and Woods [1952] 1 KB 209
Estate of Mead, Re (1964) 39 Cal Rpts 282
Evers' Trust, Re [1980] 1 WLR 1327
Eves v Eves [1975] 1 WLR 1338

F
Fairstar Heavy Transport NV V Adkins [2013] EWCA Civ 886
Falconer v Falconer [1970] 3 All ER 449
F. C. Jones (a firm) v Jones [1997] Ch 159
FHR European Ventures LLP v Cedar Capital Ltd [2014] 3 WLR 535
FHR European Ventures LLP v Mankarious [2013] EWCA Civ 17
Fine Art Society v Union Bank of London (1886) LR 17 QBD 705
First National Bank v Achampong [2004] 1 FCR 18
First National Securities v Hegerty [1985] QB 850
Firstpost Homes Ltd v Johnson [1995] 1 WLR 1567
Ford v Alexander [2012] BPIR 528
Formby v Barker [1903] 2 Ch 539
Foskett v McKeown [2001] 1 AC 102
Fowler v Barron [2003] 2 FLR 831
Fribance v Fribance (No 2) [1957] 1 All ER 357
Fry, Re [1946] Ch 312

G

Gillick v West Norfolk and Wisbech Area Health Authority [1986] AC 112
Gillett v Holt]2001] Ch 210
Gissing v Gissing [1971] AC 886
Golden Ocean Group Ltd v Salgaocar [2012] EWCA Civ 265
Goodman v Gallant [1986] Fam 186
Gore and Snell v Carpenter (1990) 60 P & CR 456
Gough v Chief Constable of West Midlands [2004] EWCA 206
Gow v Grant [2012] UKSC 29
Grafstein v Holmes and Freeman (1958) 12 DLR 727
Graham-York v York [2015] EWCA Civ 72, [2015] HLR 26
Grant v Edwards [1986] 2 All ER 426
Gresley v Cook [1980] 1 WLR 1306
Grey v Inland Revenue Commissioners [1960] AC 1
Griffiths v Williams (1977) 248 EG 947
Grindal v Hooper (1999) 96/48 LS Gaz 41
Groffman, Re (deceased) [1969] 1 WLR 733

H

Haghlighat, Re [2009] 1 FLR 1271
Hallett's Estate, Re (1880) 13 Ch D 66
Hammersmith & Fulham London Borough Council v Monk [1992] 1 AC 478
Hannah v Peel [1945] 1 KB 509
Harris v Goddard [1983] 1 WLR 1203
Harvell v Foster [1954] 2 QB 367
Hasking v Michaelides [2006] 1 BPIR 192
Haywood v Brunswick Permanent Building Society (1881) 8 QBD 403
Hazell v Hazell [1972] 1 All ER 923
Helby v Matthews [1895] AC 471
Hewer v Bryant [1970] 1 QB 357
Hewett, Re [1918] 1 Ch 458
Hibbert v McKiernan [1948] 2 KB 142
Hine v Hine [1962] 3 All ER 345
Hobson v Gorringe [1897] 1 Ch 182
Hodgson v Marks [1971] Ch 892
Holliday, Re (A Bankrupt) [1981] Ch 405
Holt's Settlement, Re [1969] 1 Ch 100
Hosking v Michaelides [2006] BPIR 1192
Hounslow London Borough Council v Pilling [1993] 1 WLR 1242
HSBC Bank plc v Dyche [2009] EWHC 2954 (Ch)
Hunt v Luck [1902] 1 Ch 428
Huntingford v Hobbs [1993] 1 FLR 736
Hypo-Mortgage Services Ltd v Robinson [1972] 2 FLR 71

I
IDC Group Ltd v Clark (1992) 1 EGLR 187
Industrial Properties (Barton Hill) Ltd v Associated Electrical Industries Ltd [1997] QB 580
Ingram v Little [1961] 1 QB 1
Inwards v Baker [1965] 2 QB 29

J
Jackson, Re (1887) 34 Ch D 732
Jackson v Bell [2001] Family Law 879
Jackson v Jackson (1804) 9 Ves 591
Jennings v Rice [2003] 1 P & CR 8
Jones v Challenger [1961] 1 QB 176
Jones v Kernott [2012] 1 AC 776
Jones v Lock (1865) LR 1 Ch App 25
Joyce v Rigolli [2004] 1 P & CR DG22
J T Developments Ltd v Quinn (1990) 62 P & CR 33
Judd v Brown [1998] 2 FLR 360

K
K, deceased, Re [1985] Ch 85, [1986] Ch 180
Keech v Sandford (1726) Sel Cas Ch 61
Keen, Re [1937] Ch 236
Kelsen v Imperial Tobacco Co. Ltd. [1957] 2 QB 334
Kewal Investment Ltd v Arthur Maiden Ltd [1990] 1 EGLR 193
Kinane v Mackie-Conteh [2005] EWCA Civ 45
Kinch v Bullard [1999] 1 WLR 423
King v Chiltern Dog Rescue [2015] EWCA Civ 581
King v Dubrey [2014] EWHC 2083 (Ch)
Kingsnorth Finance Co Ltd v Tizard [1986] 1 WLR 783
Kronheim v Johnson (1877) 7 Ch D 60

L
Laird v Laird [1999] 1 FLR 791
Lake v Jackson (1729) 1 Eq Cas Abr 290
Lall v Lall [1965] 1 WLR 1249
Laskar v Laskar [2008] 1 WLR 2695
LCC v Allen [1914] 3 KB 642
Lee v Lee [1952] 2 QB 489
Leek & Moorlands Building Society v Clark and Elison [1952] 2 QB 788
Leigh's Will Trusts, Re [1970] Ch 277
Le Mesurier v Andrus (1986) 54 OR (2d) 1
Lepel v Huthnance (1979) NZ Recent Law 269
Lillingston, Re [1952] 2 All ER 184
Linden Gardens Trust Ltd v Lenesta Sludge Disposals Ltd [1994] AC 85

Link Lending Ltd v Bustard [2010] EWCA Civ 424
Lister v Stubbs (1890) 45 Ch D 1
Lloyd v Dugdale [2002] 2 P & CR 13
Lloyds Bank plc v Byrne & Byrne [1993] 1 FLR 369
Lloyds Bank plc v Carrick [1996] 4 All ER 630
Lloyds Bank plc v Rosset [1991] 1 AC 108
Lock v Heath (1892) 8 TLR 295
Lord Abergavenny's Case (1607) 6 Co Rep 78
Lord Napier and Ettrick v Hunter [1993] 1 All ER 385
Lord Strathcona SS Co v Dominion Coal Co [1926] AC 108
Lowrie (A Bankrupt), Re [1981] 3 All ER 353
Lysaght v Edwards (1876) 2 Ch D 499
Lyus v Prowsa Developments Ltd [1982] 1 WLR 1044

M

Macleay, Re (1875) LR 20 Eq 186
Malayan Credit Ltd v Jack Chia MPH Ltd [1986] AC 549
Malory Enterprises Ltd v Cheshire Homes (UK) Ltd [2002] Ch 216
Manchester Trust v Furness [1895] 2 QB 539
Mann v Stephens (1846) 15 Sim 377
Marley v Rawlings [2014] 2 WLR 213
Marr v Collie [2017] UKPC 17
Mascall v Mascall (1984) 50 P & CR 119
Matharu v Matharu (1994) 68 P & CR 93
McCausland v Duncan Lawrie Ltd [1997] 1 WLR 38
McCormick v Grogan (1869) LR 4 HL 82
McDowell v Hirschfield Lipson and Romney [1992] 2 FLR 126
McDowell v Ulster Bank (1899) Irish Law Times 225
Mears v L & W Railway Co (1862) 11 CBNS 850
Mee, Re (1971) 23 DLR (3d) 491
Merry v Green (1841) 7 M & W 623
Midland Bank Plc v Cooke [1995] 4 All ER 562
Midland Bank Trust Co Ltd v Green [1981] AC 513
Midland Bank Trust Co Ltd v Green (No 3) [1982] Ch 829
Midland Bank Trust Co Ltd v Hett, Stubbs & Kemp (a firm) [1979] Ch 384
Mikeover v Brady [1989] 3 All ER 616
Miller Smith v Miller Smith [2010] 1 FLR 1402
Milroy v Lord (1862) 4 De G F & J 264
Ministry of Housing and Local Government v Sharp [1970] 2 QB 223
Moffatt v Kazana [1969] 2 QB 152
Moore v Regents of the University of California (1990) 51 Cal. 3d 120
Morris v C W Martin & Sons Ltd [1965] 2 All ER 725
Morrison, Jones & Taylor Ltd, Re [1914] 1 Ch 5
Morrison v London County and Westminster Bank [1914] 3 KB 356
Mortgage Corporation v Shaire [2001] Ch 743
Morton v Tewart (1842) 2 Y & C Ch 67

Moss v Cooper (1861) 1 J & H 352
Murray v Guinness, [1998] NPC 79

N
National Employers Mutual General Insurance Association Ltd v Jones [1990] 1 AC 24
National Provincial Bank Ltd v Ainsworth [1965] AC 1175
National Westminster Bank v Jones [2002] BCLC 55
Nationwide Anglia Building Society v Ahmed (1995) 70 P & CR 381
Neale v Willis (1968) 19 P & CR 839
Neilson v Poole (1969) 20 P & CR 909
Nelson v Greenway & Sykes (Builders) Ltd [2008] EGLR 59
Neville v Wilson [1997] Ch 144
Newman v Bourne and Hollingsworth (1915) TLR 209
Nichols v Lan [2007] 1 FLR 744
Nielson-Jones v Fedden [1975] Ch 222
Nisbet and Potts' Contract, Re [1906] 1 Ch 386

O
OBG Ltd v Allan [2008] 1 AC 1
Old Grovebury Manor Farms Ltd v W Seymour Plant Sales and Hire Ltd (No 2) [1979] 1 WLR 1397
Oliari v Italy (1995) Apps ns 18766/11 and 36030/11, European Court of Human Rights
Oughtred v Inland Revenue Commissioners [1960] AC 206
Owen, Re [1949] 1 All ER 901
Oxford v Moss (1979) 68 Cr App R 183
Oxley v Hiscock [2005] Fam 211

P
Paddington Building Society v Mendelsohn (1985) 50 P & CR 244
Parker v British Airways Board [1982] 1 QB 1004
Pascoe v Turner [1979] 1 WLR 531
Paul v Constance [1977] 1 WLR 527
Re Pehar [1969] NZLR 574
Pennington v Waine [2002] 1 WLR 2075
Perry v Clissold [1907] AC 731
Peter Pan Manufacturing Corporation v Corsets Silhouette [1964] 1 WLR 96
Pettitt v Pettitt [1970] AC 777
Pilcher v Rawlins (1872) 7 Ch App 259
Plimmer v Wellington Corp (1883-84) LR 9 App Cas 699
Port Line Ltd v Ben Line Steamers [1958] 2 QB 146
Poster v Slough Estates Ltd [1969] 1 Ch 495
Pritchard v Briggs [1980] Ch 338

Q
Quigley v Masterson [2012] 1 All ER 1224

R
R v Absolom The Times, 14 September 1983
R v Bentham [2005] UKHL 18
R v Kelly [1999] 2 WLR 384
R v Lynn (1788) 2 TR 733
R v Morris [1988] 58 DLR (4th) 1
R v Offley (1986) 45 Alta LR (2d) 23
R v Price [1884] 12 QBD 247
R v Rostron [2003] EWCA Crim 2206
R v Sharpe (1857) Dears & B 160
Ralli's Will Trusts, Re [1964] Ch 288
Ramsden v Dyson (1866) LR 1 HL 129
Rasmanis v Jurewitsch (1970) 70 SR NSW 407
Raval, Re [1998] 2 FLR 718
Rawlings v Rawlings [1964] P 398
Rawlinson v Mort (1905) 93 LT 555
Reading v Attorney General [1951] 1 All ER 617
Reynolds v Ashby & Son [1904] AC 466
Rimmer v Rimmer [1953] 1 QB 63
Rochefoucauld v Boustead [1897] 1 Ch 196
Rose, Re [1952] Ch 499
Rowland v Divall [1923] 2 KB 500
Royal Bank of Scotland v Etridge (No 2) [2002] 2 AC 773
Russel v Russel (1783) 1 Bro CC 269

S
Samuel Allen & Sons Ltd, Re [1907] 1 Ch 575
Schar deceased, Re [1951] Ch 280
Schobelt v Barber (1966) 60 DLR 2d 519
Scott v Southern Pacific Mortgages Ltd [2014] UKSC 52
Sen v Headley [1991] Ch 425
Shah v Shah [2002] QB 35
Shiloh Spinners Ltd v Harding [1973] AC 691
Shogun Finance Ltd v Hudson [2004] 1 AC 919
Sims v Dacorum Borough Council [2014] UKSC 63
Sinclair Investments Ltd v Versailles Trade Finance Ltd [2012] Ch 453
Smith v Morrison [1974] 1 WLR 659
Sorenson and Sorenson, Re (1977) 90 DLR (3d) 26
South Staffordshire Water Co v Sharman [1896] 2 Ch 44
Solloway Mills & Co and ors v McLaughlin [1938] AC 247
Spiro v Glencrown Properties Ltd [1991] Ch 537
Stack v Dowden [2007] 2 AC 432
Stadium Finance Ltd v Robbins [1962] 2 QB 664

xiv

Stapleford Colliery Co, Re (1890) Ch D 432
Star Energy v Bocardo [2010] UKSC 35
State Bank of India v Sood [1997] Ch 276
Steeds v Steeds (1889) 22 QBD 537
Steinfeld and Keidan v Secretary of State for Education [2017] EWCA Civ 81
Stewart v R [1988] 58 DLR (4th) 1.
Stoneham, Re [1919] 1 Ch 149
Strickland v Aldridge (1804) 9 Ves Jr 516
Strong v Bird (1874) LR 18 Eq 315
Swift 1st Ltd v The Chief Land Registrar [2015] EWCA Civ 330
Swinburne, Re [1926] Ch 38
Swiss Bank Corp v Lloyds Bank Ltd [1975] Ch 548

T
Taylor v Salmon (1838) 4 My & Cr 134
Tee v Tee & Hamilton [1999] 2 FLR 613
Tegg, Re [1936] 2 All ER 878
Thomas v The Times Book Co Ltd [1966] 1 WLR 911
Thorner v Major [2009] 1 WLR 776
Tierney v Wood (1854) 19 Beav 330
Tinsley v Milligan [1993] 3 All ER 65
Trustee of the Property of F C Jones (a firm) v Jones [1997] Ch 159
Tulk v Moxhay (1848) 2 Ph 774

U
United Bank of Kuwait plc v Sahib [1997] Ch 107
United Scientific Holdings Ltd v Burnley Borough Council [1978] AC 904
Unity Joint Stock Banking Association v King (1858) 25 Beav 72

V
Vallee v Birchwood [2013] EWHC 1449 (Ch)
Vandervell v Inland Revenue Commissioners [1967] 2 AC 291
Victoria Park Racing and Recreation Grounds Co Ltd v Taylor (1937) 58 CLR 479
Voyce v Voyce (1991) 62 P & CR 290

W
Waller v Waller [1967] 1 WLR 451
Walsh v Lonsdale (1882) LR 21 Ch D 9
Warman v Southern Counties Car Finance Corporation Ltd [1949] 2 KB 576
Wasserberg, Re [1915] 1 Ch 195
Waverley Borough Council v Fletcher [1995] QB 334
Weatherhill v Pearce [1995] 1 WLR 592
Webb v Chief Constable of Merseyside [2000] QB 427
Western Fish Products Ltd v Penwith District Council [1981] 2 All ER 204

Whatman v Gibson (1838) 9 Sim 196
Wheeler v Baldwin (1934) 52 CLR 629
White v Bijou Mansions Ltd [1937] Ch 610
White v Jones [1995] 2 AC 207
White v White [2001] 1 AC 596
Wilkes v Spooner [1911] 2 KB 473
Williams v Barton [1927] 2 Ch 9
Williams & Glyn's Bank Ltd v Boland [1981] AC 487
Williams v Hensman (1861) 1 J & H 546
Williams v Williams [1976] Ch 278
Wilson v Bell (1843) 5 Ir Eq R 501
Wilson v Wilson [1969] 1 WLR 1470
Winter v Winter (1861) 4 LT 639
Wood v Smith [1993] Ch 90
Woodward v Woodward [1995] 3 All ER 980
Wright v Gibson (1949) 78 CLR 313
Wroth v Tyler [1974] Ch 30

Y
Yaxley v Gotts [2000] Ch 162
Yearworth v North Bristol NHS Trust [2009] EWCA Civ 37
Yeoman's Row Management Ltd v Cobbe [2008] UKHL 55
Young v Bristol Aeroplane Co [1944] KB 718

Z
Zeitel v Kaye [2010] EWCA Civ 15

Table of Statutes

Administration of Estates Act 1925
Administration of Justice Act 1970
Administration of Justice Act 1973
Administration of Justice Act 1982
Anti-Social Behaviour Act 2003
Bills of Exchange Act 1882
Bodies Corporate (Joint Tenancy) Act 1899
Civil Aviation Act 1982
Civil Partnership Act 2004
Clean Air Act 1956
Clean Air Act 1993
Coal Industry Act 1994
Companies Act 2006
Consumer Credit Act 1974
Electronic Communications Act 2000
Family Law Act 1996
Family Law (Scotland) Act 2006
Firearms Act 1968
Forfeiture Act 1982
Hire-Purchase Act 1964
Housing Act 1985
Human Fertilisation and Embryology Act 1990
Human Rights Act 1998
Infrastructure Act 2015
Inheritance (Provision for Families and Dependants) Act 1975
Inheritance and Trustees' Powers Act 2014
Insolvency Act 1986
Intestates' Estates Act 1952
Land Charges Act 1925
Land Charges Act 1972
Land Registration Act 1925
Land Registration Act 2002
Landlord and Tenant (Covenants) Act 1995
Law of Property Act 1925
Law of Property Act 1969
Law of Property (Joint Tenants) Act 1964
Law of Property (Miscellaneous Provisions) Act 1989
Law of Property (Miscellaneous Provisions) Act 1994
Legal Aid, Sentencing and Punishment of Offenders Act 2012
Limitation Act 1980
Local Land Charges Act 1975
Magna Carta 1215
Marriage (Same Sex Couples) Act 2013
Married Women's Property Act 1882

Matrimonial Causes Act 1973
Matrimonial Homes Act 1967
Matrimonial Proceedings and Property Act 1970
Mental Capacity Act 2005
Misuse of Drugs Act 1971
Petroleum Act 1998
Police and Criminal Evidence Act 1984
Powers of Attorney Act 1971
Proceeds of Crime Act 2002
Requirements of Writing (Scotland) Act 1995
Sale of Goods Act 1979
Settled Land Act 1925
Slave Trade Act 1807
Slavery Abolition Act 1833
Supreme Court Act 1981
Supreme Court of Judicature Act 1873
Supreme Court of Judicature Act 1875
Theft Act 1968
Torts (Interference with Goods) Act 1977
Town and Country Planning Act 1947
Town and Country Planning Act 1990
Treasure Act 1996
Tribunals, Courts and Enforcement Act 2007
Trustee Act 1925
Trustee Act 2000
Trustee Delegation Act 1999
Trusts of Land and Appointment of Trustees Act 1996
Statute of Frauds 1677
Wills Act 1837
Wills Act 1968
Wills (Soldiers and Sailors) Act 1918

Chapter 1

WHAT IS PROPERTY?

Anyone embarking on the study of the law of property has two principal challenges. The first is the use of technical and sometimes arcane language to describe and apply established legal principles; this can be overcome with practice and perseverance. Do not be put off by the language but try to tie descriptor to concept; with practice you will become more proficient as when learning any new language. The second challenge is that unlike other areas of law, where a succinct definition may be given of, say, what is a contract, tort or crime, property is harder to define. Broadly we all tend to have an intuitive sense of what property is, as J.W. Harris[1] suggests "(w)e get by in daily life with a range of conventional property talk which has no problem 'knowing' who owns a particular book or a car or a house or a ten-pound note. Otherwise we could not borrow or lend or sell...". However, an accurate description of the concept is much more difficult and British lawyers tend to struggle with the concept of 'ownership', which we will come back to in the next chapter.

Whilst lay people and lawyers inhabit the same world and have mostly similar preoccupations, their technical view of what is happening in particular contexts or transactions can vary markedly. A lay person seeing my watch might describe it as 'property', to a lawyer it is just a thing—a watch. To lawyers it is a trite observation that 'property' is the relationship between individuals over things[2]. The thing or object of these rights and duties can be tangible or intangible, movable or immovable, real (land) or personal (non-land). Whilst the thing or object of the rights and duties may help you to understand the precise nature of the rights and duties that may exist between individuals (or even who might hold competing claims and of the nature/importance of those claims), the thing or object is very often the least interesting aspect of any 'property' based enquiry. Consequently, any lawyerly discussion of property will always revolve around the identification of the rights and duties that specifically exist over the thing before a critical examination can take place. It is for this reason that, while a lay person might

---

[1] J.W. Harris, *Property and Justice* (1996), p. 424.
[2] C.B. Macpherson (ed) Property, Mainstream and Critical Positions (1978), p. 202.

be happy to discuss the 'ownership' of my watch, for any real understanding about what that 'ownership' means in practice a lawyer would look at the claims explicitly or implicitly being made.[3] For example, normally when a lay person says that they 'own' a watch they are asserting a right of possession, a right to exclude the world from it, a right to alienate it, a right to destroy it, a right to be recognised by the law as the title holder, a right to use it, and so on. At the same time there are implicit duties that exist, for example not to use it to kill or maim another, to dispose of it in a legally compliant manner, etc. The practical importance of this position is that it allows for multiple concurrent interests to exist over a thing and yet be conceptually frameable. In the case of my watch, although I might have most of the important rights, I do not have all of them. I do not have the design rights that exist over it, nor any patent or trade mark rights; I could not use it as a template to produce more watches for example. 'Ownership' is therefore a metaphor, a symbol to represent often unspecified rights and duties, rather than a descriptor. On its own it is insufficient to convey a real understanding of what claims are being made, although in day to day life it is an adequate short hand that is operable by those who do not really need to dwell on the rights and duties in play. In everyday situations there is sufficient understanding (even though this is apparent rather than real) for lay people to have 'ownership' of a watch. Whilst lay people may safely live with the imprecision, it is essential that the legal system be able to identify and characterise the rights and duties which attach to things; essentially property lawyers are only ever interested in the creation, transfer or destruction of these rights and duties over things.

Property rights can exist in a very wide range of situations and we can describe many rights as proprietary that seem to have no obvious connection. For example, if my aunt dies leaving all her property to me as sole beneficiary of her will, I might stand to inherit a house, car, furniture, stocks & shares, £100 in banknotes, £5,000 in her deposit account at the bank and the copyright to the bestseller that she authored. The house is 'real property' (land); the car and furniture are tangible and might be described as 'chattels' (non-land); stocks & shares are intangible (I would only need the share certificate to prove ownership, they have value and may be transferred); money is tangible to a certain extent but the value is intangible (so the £100 is partly tangible and partly intangible), the money on deposit is not the same as cash: my aunt is

---

[3] See further ch 2, "Ownership".

owed the money by the bank; as a creditor of the bank she is owed a debt (so this is intangible property); and the copyright is a valuable, intangible, intellectual property right. So do these items that we might wish to call property have some common characteristic(s)? One common characteristic is that the rights can be transferred from one person to another. Transfer may be outright, a total, absolute transfer or it may be partial, eg lending a book.

Perhaps another way to consider this is to ask what makes a property right different from a personal right. Whilst personal rights are only exercisable against an individual or individuals (rights *in personam*), property rights are valid against the world (rights *in rem*). The fact that the rights may be exercised against third parties may be said to be characteristic of property rights.

In *National Provincial Bank v Ainsworth*[4] the court had to decide whether Mr Ainsworth's legal duty to provide a home for his wife and children was a personal or property right. Mr Ainsworth was the sole owner of the house in which he and his wife and children lived. He was a businessman and used the house as security for a loan with National Provincial Bank in the form of a mortgage. After the marriage had broken down (he deserted his family and went to live elsewhere), he defaulted on the loan. The bank wished to evict Mrs Ainsworth and the children to gain possession of the house so that they could realise their security. Mr Ainsworth was under a legal duty to provide a home for his family; could that duty be exerted against the bank? (Since Mr Ainsworth could not evict them, did this affect the bank's ability to evict them?) Previously it had been held that deserted wives had a right to remain in the former marital home, but the House of Lords overturned this line of case law by holding that the wife's right to have a roof over her head was a personal right, only enforceable against her husband, not a proprietary right which could be enforceable against a third party. As a result Mrs Ainsworth and children lost their home. As you will see in Chapter 8, the Matrimonial Homes Act 1967 (substantially re-enacted by the Family Law Act 1996) was passed in response to the public outcry following the decision in *Ainsworth*. Where one spouse owns the matrimonial home this Act gave the non-owning spouse a statutory right of occupation (this could be registered and hence protected against third parties).

---

[4] *National Provincial Bank v Ainsworth* [1965] AC 1175.

Commenting on the 'broad or penumbral band' dividing personal from property rights, Lord Wilberforce was clear that "(b)efore a right or an interest can be admitted into the category of property, or of a right affecting property, it must be definable, identifiable by third parties, capable in its nature of assumption by third parties, and have some degree of permanence or stability"[5]. Although the effect of the decision in *Ainsworth* has been modified by statute, this idea about how to recognise a property right is still employed.

Lord Wilberforce's explanation is sufficient as a minimal definition of this distinction. It does not purport to set out general criteria by which the distinction is to be made, in the many different contexts in which it may arise. Kevin Grey, having made scathing criticisms of Lord Wilberforce's reasoning, made some positive progress in delineating such criteria, in his landmark article, "Property in Thin Air"[6]. His analysis centres on the decision of the High Court of Australia in *Victoria Park Racing and Recreation Grounds Co Ltd v Taylor*[7]. There, the respondent owned a house overlooking Victoria Park's horse racing course. He arranged with a broadcasting company for live commentaries to be broadcast on the progress of the races, and there arose an extensive off-course betting industry. The respondent's activities caused significant financial detriment to Victoria Park, which sought an injunction to restrain those activities, based on allegations of nuisance and breach of copyright. The Court held by a majority that the claim failed, because Victoria Park had no recognisable proprietary interest in the activities of the racecourse: the spectacle of the races and the profits thereby generated. Building on that, Grey's central idea is that, for a resource to be treated as property, it must be "excludable"[8]. As he explains: "A resource is 'excludable' only if it is feasible for a legal person to exercise regulatory control over the access of strangers to the various benefits inherent in that resource."[9] This is a fruitful notion, which Grey develops very perceptively. However, it too has its limitations. It is directed at the question of treating a resource as property as against a stranger who has no pre-existing legal relationship with the claimant. It appears not to assist in drawing the dividing line where there is such a pre-existing relationship, either between the parties, as in *Ashburn Anstalt* and

---

[5] *National Provincial Bank v Ainsworth* [1965] AC 1175, at 1247-1248.
[6] [1991] CLJ 252.
[7] (1937) 58 CLR 479.
[8] An "ugly but effective word": [1991] CLJ 252 at 268.
[9] Ibid.

FHR European Ventures (discussed in the following paragraphs), or between one of those parties and another, as in *Ainsworth* or *Tulk v Moxhay*[10]. Indeed, in those contexts, Lord Wilberforce's criteria are more helpful than Grey's.

The idea that the defining feature of a proprietary right is the holder's ability to exert it against a third party can be seen in *Ashburn Arnstalt v Arnold*[11]. One of the questions that the court faced was whether a person with a contractual right to occupy could enforce it against a third party (if the person they had entered the contract with transferred the land to the third party). The Courts had previously said, somewhat contentiously, that a contractual licence created a proprietary right,[12] but in *Ashburn Anstalt* the Lord Denning line of cases was overruled and the old understanding that a contractual licence to occupy did not form a proprietary right was re-established. This meant that the contractual licence could be enforced against the original party to it as a personal right but could not be enforced against a third party who had later acquired the land.

From this it seems axiomatic that property rights may be transferred and the proprietary rights not cut down in the process (an exception to this is that spouses' rights of occupation under the family legislation cannot be transferred to anyone else). However, there are also instances where property rights can be transferred but which cannot be held against a third party. For example the benefit of a debt can be assigned to someone other than the original creditor, hence a debt is property; a contrasting example would be the benefit of an easement (such as a right of way) over a neighbour's land, this may be conveyed (transferred) from one owner of a piece of land to the next, preserving the easement over the neighbour's property during the process.

The importance of being able to determine whether an interest is personal or proprietary in nature goes well beyond just a simple understanding of whether or not it is enforceable against a third party. In some situations, for example in cases of insolvency or a breach of trust, the difference is important because of extrinsic legal rules and the limits on the jurisdiction of the court. For example, in *FHR European Ventures LLP and others v Cedar Capital Partners*

---

[10] (1848) 41 ER 1143: Restrictive covenants run with the land and are binding on landowners who acquire the land with notice of the restriction.
[11] *Ashburn Arnstalt v Arnold* [1989] Ch 1.
[12] *Errington v Errington and Woods* [1952] 1 KB 290; *Binions v Evans* [1972] Ch 359.

LLC[13] the Supreme Court had to decide whether an agent who had taken a bribe or secret commission held it on trust for the agent's principal (giving the principal a proprietary claim) or if the principal merely had an equitable claim for compensation in a sum equal in value to the bribe or secret commission. The Supreme Court found the former (somewhat clarifying conflicting case law that had been generated over a period of well over 100 years). Lord Neuberger PSC[14] cited with approval examples where the principal affected by a breach of fiduciary duty had been found to have a proprietary claim. This means that in such cases the claimant has an equitable right to trace or follow everything that arises (such as interest or profits made from investments) from the bribe or secret commission taken by the fiduciary and not just the exact sum taken.

Functions and 'types' of property
In her book, *Property; Meanings, histories, theories,* Davies argues "(l)egally, property is not proper, that is, it has no special, distinct, and essential characteristics. It is more or less a concept in circulation, which changes according to the context in which it finds itself"[15]. This is a consequence of the practical nature of the law of property and the multiplicity of functions it serves. These functions include amongst others: housing and manufacturing (land used for dwellings and industry); commerce (buying/selling); endowment (arrangement whereby property is used for a continuing purpose, for example a competition prize or university scholarship); investment (use of property for interest or income generation); currency (universal means of exchange such as money); security (for example a mortgage or loan which vests in the lender a right to take possession of something of value such as land or stocks & shares); recreation (for example tracts of land for walking like 'heritage land' held by the National Trust); agriculture & forestry (growing crops, trees etc). There will be circumstances where the functions may conflict; for example, a conflict may arise when a house is used for both accommodation and as security for a loan. When there is a conflict the law must have mechanism(s) to resolve the conflict.

---

[13] *FHR European Ventures LLP and others v Cedar Capital Partners LLC* [2014] UKSC 45.
[14] Ibid at [48].
[15] M. Davies, *Property*, Routledge-Cavendish, 2007, p 21-22.

The traditional classifications of different 'types' of property arose from the nature of the 'things' over which the rights/duties existed or the method for enforcing those rights. For example distinct categories such as Real/Personal; Movable/Immovable; or Tangible/Intangible were drawn. Real property (land) as a concept is drawn from the action in court whereby you could recover your property and not merely financial compensation for its loss, for example freehold land; personal property was all other property that was ineligible for the 'real action'. This distinction leads to some apparent anomalies; for example, leasehold land is land that is held under a lease for a defined period of time, the concept of the lease was not developed before real actions were abolished, so leasehold land is personal property. Immovable property is land (all kinds) and interests in land. Tangible property is derived from choses in *possession* (things that can be possessed or held) and intangible property from *choses in action* (things that could be enforced in court such as a debt). These categories are not definitive but rather descriptive and indicate the kind of approach a court will take in resolving conflicts involving them.

English law has traditionally recognised many different kinds of property. These include:
Land — this is probably the most basic commodity and source of the most disputes. It is permanent and indestructible (this is not always true, land can be eroded by the sea); however it is practically finite and the basis of all human life and activity. Because of the importance of land throughout English history and its control the source of wealth, power and status, the law lays down testing formalities for transactions over it. The range of rights that exist or co-exist is probably greatest with respect to land. For example a piece of land may support a complex array of rights which are attached to it eg leases, mortgages, easements etc.

Goods or Chattels — tangible property other than land. May be bought and sold or transferred with much less formality in most instances.

Intangible movables (debt or other *choses in action* / commercial documents) Debt or other *choses in action* — for example in the case of a will, the personal representative of the deceased sends the will to the probate registry for a grant of probate (essentially to check that the will is valid and to enable effective tax collection): this gives the personal representative authority to collect together all the deceased's assets, to pay off any debts and distribute the balance to the beneficiary. If there is no executor named (or willing to act) a family member can apply for a grant of administration (becomes administrator rather than executor). Whilst this process is going on the beneficiaries do not have any rights over the property in the deceased's estate, these are held by the executors/administrators. The beneficiaries do have a right to compel proper administration of the estate which is a *chose in action*. This is explained in more detail in chapter 5 under the heading "Dispositions on death".

Commercial documents : negotiable instruments (for example a cheque) and bills of lading — negotiable instruments and (uncrossed) cheques may be transferred. These are noteworthy because like money they provide a limited exception to *nemo dat* (an extremely important property rule). *Nemo dat quod non habet* means that nobody can give what they don't have. For example, if a thief steals a car and then sells it to an innocent party who has absolutely no knowledge of the theft, in English law the innocent buyer does not get good title to the car. In the case of an uncrossed cheque which is made out to 'bearer' (this orders the bank to pay whoever has the cheque), if the cheque is lost or stolen the finder/thief can cash the cheque. In many contexts a cheque is the equivalent of money, provided that there are sufficient funds in the bank account to meet the value of the cheque. However, it is established that, on analysis, a cheque is merely a mandate to the bank to pay, and that mandate can be revoked. If, for example, the drawer of the cheque dies before the cheque is presented for payment, the mandate is automatically revoked[16]. Like money, a cheque is partly tangible property (the paper on which it is written) and partly intangible property (the amount for which it is written). As tangible property, it can be stolen and can be made the subject of a civil claim in the tort of conversion. Financial compensation is the normal remedy for conversion; in the case of a cheque the damages awarded will be the value of the cheque, not merely of the paper: the "face value" rule.[17] On the other hand, a debt, although a chose in action and in some contexts treated as an item of property, is purely intangible and cannot be the subject of a conversion.[18]

---

[16] *Re Swinburne, Sutton v Featherley* [1926] Ch 38.
[17] *Morison v London County and Westminster Bank* [1914] 3 KB 356. The same rule applies to the conversion of other documentary items of property, for example postal orders: *Fine Art Society v Union Bank of London* (1886) LR 17 QBD 705, and share certificates: *Solloway Mills & Co and ors v McLaughlin* [1938] AC 247.
[18] *OBG Ltd v Allan* [2008] 1 AC 1.

Bills of lading are documents which describe cargo. Three copies are made; one copy is retained by the person sending the cargo (the Consignor), one copy is kept by the captain of the vessel, the third copy is sent to the ultimate recipient of the goods (the Consignee). The underlying principle is that the Consignee presents their copy of the bill of lading to show their entitlement to receive the goods (the bill of lading represents the goods). The Consignee can sell the goods whilst they are in transit using the bill of lading as a document of title to transfer the goods (hence the bill of lading has a value equivalent to the value of the goods). It should be noted that in some states of the USA bills of lading are a negotiable instrument, in the UK the *nemo dat* rule applies and so in English law you have to prove ownership.

Goodwill of a business — this is the reasonable hope or expectation that customers would stay with, say, a shop if the business were transferred to new owners. This can be sold or transferred as a separate item (so one might sell the land or building, stock and goodwill).

Stocks & shares — these represent rights in relation to a company to participate in decisions, dividends or ultimately a share out of the liquidated assets.

Money — this also is an example of an exception to the *nemo dat* rule. If a thief steals money and uses the money to buy something in a shop, the shopkeeper has good title to the cash provided they are an innocent recipient.

Intellectual property — this includes patents, trademarks and copyright. Patents allow an inventor to protect rights in their invention for a maximum of 20 years from the date of grant of the patent (this is not necessarily true for certain medical patents that have to go through mandatory testing). Their time-limited monopoly allows the patent holder to decide what is done with the invention covered by the claims of the patent. The specification used in the application for grant becomes a public document and is available to the public at large. Trademarks are another example of a state granted right available through a registration process. They allow commercial entities protection against anyone else using identical or similar marks. Copyright is an unregistered right and subsists automatically in, amongst other things, literary, dramatic or musical works as soon as they are created. It allows the copyright holder to prevent others from copying the form of expression used for a period of time (life plus 70 years in the case of the works mentioned).

One thing that should be noted is that the examples listed above do not constitute a closed list of 'types' of property and that any such list would change with time and would depend on where in the world we were. Some centuries ago it was perfectly lawful to own human beings in the UK (until the Slave Trade Act was passed in 1807 and the Slavery Abolition Act in 1833); if you were to suggest it today most people would be rightly horrified. Other 'things' which society currently seeks to control include nuclear material, weapons and explosives; these all pose a threat to society if misused, so their acquisition, possession and transfer are tightly regulated. In this sense "ownership is not a necessary legal concept. The problem of ownership remains, but it is not a legal problem; it is the concern of the politician, the economist, the sociologist...".[19] So 'what' can be owned may change with time and the possession or use of various things may be regulated by society for a variety of reasons. Whilst such regulation may be most appropriately conducted through
Parliament, occasionally the courts must consider the boundaries of the 'what is property' question. Although there might be a general reluctance, new property rights are occasionally recognised; for example in *Armstrong DLW GmbH v Winnington Networks Ltd*[20] the right to property in carbon emission allowances was accepted.

The boundaries of what might be thought of as property are occasionally tested by academics too. Reference has already been made to Kevin Grey's article 'Property in Thin Air'[21] where the ability to exclude others from a resource was argued to be the boundary between property and non-property. Charles Reich wrote a very influential article 'The New Property'[22] which advocated that a right to state welfare payments or other forms of public largesse should be thought of as a right to property (as a mechanism to control the expansion of State power and to secure the independence of citizens).

---

[19] A.D. Hargreaves, *Modern Real Property* (1956) 19 Modern Law Review 14, at 17. See further ch 2, "Ownership".
[20] [2012] EWHC 10 (Ch).
[21] Supra n4.
[22] C. Reich, *The New Property*, (1964) 73 YLJ 733.

Harris was amongst those who rejected Reich's suggestion that welfare payments be tagged with a 'property' label; "'The New Property' was a catchy title for an article which highlighted important dangers of the wealth-allocating State. But it is possible to support any or all of Reich's remedial proposals without any expansion in the concept of property".[23] Just because something might be conceived of as 'property' does not necessarily mean that it is a good idea to do so.

Trade secrets are a particularly good example of some of the difficulties in *ad hoc* judicial redrawing of the categories of property and the use of proprietary language obscuring the legal situation. It no doubt stems from the interesting dichotomy in the way that confidential information is treated by the law on the one hand and the public at large on the other. Individuals with secrets invariably conceive of them as their own property. Companies with trade secrets view them in much the same way, as assets of the company which may be bought, sold or exploited in any manner of their choosing. Control over confidential information is often jealously guarded; if it is misappropriated in some way then the "owner" will often feel a sense of violation closely associated with a view that the information had been stolen. Indeed, Sir Edward Boyle MP, speaking to introduce his Industrial Information Bill to Parliament in 1968, said; "It is not too much to say that we live in a country where...the theft of the board room table is punished far more severely than the theft of board room secrets."[24]

In *Peter Pan Manufacturing Corporation v Corsets Silhouette*[25] the claimant disclosed various designs and manufacturing methods for lycra garments to the defendants whilst negotiating with them. After the negotiations had broken down, Corsets Silhouette started to use the information for their own business. It was held that the information was confidential and Peter Pan were given various remedies (an injunction to stop the defendants manufacturing from the claimant's designs and an order for delivery up of all the unlawfully manufactured stock and all profits which had been earned unlawfully). This was taken to show that confidential information is an item of intangible property; it has a value and can be protected.

---

[23] Supra n1 at 151.
[24] HC Deb 775, col 806, 13 December 1968.
[25] [1964] 1 WLR 96.

Judicial attempts to rationalise upholding duties of confidence with respect to certain information by applying a proprietary analysis (often where it was not needed at all) greatly shaped the debate. Of particular note is the case of *Boardman v Phipps*,[26] where a trustee had derived some benefit through the use of information which he had gained in his position as trustee. Lord Hodson was of the opinion that the nature of information did not necessarily preclude its being described as property. He thought that each case should depend on its own facts and he gave the example of know-how, which might constitute a valuable asset, as being property in a commercial sense.[27] Lord Guest also saw no reason why information and knowledge should not be trust property.[28] In a strong dissenting judgment though, Lord Upjohn acknowledged that confidential information was often treated as if it were property but that;[29] "the real truth is that it is not property in any normal sense but equity will restrain its transmission to another if in breach of some confidential relationship".

It is ironic that the majority decision in *Boardman v Phipps* is often cited as grounds for the proposition that confidential information can be property because the question of whether the information constituted trust property really need never have been considered. Mr Boardman had put himself in a position where there was the potential that a conflict could arise between his own interests and those of the trust. This in itself was a breach of his fiduciary responsibilities to the trust for which he was answerable.

The civil law of confidence was clarified soon afterwards. Confidential information is not protected *per se*, but a civil action is available, according to Megarry J in *Coco v A. N. Clark*[30], when three conditions are met; information having the necessary quality of confidence, which has been disclosed under circumstances giving rise to an obligation of confidence, is (or is anticipated to be) used or disclosed without authorisation to do so. The basis of the action is to restrain the breach of the duty of confidence, not to protect the 'property' in the information.

---

[26] [1967] 2 AC 46.
[27] Ibid at 107.
[28] Ibid at 115.
[29] Ibid at 127.
[30] [1969] RPC 41.

Despite the judicial uncertainty in the civil courts, the criminal courts do not regard information as constituting property. In the case of *Oxford v Moss*[31] an engineering student at the University of Liverpool gained access to an exam paper before the examination which he copied before returning the original paper. He had not stolen the physical property (the examination paper) as that had been returned. He was charged with stealing the information on the paper. He was found not guilty on a point of law. It was held that confidential information did not constitute "property" within the meaning of the Theft Act[32] and that for theft to be proven, the appropriation must be "with the intention of permanently depriving the other of it".[33] In this instance, the court was of the view that the University had not been permanently deprived of the information, since it still had what it started with. It would be interesting to see if a court would reach the same conclusion today since the broadening of the definition of theft under *R v Morris*[34], such that theft takes place if there is dishonest appropriation of *one* of the property rights of the owner.

The potential impact of the ruling in *Oxford v Moss* on the commercial world could be seen when it was followed in *R v Absolom*[35]. A geologist obtained and tried to sell geological information contained in a 'graphalog' to the rivals of the company who had already spent £13 million as the sole oil explorers in the area. The court was told that the information had a sale value of between £50,000 and £100,000. Although the judge found that the geologist had acted in 'utmost bad faith', he directed the jury that the graphalog information did not fall within the definition of property for the purposes of the criminal law. This was a case where the actions of the defendant were felt to be wholly wrong and direct criminal censure to deter others from acting in such a reprehensible way was conspicuously absent. The lack of criminal response was particularly felt to be unsatisfactory where civil actions were unlikely due to a defendant's lack of resources.

---

[31] (1978) 68 Cr App R 183 DC. A similar conclusion was reached by the Supreme Court of Canada in *Stewart v R* [1988] 58 DLR (4th) 1 which held that confidential information was not anything 'animate or inanimate' within the Canadian Criminal Code.
[32] Theft Act 1968 s 4(1) defines property as including money and all other property, real or personal, including things in action and other intangible property.
[33] Ibid s6(1).
[34] *R v Morris* [1983] 3 WLR 697.
[35] *R v Absolom* The Times, 14 September 1983.

More recently in *Fairstar Heavy Transport NV V Adkins*[36] Mummery LJ determined that there was no proprietary claim to the contents of some emails,[37] "(t)he claim to property in intangible information presents obvious definitional difficulties, having regard to the criteria of certainty, exclusivity, control and assignability that normally characterise property rights and distinguish them from personal rights".

Another area which exposes the dichotomy of public expectation and legal position is the law relating to 'ownership' of body parts. Whilst most people would intuitively assert that they owned their own bodies and any excised parts of their body, the starting point for the law in the UK (and much of the world) is that there are no property rights in the human body[38]. Partly this is a response to the abolition of slavery and the pervading view that owning humans (and likewise body parts) is an affront to human dignity. The legal status of the human body has developed *ad hoc* over many years and the sometimes inconsistent approach to the developing jurisprudence is a particular difficulty to those researching and developing new treatments in the field of medicine. The general position that there is no property in human bodies was confirmed to include living human body parts by the House of Lords in *R v Bentham*[39]. During an attempted robbery the defendant put his hand inside his zipped-up jacket with the material forced out by his hand to give the impression that he had a gun. The court decided he was not in possession of an imitation firearm within the meaning of section 17(2) of the Firearms Act 1968 because he had used his hand as the imitation firearm and he could not be in possession of his own hand.

One of the first exceptions to the idea that there could not be property in body parts was established in the Australian High Court case of *Doodeward v Spence*[40]. The Court held that the lawful exercise of work and skill used to preserve the two-headed foetus distinguished it from being a mere corpse and so founded a proprietary right of possession to the person who performed the preservation process allowing them to keep it.

---

[36] [2013] EWCA Civ 886
[37] Ibid at [47].
[38] See *R v Lynn* (1788) 2 TR 733; *R v Sharpe* (1857) Dears & B 160; *R v Price* [1884] 12 QBD 247; *Dobson v North Tyneside Health Authority* [1996] EWCA Civ 1301.
[39] *R v Bentham* [2005] UKHL 18.
[40] *Doodeward v Spence* [1908] HCA 45.

This idea that bodies or elements of them might be capable of becoming property if sufficient work or skill changed them in some way was considered in an American case, *Moore v Regents of the University of California*[41]. Mr Moore brought a claim after finding out that the doctors treating him for cancer of the spleen, together with other researchers, had applied for and been granted a patent over a cell line developed from tissue removed from him during treatment. Whilst observing that granting property rights to Mr Moore would hinder research by restricting access to the necessary raw materials, the court held that the patent was "factually and legally distinct from the cells taken from Moore's body"[42]. Whilst Mr Moore had neither rights over the tissue taken from him, nor the patent developed from access to that tissue, the researchers could lawfully obtain property rights (the patent) over the cell line developed.

This formulation of the exception to the general prohibition of property rights in body parts found its way into UK law in *R v Kelly*[43] where it was held that excised human body parts could be property for the purposes of the Theft Act 1968 if they had been changed due to the application of skill in processes of dissection and preservation. This position was more recently revisited in *Yearworth v North Bristol NHS Trust*[44]. Faced with the prospect of damaged fertility from proposed courses of chemotherapy, six men produced sperm samples which were frozen and stored by the hospital undertaking their treatment as an insurance against any treatment effects on their fertility. (The hospital held the relevant regulatory licence under the Human Fertilisation and Embryology Act 1990.) However, the hospital failed to maintain the storage facility correctly and the sperm samples were destroyed. The claimants brought negligence claims against the hospital and in order to prove one strand of their claim they had to prove that their sperm was property (in order to satisfy the requirement for loss of property). Lord Judge LCJ observed that advances in medical science require a re-analysis of the common law's approach to the ownership of human body parts and products of living bodies. He accepted that the processing and storage of the sperm met the change of attribute requirement due to application of skill but was:[45]

---

[41] *Moore v Regents of the University of California* (1990) 51 Cal. 3d 120.
[42] 51 Cal. 3d 120 at 141.
[43] [1999] 2 WLR 384.
[44] *Yearworth v North Bristol NHS Trust* [2009] EWCA Civ 37.
[45] Ibid at [45].

"...not content to see the common law in this area founded upon the principle in *Doodeward*, which was devised as an exception to a principle, itself of exceptional character, relating to the ownership of a human corpse. Such ancestry does not commend it as a solid foundation. Moreover, a distinction between the capacity to own body parts or products which have, and which have not, been subject to the exercise of work or skill is not entirely logical."

The Court took a broader view and held that, for the purposes of their claims in negligence, the men owned the sperm which they had produced. The men had generated it from their bodies solely so that it might be used at some later time for their own benefit. Following on from this the Court held that there was a bailment between the men and the Trust.

In *Yearworth* the Court made it clear that its decision relating to the existence of property interests was confined to the specific circumstances of the case, but the judgment undoubtedly demonstrates that prohibition against owning body parts or products is not absolute.

As we saw earlier, property rights exist in many different situations and perform different functions. When asserting that I own my watch I am (probably) unable to assert all the rights that exist over it. The exact nature of the rights that a proprietor may be able to claim will obviously depend on the nature of the acquisition of the 'thing' (*nemo dat*) but will also depend on the usual use or enjoyment or nature of that 'thing'. For example, in the context of land, section 205 (1)(ix) of the Law of Property Act 1925 defines land very broadly to include mines and minerals as well as any buildings that are physically on the land. However, what are the normal limits of physical control over this? When enquiring what rights a landowner has to the land, reference is often made to the judgment of Sir William James V-C in *Corbett v Hill*[46]; "now the ordinary rule of law is, that whoever has got the *solum* - whoever has got the site - is the owner of everything up to the sky and down to the centre of the earth". This may be all very well in theory but in practice what are the limits to a landowner's enjoyment of their land? Sir William James did allow[47] "(b)ut that ordinary presumption of law, no doubt, is frequently rebutted, particularly with regard to property in towns". In

---

[46] (1870) LR 9 Eq 671
[47] Ibid at 673.

Bernstein v Skyviews & General Ltd.[48] Griffiths J thought that a reasonable balance between landowner and public access to airspace above the land to allow overflight by aeroplanes was stuck by construing the right of the landowner as a right "to such height as is necessary for the ordinary use and enjoyment of his land and the structures upon it"[49]. (The overflight of land is also authorised by section 76(1) of the Civil Aviation Act 1982.) However, a sign projecting into the airspace above land can be a trespass to that land[50] (even though it does not touch it)[51]. Likewise an interference with the subsoil or strata below land will be an actionable trespass to land. In *Star Energy v Bocardo*[52] drilling horizontally under another's land even at substantial depths (such that it was not in practical terms interfering with the landowner's use or enjoyment of the land) was an actionable trespass. That is not to say that no drilling can take place under another's land. The Coal Industry Act 1994 and the Petroleum Act 1998 are examples of a statute that reserves rights in underground resources for the Crown. The government is thus enabled to sell licences for the extraction of the specific resource (which belongs to the Crown rather than the landowner). More recently, in order to facilitate fracking, the Infrastructure Act 2015 was passed. Section 43(1) grants a statutory right of access to drill under 'deep-level' land (over 300 metres deep) to enable extraction of shale gas or deep geothermal energy. This right allows for drilling, boring, fracturing or otherwise altering the deep-level land, installing infrastructure and removing any substances without the overlying landowner's consent.

---

[48] [1978] QB 479
[49] Ibid at 488.
[50] *Kelsen v Imperial Tobacco Co. Ltd.* [1957] 2 QB 334.
[51] One question that the law will need to answer in due course concerns the legal reaction to the phenomenon of drones (low altitude flying machines controlled by land-based controls). At the moment there is only regulation of commercial drones (weighing over 20kg).
[52] [2010] UKSC 35.

Chapter 2

OWNERSHIP, ITS REGULATION AND ITS FRAGMENTATION[53]

In our everyday language, when we talk about property, we commonly use the term "ownership". Celia may say, "I own this watch"," I own this desk", "I own this money", "I own the house where I live". Let us examine the latter statement, about ownership of the house. It might mean that Celia owns the house without any limit of time, ie, for ever; but many houses are owned on a very long lease, typically 900 or even 999 years.[54] Any lease must begin on a particular date, and therefore, according to its length, will end on a particular date, which may be long in the future. By contrast, an apartment or flat will typically be held on a much shorter lease, and a student let may well be for just one year. Between these two extremes, many business premises are held on a lease for 7 or 8 years.

These examples demonstrate that time (or duration) is an ingredient in the concept of ownership, in contrast to our everyday assumption that ownership lasts for ever. Further ingredients can be identified. The simple sounding statement, "I own this house" or "I own this watch", contains a number of elements which can be distinguished one from another. Firstly, Celia asserts that no one in the world can successfully challenge her right to the item, and therefore she can recover the item, or its value, from anyone who takes it without her consent. Secondly, she asserts that she can use and possess the item (or even destroy it). Thirdly, she asserts that she can dispose of the item, during her lifetime by sale or gift, or, since her ownership will last for ever, on her death. Thus, there are several different rights contained in the concept of ownership, and ownership can be described as a bundle of rights; the process

---

[53] The classic account is Professor Honoré's essay, "Ownership", in A. G. Guest (ed), *Oxford Essays in Jurisprudence* (1961), p. 107. Honoré defines ownership as "the greatest possible interest in a thing which a mature legal system recognises" and defines the elements of ownership as "the right to possess, the right to manage, the right to the income of the thing, the right to the capital, the right to security, the rights or incidents of transmissibility and absence of term, the prohibition of harmful use, liability to execution, and the incident of residuarity."
Some commentators would have us believe that there is no room in English law for the concept of ownership; see the discussion in Green and Randall, *The Tort of Conversion*, pp. 80 *et seq*. This is not the place to debate the issue; the present authors can say only that they disagree.

[54] In Sheffield, in many cases, the great landed estates, for example those of the Duke of Norfolk and the Duke of Devonshire, own the freehold out of which the long residential leases are derived.

of separating those various rights into different people is termed "fragmentation of ownership".

However, before fragmentation of ownership is examined in detail, it needs to be observed that the right to the use and possession of an item of property is not in all cases unrestricted. The law regulates in many different ways the use and possession of different kinds of property. Take firstly the use of land. The common law tort of private nuisance seeks to prevent the unreasonable use of a piece of land causing substantial interference with the enjoyment of neighbouring land. Examples are nuisance by creating excessive noise or noxious odours, by interfering with an easement, such as a right of way, or by overhanging tree branches. There are also statutes which control some aspects of the use of land, such as the clean air legislation, commencing with the Clean Air Act 1956[55], and legislation controlling the height of hedges.[56] The most comprehensive system controlling the use of land has been created by the town and country planning legislation, commencing with the Town and Country Planning Act 1947.[57] Subject to exceptions, any development of land, including any material change of use, requires planning permission granted by the local planning authority. So comprehensive is this system of control that, following the Act of 1947, some commentators put forward an extreme argument that the ownership of land had been abolished, replaced by ownership of the current use. That argument was firmly rejected by the House of Lords in *Belfast Corporation* v *O D Cars Ltd*.[58] The decision was that the statutory restrictions on the use and development of land were regulatory only, and did not amount to a deprivation of ownership. They therefore did not breach constitutional principles designed to prevent the State from "taking" property from its owner, and did not trigger a general constitutional requirement to pay compensation on a taking.[59]

In the case of property other than land, there are many situations where the law restricts the use, or even the possession, of an item of property. Examples abound. There are age restrictions on the sale of alcohol and tobacco products.

---

[55] See now the Clean Air Act 1993.
[56] See Part 8 of the Anti-Social Behaviour Act 2003.
[57] See now the Town and Country Planning Act 1990 (as amended). There is a huge body of law on this subject; *The Encyclopaedia of Planning Law* runs to six loose-leaf volumes.
[58] [1960] AC 490. See the excellent analysis of various philosophies of land ownership in Gray and Gray, *Elements of Land Law* (5th edition), para 11.2.
[59] See ch 3, Magna Carta (1215); Art 1, First Protocol, European Convention on Human Rights.

The use or possession of dangerous drugs is a criminal offence, and the drugs may be forfeited.[60] The use of motor vehicles on public highways is regulated in many different ways, for example by the requirement that the driver is licensed after passing a driving test, that the vehicle is covered by a road fund licence, that the driver is covered by third party insurance, and that the vehicle is driven within speed limits. A final example is the control of the use of certain firearms, with age restrictions and the requirement to obtain a firearms certificate.

What all of this demonstrates is that the law's regulation of the use or possession of various items of property is perfectly compatible with a person's ownership of that property. Ownership is, in such cases, a residual concept.

Now let us examine in detail fragmentation of ownership, starting with the idea that ownership lasts for ever. The situation is in fact not so simple. In the case of both land and other property, ownership can be divided into segments of time. We have already seen that, in the case of land, the owner can create a lease for a certain duration of time. She can also create a tenancy for a period of time, a week, a month, a quarter, a year, which will automatically continue from one period to another until terminated by notice to quit. It is also possible to create a lease of indefinite duration, a tenancy at will. Such a tenancy can be terminated by either party at any time without notice, and will terminate automatically if either party disposes of her rights.[61] A lessee can create a sublease, for any period of time less than the original lease. The original owner's rights are termed a fee simple: "fee" meaning rights that can be inherited, "simple" meaning that the rights are unqualified and can be inherited by anyone. But that is not all. Celia as fee simple owner can transfer rights of use and possession to a person for her lifetime, "To Helen for life". Further, it was possible, until 1997[62], to transfer the rights to a person and her lineal descendants: a fee tail estate or entailed interest.

In land law the accepted terminology for these interests of varying length is "an estate in land" (an estate in fee simple or freehold estate, a leasehold estate, a life estate or life interest, and a fee tail estate, or entailed interest). In personal property the accepted terminology is ownership, out of which may

---

[60] S 27, Misuse of Drugs Act 1971.
[61] For other species of lease or tenancy see Megarry and Wade, *The Law of Real Property* (7th edition), paras 17-079 *et seq*.
[62] Sch 1, para 5(1), Trusts of Land and Appointment of Trustees Act 1996.

be created a life interest, and out of which it was in the past possible to create an entailed interest.[63] With tangible personal property (chattels) it is also possible in another way to sever ownership and possession. Take a simple example: Celia lends her book to Helen, or a student borrows a book from the University library. The transaction is called a bailment, the transfer of possession but not ownership, and it may be for a definite period of time, or indefinitely (a bailment at will). It may be for a consideration (contractual) or gratuitous. The concept of a bailment covers a wide variety of scenarios; for example, leaving clothes to be dry cleaned, depositing furniture to be stored while moving house, hiring a car for a holiday, loaning an old master painting for display in an exhibition, renting a mobile telephone, or depositing an item as security for a loan.

Since a bailment involves the transfer of possession but not ownership, it follows that the original owner (the bailor) has retained ownership, but her ownership is reduced by the transfer of possession. Her ownership is now described as being in reversion, because the right of possession will in time revert to her; she has a reversionary interest.

The reversionary interest on a bailment is a proprietary interest in its own right. If the chattel is damaged by negligence during the course of the bailment, the owner (the bailor) may recover compensation for any long term damage affecting the reversionary interest.[64] The benefit of a bailment may be assigned as a chose in action, unless assignment is precluded by the terms of a contract. [65] A bailee, with the authority of the bailor, may create a sub-bailment.[66] The reversionary interest may be transferred to another person. The question then arises whether the transferee takes subject to the bailment. Surprisingly, there is no definitive answer to that question. The consensus of opinion among the commentators is that a bailment does create a proprietary interest binding on the transferee, at least in the case of long-term leases of

---

[63] From 1 January 1926 to 31 December 1996: s 130(1), Law of Property Act 1925; sch 1, para 5(1), Trusts of Land and Appointment of Trustees Act 1996.
[64] *Mears v LSW Railway Co* (1862) 11 CBNS 850.
[65] Such a contractual term is valid: *Linden Gardens Trust Ltd v Lenesta Sludge Disposals Ltd* [1994] AC 85.
[66] See, for example, *Morris v C W Martin & Sons Ltd* [1965] 2 All ER 725, where the claimant deposited her fur with a furrier for cleaning. With her consent he sub-contracted the work to the respondent company, who specialised in such work. The company thus became a sub-bailee. The fur was stolen by the company's employee to whom the cleaning work was entrusted. The Court of Appeal held that the company owed a duty of care directly to the claimant and was vicariously liable for its employee's theft.

chattels.[67] Such leases are common in the case of cars, ships, aircraft, office equipment and railway rolling stock. It is not clear where or on what basis the dividing line between short-term and long-term bailments could be drawn.

It is clear that a pledge, or pawn, does create a proprietary interest. A pledge is a deposit of a chattel as security for a loan. Suppose, for example, that Celia owns a gold watch worth £1,000 but is short of immediate cash. She may arrange with David a loan of £500 for 6 months at an interest rate of 20%, secured by the deposit of the watch. Celia retains a reversionary interest, now comprising her right to redeem the watch on payment of £600, and she may transfer that interest subject to the pledge. David has a power of sale in default of payment according to the contractual terms, so that, if Celia defaults, David may sell the watch. He has a duty to obtain the best price reasonably obtainable. If he sells the watch for its original value of £1,000, he will hold the surplus (£400 less the expenses of the sale) subject to a duty to account to Celia (or her successor).[68]

In all cases where the owner of property creates a right of possession which is limited in time, such as a life interest, a lease or tenancy, or a bailment, the owner (Celia) therefore retains her residual rights of ownership Alternatively, Celia may fully dispose of her ownership, but by creating a limited interest followed by a disposition of her residual rights. For example, Celia may give her land to Rachel for life, and then to Sarah in fee simple. Rachel is said to have a life interest in possession, and Sarah is said to have the fee simple in remainder, because the fee simple remains away from Celia. If the disposition were to Rachel for life, then to her daughter Hannah for life, and then to Sarah in fee simple, Rachel would have a life interest in possession, Hannah a life interest in remainder, and Sarah the fee simple in remainder.

The same kind of thinking applies to the creation of leases and subleases. Suppose that Celia, the fee simple owner, grants a lease for 100 years to Rachel, and that Rachel then grants a lease for 50 years to Sarah. Celia now has a fee simple in reversion, but Rachel also has a reversion, the residue of her original 100 year lease: there is a freehold reversion vested in Rachel and a leasehold reversion vested in Sarah.

---

[67] There is a very useful summary of the present position in Smith, *Plural Ownership*, pp. 211-212.
[68] This is an example of overreaching, considered in ch 6 : Celia's right to the watch is converted by David's sale into a right to the surplus money.

23

There is an important distinction between vested and contingent interests in property. For an interest to be vested the owner of that interest must stand ready to take that interest as soon as any prior interest has come to an end, without satisfying any condition. For example, if land is given to Rachel for life and then to Sarah in fee simple, both Rachel and Sarah have an interest which is vested; Rachel's life interest is vested in possession, and Sarah's fee simple is vested in remainder. A reversion is necessarily vested. But suppose that the disposition is to Rachel for life if she reaches the age of 25. Rachel in that case has an interest which is contingent (or conditional) on her reaching the specified age. It is subject to a condition precedent. Her interest will vest when she reaches that age. Or the condition may be a condition subsequent. For example, the property may be transferred to Rachel immediately, but if she fails to reach the age of 25 then it shall go to Louise. The result is that Rachel has an immediate vested interest, but subject to the possibility that it might be divested. Take another example. Suppose that Celia transfers property to all her children, whenever born, who reach the age of 21. The result is that, when her first child reaches the age of 21, that child will acquire a vested interest in the whole property. Yet the possibility exists that another child, or other children, may reach that age, and each such child will then acquire a vested interest. If, for example, three of Rachel's siblings reach the age of 21, the four children will each receive a quarter share. So, before that event, Rachel may be described as having an interest which is vested subject to the possibility of being partially divested

Reversions and remainders are proprietary interests in their own right, and may be transferred in familiar ways. They may be described as future interests, since they confer a right of possession in the future, but they are also existing rights: they are, therefore, present rights to future possession.

So far, this analysis of ownership has focused on the element of time. Another element is the power of disposition: the owner of the property may dispose of the property, or of her interest in it, in any way that the law recognises. Indeed, so strong is the link between ownership and the power of disposition that some attempts to exclude that power are held void. A blanket exclusion is certainly void, but a partial restraint may be valid, depending on the extent of the restraint. The distinction is not very clearly defined in the case law. We can be certain that a condition that the owner shall not dispose of the property to Alan (one individual in the whole world) would be held valid. In a borderline case the court has upheld a restriction on disposition to four sisters or their children.[69] These principles were mainly worked out in relation to dispositions of land, but, as would be expected, they apply equally to dispositions of personal property.[70]

The position is different in relation to leases and tenancies. There, the lessor's continuing interest in the land is considered sufficient to allow her to control any assignment of the lease or the grant of a sublease. Disposition may be completely prohibited, or, typically, to any person only with the lessor's consent, which statute modifies to provide that the consent may not be unreasonably withheld.[71] Even so, a disposition in defiance of such a restriction is valid and effective, though it may amount to a breach of covenant and may trigger a forfeiture clause included in the lease.[72]

The position is different again in relation to assignments of a chose in action. Assignment may be validly excluded, and the result is to exclude completely the power of disposition.[73]

It is possible to separate the power of disposition from ownership. This may be achieved by creating a power of appointment or a discretionary trust. Suppose that Celia gives property to Rachel and then to such persons as Rachel shall appoint. This is an example of a general power of appointment: Rachel may give the property to any person in the world, including herself. It is the equivalent of absolute ownership. If the power is to appoint to any person whom Rachel shall by her will appoint, it is still regarded as a general power of appointment, but Rachel may give the property to any person in the world other than herself. The power may be more restricted, for example to such of her children as Rachel shall appoint. This is a special power of appointment. Slightly different is a discretionary trust, where property is transferred to trustees who are given a discretion to decide who, from within a restricted class, shall be the beneficiary, or beneficiaries, of the trust.

---

[69] *Doe d Gill v Pearson* (1805) 6 East 173. See also *Re Macleay* (1875) LR 20 Eq 186, where a condition that the owner should never sell the property out of the family was held valid. There are other situations where a condition is void as contrary to public policy, for example a condition in restraint of marriage; for a full discussion see Megarry and Wade, op cit, paras 3-056 *et seq*.
[70] See, for example, *Re Hewett* [1918] 1 Ch 458; *Re Borwick* [1933] Ch 657; *Re Tegg* [1936] 2 All ER 878.
[71] S 19(1), Landlord and Tenant Act 1927.
[72] *Old Grovebury Manor Farm Ltd* v *W Seymour Plant Sales and Hire Ltd (No 2)* [1979] 1 WLR 1397.
[73] *Linden Gardens Trust Ltd* v *Lenesta Sludge Disposals Ltd* [1994] AC 85.

One final example of fragmentation. Houses and other property are commonly bought with the aid of a loan secured on the property. This means that, if the loan is not repaid according to its contractual terms, the lender will be able to take action against the property, typically by selling the property. The secured lender therefore has, to the extent of the value of the property, priority over unsecured creditors in the event of the borrower's insolvency. In the case of land, the type of security will be a mortgage or charge.[74] What about the purchase of major domestic items, such as furniture, washing machines or cookers?

The favoured loan vehicle is a credit sale or hire-purchase. Hire-purchase illustrates many of the present themes and is therefore considered here.[75] The essence is that the seller of the goods sells them to a finance company, which then hires (bails) the goods to the purchaser, who is granted an option to purchase the goods after paying the hire charges, which are calculated to equal the purchase price plus the agreed rate of interest. The economic, or functional, effect of the transaction is to bring about a sale of the goods, coupled with a secured loan in favour of the finance company. However, the legal effect is wholly different: the purchaser has only the benefit of a bailment until the option to purchase is exercised on full payment. Therefore, the goods cannot be sold; the only right that the purchaser has is a contractual right to the bailment, which can be assigned as a chose in action, unless the power of assignment is excluded, which is commonly the case.[76] In that event, the finance company's hold over the goods is complete.[77]

So, we can conclude that the notion of ownership is by no means as simple as might appear. On the contrary, owing to the various means of regulation and the different means of fragmentation, it is fairly complex.[78]

---

[74] Considered in more detail in ch 4, "The Contribution of Equity", under the heading "The equity of redemption".
[75] Note: hire-purchase, and *not* higher purchase, as sometimes seen in examination scripts!
[76] Such an exclusion is valid: *Linden Gardens Trust Ltd* v *Lenesta Sludge Disposals Ltd* [1994] AC 85.
[77] See, however, the protection of a private purchaser of a motor vehicle, considered in ch 6, "Protection of the Purchaser".
[78] There are further instances of fragmentation: co-ownership, incumbrances, title, and legal estates and equitable interests, which are considered elsewhere in this book.

Chapter 3

POSSESSION AND TITLE

If Celia says that she owns a book, implicit in that statement is a claim that there is no one in the world who can successfully challenge her ownership, and that, therefore, she can recover the book, or its value, from anyone who takes it without her consent. However, if she brought a court action against a person who did wrongfully acquire the book, for example a thief, how could she prove her ownership? It is unlikely that she would have any documentary evidence. Exceptionally, there are some items of property where a register of ownership or of provenance is kept. Such items include ships, aircraft, thoroughbred racehorses, old master paintings, and valuable pieces of furniture and silver. Those examples are truly exceptional. In the ordinary case of Celia and her book, her verbal evidence will have to suffice. She might be able to say, for example, that she bought the book from a respectable bookshop, and she might even have a receipt to prove that transaction. If the book was a used copy when she bought it, she might be able to say that she bought it from a fellow student or in a car boot sale. She might be able to say that her father gave it to her. None of these statements, however, proves an irrefutable title. It is possible, for example, that the book was stolen at some point in its devolution through to Celia. However, a vital factor is that she had undisturbed possession of the book; the result is that anyone who disputes the lawfulness of her possession has to prove the unlawfulness of that possession The hypothetical theft therefore fades from view. As the everyday phrase has it, "possession is nine parts of the law".

Much the same would be true if Celia wished to sell her book. The buyer would have to be satisfied with whatever verbal evidence Celia could give to prove her ownership. However, a condition is implied into the sale contract that Celia has a right to sell the book, and the buyer will have contractual remedies if it turns out that Celia's claim to ownership is in some way defective.[79]

---

[79] S 12(1), Sale of Goods Act 1979. A breach may affect the seller quite drastically: for examples see *Rowland v Divall* [1923] 2 KB 500; *Warman v Southern Counties Car Finance Corp Ltd* [1949] 2 KB 576.

Proof of ownership of land is somewhat different. Firstly, there is normally a documentary title.[80] Secondly, there is a major distinction between registered and unregistered land. Let us take unregistered land first. If Celia wishes to sell her house in the unregistered system, she needs, in the first place, to prove her title to the legal estate, freehold or leasehold, by producing title deeds going back at least 15 years.[81] For example, she may produce a deed by which the fee simple was conveyed on sale by Alan to Brian in 1980, followed by a deed of gift by which the fee simple was transferred by Brian to Celia in 2010. That title is by no means irrefutable; it could, for example, be affected by some kind of fraud in either of the transfers. 15 years is no more than the blink of an eye in the history of a piece of land. Celia's undisturbed possession since she bought the house is again a vital factor, meaning that her ownership is presumed in the absence of proof to the contrary. Celia is said to have a good marketable title, any theoretical risks being ignored. Of course, a purchaser will also be concerned to ascertain whether any incumbrances or other burdens affect the property. Some burdens may be revealed by the title deeds. Beyond that it is the purchaser's task to search the land charges register and the local land charges register, and she will be bound by any interests there registered.[82] A prudent purchaser will also physically inspect the property and make inquiries of any person found to be in occupation, seeking to discover whether there are any informally created interests affecting the property.[83] Unless the contract between Celia and the purchaser provides otherwise, the purchaser's task will be aided by two duties of disclosure imposed on Celia: (1) to disclose, before the contract, any latent (ie, non-apparent) defects in her title, and (2) to disclose after the contract any latent and irremovable incumbrances.

---

[80] A title to land may also be acquired solely by adverse possession: see pp. 32-33 later in this chapter.
[81] S 44, Law of Property Act 1925, as amended by s 23, Law of Property Act 1969.
[82] However, a purchaser is protected against land charges by the result of an official search: s 10(4), Land Charges Act 1972. Therefore, a registered charge not revealed by an official search will not bind the purchaser, leaving the defeated owner of the charge to seek damages for negligence against the Chief Land Registrar: see *Ministry of Housing and Local Government* v *Sharp* [1970] 2 QB 223. Compare the position with respect to local land charges, where an official search does not defeat the charge but gives the purchaser a right to statutory compensation: s 10, Local Land Charges Act 1975.
[83] *Hunt* v *Luck* [1902] 1 Ch 428. Any unregistrable equitable interests will be defeated by a purchaser for value of the legal estate who has made all reasonable inquiries and has no knowledge of those interests, ie, a purchaser without notice.

If Celia has no reason to doubt her title to the land, she is likely to sell "with full title guarantee", which means, in summary, that she guarantees that she has the right to dispose of the land free from all incumbrances, other than those to which the transfer is expressly made subject, and those of which she neither knew nor could reasonably be expected to know.[84] Alternatively, Celia may sell "with limited title guarantee", in which case her liability for incumbrances is limited to those which she has created, or allowed to be created, since the last disposition for value.[85]

Celia's sale of the land, with unregistered title, will now trigger a requirement of first registration.[86] The purchaser from Celia of the legal estate, freehold or leasehold, will be registered as the proprietor of that estate, and incumbrances affecting that estate will be protected on the register. Transactions thereafter will be by reference to the register. However, some interests in the land are not required to be registered. These are known colloquially as overriding interests, but there is a distinction between those interests which override first registration[87] and those interests which override a registered disposition.[88]

The registration of the purchaser as the proprietor of the legal estate, freehold or leasehold, will actually vest that estate in its proprietor, thus overcoming any previous defects in the title.[89] Even so, the registered title is not indefeasible, because the register can be altered in order to keep the register up to date or to correct a mistake.[90] Some alterations may be fairly innocuous, such as the correction of a name or an address. However, the power of alteration goes further, so as to embrace situations where the alteration prejudicially affects the title of the registered proprietor. The Land Registration Act 2002 calls such an alteration "rectification".[91] Particular protection against rectification is given to a registered proprietor in possession; there shall be no rectification unless the registered proprietor has consented,

---

[84] Ss 1-6, Law of Property (Miscellaneous Provisions) Act 1994.
[85] S 3(3), Law of Property (Miscellaneous Provisions) Act 1994.
[86] S 4(1)(a)(i), Land Registration Act 2002. S 4 contains a list of transactions with a legal estate which will trigger first registration. A striking exception is the grant of a lease for a term not exceeding seven years, or the assignment of a lease having not more than seven years to run at the date of the assignment. Such a lease does not trigger first registration, and will override first registration of the title to the reversion and the registered disposition of that title.
[87] S 11(4) and (5), and Sch 1, Land Registration Act 2002.
[88] S 29(2) and Sch 3, Land Registration Act 2002.
[89] Ss 11 and 12, Land Registration Act 2002.
[90] S 65 and Sch 4, Land Registration Act 2002.
[91] Sch 4, para 1.

or he has caused or substantially contributed to the mistake by his fraud or lack of proper care, or it would be unjust for any other reason for the rectification not to be made.[92]

If a mistake is established and rectification is ordered, the registered proprietor will be compensated for his loss, unless he has by fraud or lack of proper care caused or substantially contributed to the loss. Alternatively, if a mistake is established but the register is not rectified, the disappointed claimant will be compensated for the loss, unless the loss was wholly or partially caused by his fraud or lack of proper care.[93]

Celia has a legal remedy if the book, or any other chattel, is wrongfully taken from her; similarly, if she is unlawfully dispossessed of any of her land. In the case of a chattel she may sue the wrongdoer in the tort of conversion. In the case of land she has an action for the recovery of land. In neither case is it necessary for her to prove ownership of the property, in the sense of having rights against the whole world. She need only prove that she has a right to immediate possession against the alleged wrongdoer. The respondent cannot rely on a plea that some third party has a better right to possession than Celia (a jus tertii).[94] This leads to the concept of relative title: Celia may have a better title than the alleged wrongdoer, but some third party may have a better title than Celia.

An immediate right to possession will usually be proved by Celia's possession of the property immediately before the alleged wrongdoing.[95] This is extended, however, to include a right to recover possession under a bailment at will (which may be terminated at any time without notice), and presumably the reversion on a tenancy at will (which may be similarly terminated). Any possessory title[96] which Celia may have can be transferred in exactly the same

---

[92] Sch 4, para 6(2). Note the remarkable four negatives involved in para 6(2)(b)!
[93] Sch 8, para, 5(1). Where the loss was caused partly by the claimant's own lack of proper care, the indemnity will be reduced proportionately: ibid, para 5(2).
[94] There is a limited exception in the case of chattels, created by s 8(1), Torts (Interference with Goods) Act 1977, supplemented by rule 19.5A , Supreme Court Rules: the alleged wrongdoer may name a third party believed to have a better title than Celia and may join that person as a party to the action. The purpose is to avoid multiplicity of claims and to avoid the alleged wrongdoer being held liable to more than one claimant.
[95] Even possession apparently obtained dishonestly will found a claim: *Costello* v *Chief Constable of Derbyshire Constabulary* [2001] 1 WLR 1437 (summarised in Appendix 1).
[96] A possessory title is one of the four classes of title which may be granted to the proprietor of registered land: ss 9(1) and 10(1), Land Registration Act 2002.

way as full ownership. She may, for example, dispose of it by way of sale[97] or gift, and it will pass under her will or on intestacy.[98]

The importance of possession is reinforced by provisions contained in the Limitation Act 1980. There is a time limit within which an action for the recovery of property must be commenced, six years in the case of chattels[99], twelve years in the case of land.[100] Time never runs in favour of a thief, but will run in favour of a person who buys a chattel in good faith from a thief.[101] Time usually runs from the date of the alleged wrongdoing.[102] When the relevant time limit has expired, the claimant's title is extinguished.[103]

If, while the relevant period of limitation is still running, the alleged wrongdoer disposes of his title, the person acquiring that title can add his own period of possession to that of the first alleged wrongdoer. So, for example, if Brian dispossesses Celia of her land, remains in possession for eight years and then sells his title to David, Celia's claim will be barred, and her title extinguished, after four more years. Similarly, if Brian after eight years is dispossessed by David, Celia's claim will again be barred, and her title extinguished, after four more years. However, in this case, Brian still has a claim against David, and the limitation period against Brian has eight more years to run.

All of this applies without qualification to unregistered land, and originally applied also to registered land. However, Parliament, in enacting the Land Registration Act 2002, decided that, for the future, a greater degree of protection should be conferred on the proprietors of registered titles. The Limitation Act 1980 no longer applies to registered titles. Instead, the Land Registration Act contains a substantially new scheme[104], which may be described as follows. If Brian dispossesses Celia of her land and remains in adverse possession for ten years, he may then apply to be registered as

---

[97] Where Celia knows or suspects that her title to a chattel may be imperfect, she may contract to sell only such title as she or a third party may have: s 12(3)-(5), Sale of Goods Act 1979.
[98] Asher v Whitlock (1865) LR 1 QB 1; Perry v Clissold [1907] AC 731; Wheeler v Baldwin (1934) 52 CLR 629; Allen v Roughley (1955) CLR 98.
[99] S 2, Limitation Act 1980.
[100] S 15(1).
[101] S 4.
[102] The position is different where the claimant has a future interest at the date of the alleged wrongdoing: s 15(2) (land), and also where the claimant, at that date, is a minor or is of unsound mind: ss 28 and 38(2).
[103] S 17 (land).
[104] Ss 96-98 and Sch 6, Land Registration Act 2002.

proprietor in place of Celia. The Chief Land Registrar will notify Celia and any other interested party (for example, a mortgagee or a landlord) of Brian's application. There is then an opportunity to serve a counter-notice objecting to Brian's application. If no counter-notice is served, Brian is entitled to be registered as proprietor in place of Celia. If, on the other hand, a counter-notice is served, Brian's application must be rejected unless he satisfies one of the following three conditions:

(1) he is entitled to the benefit of a proprietary estoppel, which would make it unconscionable for Celia to seek to dispossess Brian;

(2) he is for some other reason entitled to be registered as proprietor;

(3) he is the owner of adjacent land and he, or his predecessor(s) in title, reasonably believed that the land in question belonged to him (or them), ie, the question is about defining the boundary.[105]

If Brian satisfies one of these conditions, he is entitled to be registered as proprietor. If he does not, he may apply again after being in adverse possession for two more years, and this time his application will succeed; the effect is that Celia is given two years' notice that she must evict Brian if his application is to be defeated.

In calculating these two periods of adverse possession, a successor in title (for example, a donee or purchaser) may add on his period of adverse possession to that of Brian. This replicates the position under the Limitation Act 1980. However, a person who unlawfully dispossesses Brian and acquires adverse possession is not a successor in title of Brian, and may not add on his period of adverse possession to that of Brian.[106] This differs from the position under the Limitation Act 1980.

In *Best v The Chief Land Registrar*[107] the Court of Appeal had to consider whether, following section 144 of the Legal Aid, Sentencing and Punishment of Offenders Act 2012, (which outlawed being in a residential building as a squatter while living or intending to live there having entered as a trespasser), a person committing a criminal offence under the Act could still acquire the land through adverse possession. The Court found that section 144 had been

---

[105] This accords with the "general boundaries" rule in s 60, Land Registration Act 2002.
[106] Sch 6, para 11(2), Land Registration Act 2002.
[107] [2015] EWCA Civ 17.

introduced to deal with the problem of short-term squatting and, had Parliament intended to interfere with the operation of the law on adverse possession, then that point would have been expressly dealt with by the Act. The Court found that the strong public policy reasons for allowing land to be acquired through long-term adverse possession (preventing land becoming stagnant and 'falling out of ownership') outweighed the concern that individuals might benefit from their own wrongdoing in acquiring the land.

APPENDIX 1

The Finding Cases

Finding a chattel which belongs to another person is a striking example of acquiring title by taking possession.[108] The basic proposition has been clarified and refined in a sequence of reported cases stretching back to 1722. The principal cases are presented here mainly in chronological order, since they well demonstrate the process of following and distinguishing precedent.

The foundation case is *Armory* v *Delamirie*[109]. The claimant was a boy who found a jewelled ring in another person's house. He took it to a goldsmith, the respondent, who removed the stones. The claimant was held entitled to be compensated for the value of the stones. Pratt CJKB ruled that "the finder of a jewel, though he does not by such finding acquire an absolute property or ownership, yet he has such a property as will enable him to keep it against all but the rightful owner."[110]

That proposition is encapsulated in the everyday maxim, "Finders keepers" (to which may be added "Losers weepers"). However, the law is considerably more subtle. It will be noticed that in *Armory* v *Delamirie* no claim was made by the owner or occupier of the house where the ring was found. That contest, occupier against finder, has been considered in several later cases. In *Bridges* v *Hawkesworth*[111] the claimant, a sales representative, called at a bookshop, and on the floor where he was standing he found a parcel containing £64 in banknotes. He handed the notes to the shopkeeper, the respondent, with a request that the notes should be kept safely for their owner. The respondent advertised the find, but the notes were never claimed. Three years later the claimant requested the return of the notes, offering to pay for the advertisement and to indemnify the respondent against any future claim from the rightful owner. The request was refused. The Queen's Bench Divisional Court held in favour of the claimant: "The notes were never in the custody, nor in the protection of [the respondent's] house, before they were found..."[112]

---

[108] There is an excellent monograph: Hickey, *Property and the Law of Finders* (Hart Publishing, 2010).
[109] (1722) 1 Stra 505.
[110] Ibid.
[111] (1851) 15 Jur 1079.
[112] Ibid per Patteson J.

34

In modern terminology, the respondent did not have prior possession of the notes because he had not exercised sufficient control over them.

Hannah v *Peel*[113] is a similar case. A house owned but never occupied by the respondent was requisitioned during war time for use as a sick bay by the army. The claimant, Lance Corporal Hannah, found a brooch on a window frame in a bedroom of the house. A few months later he reported the find to his commanding officer and then delivered the brooch to the police. The police in due course delivered the brooch to the respondent, who sold it for £66; a month later the brooch was resold for £88. Birkett J held for the claimant, following *Bridges* v *Hawkesworth*. The important point is that the respondent was never in possession of the house and therefore never had possession or control of the brooch.

In both of these latter cases the chattel was found loose, lying on the ground by its own weight. Would it make any difference if the chattel was found in the ground? That issue arose in *Elwes* v *Brigg Gas Co*.[114] The respondent company was the lessee of land from the claimant, who was the tenant for life in possession of the Elwes family estates. During excavations permitted by the lease the company found a prehistoric canoe embedded in the land. The company claimed title to the boat, but that claim was resisted by the claimant. Chitty J gave judgment for the claimant, reasoning that at the date of the lease the claimant had a title to the boat, that nothing in the lease transferred that title to the company, and that therefore the claimant's title prevailed.

The next case is *South Staffordshire Water Co* v *Sharman*.[115] The claimant company owned the Minster Pool. They engaged the respondent to clean the pool. The respondent's employee found two rings embedded in the mud at the bottom of the pool. The respondent refused to deliver the rings to the claimant company, but delivered them to the police. The owner was never traced. Lord Russell of Killowen CJ gave judgment for the claimant company; they had possession (control) of the rings before they were found, despite not knowing about them. He distinguished *Bridges* v *Hawkesworth* on the basis that there the notes were found in the public part of the shop.

---

[113] [1945] 1 KB 509.
[114] (1886) LR 33 Ch D 562.
[115] [1896] 2 QB 44.

Sharman was decided in 1896. After that we need to fast forward to 1963, when the next significant case, *City of London Corporation* v *Appleyard*,[116] was decided. The claimant corporation was the freehold owner of land in the City of London. A building lease became vested in 1964 in Yorkwin Investments Ltd. By virtue of that lease Yorkwin were entitled to demolish the building and to erect a new one. Clause 15 of the lease reserved "articles of value" to the claimant corporation. Yorkwin engaged Wates on the demolition and erection contract. During the process of demolition two employees of Wates found a wall safe which when opened revealed a wooden box containing bank notes to the value of £5,278. All the notes were issued in 1943 or 1944. The true owner of the notes was never found. The judge held: (1) that the two employees could not claim the notes against their employers, Wates; (2) that Wates were independent contractors engaged by Yorkwin and that Yorkwin had the better title; (3) that the safe and its contents were part of the land owned by the claimant corporation and comprised in the lease, but the articles were "articles of value" within Clause 15 and therefore reserved to the corporation. It followed that the corporation had a better title than all but the true owner.

Moffatt v *Kazana*[117] also concerned the finding of a quantity of banknotes, on this occasion to the value of £2,987. The notes were found in a biscuit tin which was dislodged from the loft space in a house then owned by the respondent. The house was previously owned by Mr. Russell (the claimant was the personal representative of Mr. Russell), and the judge found that, on the balance of probabilities, Mr. Russell had placed the notes in the loft space. Mr. Russell was entitled to the notes at that time, and had probably forgotten about them. The question, therefore, was whether the title to the notes had passed to the respondent when he bought the house from Mr. Russell. The judge held that it did not; the conveyance did not expressly refer to the notes, and no reference to the notes could be implied. The claimant therefore succeeded.

---

[116] [1963] 1 WLR 982.
[117] [1969] 2 QB 152.

The next case is *Parker* v *British Airways Board*.[118] This is the leading modern case on finding, important because the three members of the Court of Appeal made a determined attempt to explain and rationalise the previous authorities. The claimant, Mr. Parker, was a passenger at Heathrow Airport, holding a ticket which entitled him to use the executive lounge. In that lounge he found a gold bracelet on the floor. He picked it up and handed it to an employee of British Airways, asking him to search for the true owner but in default to return the bracelet to Mr. Parker. The true owner was not found, but British Airways sold the bracelet for £850. Mr. Parker's action to recover that sum was successful. The court unanimously held that there is a distinction between a chattel found in the land and a chattel found on the land: the in/on distinction. Where a chattel is found in the land, the person who has possession of the land will also have possession of the chattel, so that person has prior possession of the chattel, which will prevail over the subsequent possession of the finder. Where, however, a chattel is found on the land, the person who has possession of the land must prove that he had prior possession of the chattel by showing that he had a manifest intention to exercise control over things found on the land. This can be recognised as the distinction between, for example, *Bridges* v *Hawkesworth* and *South Staffordshire Water Co* v *Sharman*. Applying that distinction to the facts of *Parker*, the court held, obviously, that the gold bracelet was found on the land, lying loose on the floor. British Airways had not manifested an intention to exercise control over things found in the executive lounge, since, although access was to some extent restricted, a fairly large cross-section of the public was entitled to use that facility. However, that issue of manifest intention is highly fact specific. The necessary intention can be inferred from the nature of the premises. A bank vault would be likely to suffice, as would a private house.[119] Presumably a private car would also fall on that side of the line, but probably not a taxi cab, or a bus, train or aeroplane.

Donaldson LJ went on to formulate, obiter, a further series of propositions. These include: (1) a finder is under a duty to take reasonable steps to discover the true owner; (2) a trespassing finder will fail against the occupier; (3) a person who finds in the course of employment or agency will fail against the

---

[118] [1982] 1 QB 1004.
[119] Ibid, at 1019.

employer or principal.[120] Each of these propositions is debatable. As to (1), the postulated duty to take reasonable steps to discover the true owner, it must be remembered that the true owner, subject to the limitation period, will always succeed in a claim against the finder. The postulated duty seems not to add anything, and it is not easy to see what would be the remedy for breach of the supposed duty. It is difficult to believe that the finder must incur expense in performing such a duty, for example, by paying the cost of a newspaper advertisement. The decided cases seem to assume that handing the found item to the police, or to the occupier of the place of the finding, is sufficient. Are those to be considered reasonable steps to discover the true owner? It is quite possible that neither of those parties will be interested in taking any further steps to discover the true owner. There is certainly an obligation on the finder to take reasonable care of the chattel until such time as the true owner might be found. The finder will be liable if the chattel is lost or damaged by his negligence while the chattel is in her possession.[121] A further obligation might arise if the object found is a live animal, for example a cat or a dog. There must be an implied duty to take reasonable steps to keep the animal alive by feeding and nurturing. But what of veterinary fees, which can be very expensive? It may well be that such payments could not be reasonably expected. Finally, it is now known, since *Parker*, that even a person who acquires possession by dishonesty, for example by theft, may acquire a title against all but the true owner[122], a result which is quite inimical to the postulated duty. As to (2), that a trespassing finder will fail against the occupier, there are certainly cases where that proposition was accepted. A vivid example is *Hibbert* v *McKiernan*[123], where the appellant had been convicted of theft of golf balls from the owners of the golf course. The owners had shown their intention to exercise control by, inter alia, having a police officer present on the course with the special duty of warding off or arresting persons taking lost golf balls. The conviction was upheld by the Queen's Bench Divisional Court. It can be readily accepted that an occupier manifests an intention to control premises to which others have no right of access. However, it is uncertain whether that principle will be applied rigorously. Suppose, for example, that Mr. Parker had only an economy class airline ticket,

---

[120] Ibid, at 1017.
[121] *Newman* v *Bourne and Hollingsworth* (1915) TLR 209.
[122] *Costello v Chief Constable of Derbyshire* [2001] 1 WLR 1437.
[123] [1948] 2 KB 142. See also *R* v *Rostron* [2003] EWCA Crim 2206.

but had inadvertently managed to enter the executive lounge at Heathrow; or suppose that a person approaching the front door of a private house had picked up an object lying inches outside the path to that house. Is there a distinction between intended and unintended trespass?[124] Such questions are for the future. As to (3), that a person who finds in the course of employment or agency will fail against the employer or principal, the decided cases are inconclusive. There are cases which support that view. For example, in *McDowell* v *Ulster Bank*[125] a porter in a Belfast bank, while sweeping the floor, found a parcel containing notes to the value of £25. He handed the notes to the branch manager, asking him to try and find the owner. The owner was not found, and the bank refused to return the notes to the porter. The porter's claim failed on the employer/employee point. Various dicta support this view, for example Donaldson LJ in *Parker* and McNair J in *Appleyard*. A contrary case is *Byrne* v *Hoare*[126], where a police officer who found a gold ingot while on special duty at a drive-in movie theatre was held to be entitled. If the postulated rule is to be supported, there is an implied distinction between findings in the course of employment, or agency, and those ancillary or collateral to that relationship. Down that line, there is ample case law in the context of vicarious liability in the law of torts, though the distinction is not well developed in the context of finding. Setting all that aside, a better approach might be to concentrate on the employee's, and agent's, duty of loyalty, which precludes the retention of profits acquired in breach of that duty (invoking the law of restitution or unjust enrichment). A prime example is *Reading* v *Attorney-General* [127]. The appellant was a sergeant in the British army. He had, while in uniform, regularly taken bribes to enable lorries to pass through police lines without being inspected. The House of Lords held that he could not keep the money but must give it up to his employer, the Crown. That decision clearly involves a gross abuse by Reading of his position. If that principle were to be applied in the context of finding, the law

---

[124] See Marshall, *The Problem of Finding* (1949) 2 Current Legal Problems 68.
[125] (1899) 33 Irish Law Times 225. A similar Irish case is *Crinion* v *Minister of Justice* (1959) 25 Irish Jurist Reports 15.
[126] [1965] Qd R 135.
[127] [1951] 1 All ER 617.

would be far more generous to finders who happen to be employees or agents, a result to be welcomed.[128]

After that long digression based on *Parker*, it is necessary to revert to the chronological presentation of the decided cases. The final case in the sequence is *Costello* v *Chief Constable of Derbyshire*,[129] where the Court of Appeal considered the position of a person who acquires possession dishonestly, for example in the course of theft. The claimant was in possession of a car which the police believed he had stolen. The police seized the car and detained it for the purposes of their inquiry, pursuant to their powers under sections 19 and 22 of the Police and Criminal Evidence Act 1984. On the conclusion of their inquiries the police refused to return the car to the claimant. The claim was successful; in the absence of the true owner, the claimant had a better title than the police, whose powers of detention had expired. That result might, at first glance, seem counter-intuitive, because it rewards criminality. However, the decision is certainly correct: Parliament had deliberately given the police only limited powers of detention, and it would have been constitutionally improper for the courts, in effect, to extend those powers by conferring on the police an unlimited power of confiscation.[130] The point can be tested in a different way. Mr. Parker was obviously an honest finder of the gold bracelet, but what if he had been a dishonest finder? Suppose, for example, that he had put the bracelet in his pocket, told nobody about his find, and treated the bracelet as his own. That would have constituted theft. Would the decision have been different? Surely not, because the hypothetical dishonest conduct of Mr. Parker does nothing to improve the claim of British Airways to have acquired prior possession.

---

[128] If the employer/principal succeeds under this principle, the remedy will be the imposition of a constructive trust on the item found: *FHR European Ventures LLP* v *Cedar Capital Partners LLC* [2014] 3 WLR 535; see also ch 1, n 13 and text thereto and ch4, n178 and text thereto.

[129] [2001] 1 WLR 1437, following *Webb* v *Chief Constable of Merseyside* [2000] QB 427 (allegation of drug trafficking, but claimants never convicted of offence, and therefore statutory powers of confiscation not triggered). Both *Costello* and *Webb* have been followed by the Court of Appeal in *Gough v Chief Constable of West Midlands Police* [2004] EWCA Civ 206. Mr. Costello was released on bail and no criminal proceedings were brought against him. See also the Canadian cases *Bird v Fort Frances (1949) 2 DLR 791* and *Grafstein v Holme and Freeman* (1958) 12 DLR 727.

[130] There are several modern statutes which provide for the confiscation of property obtained by crime. The most comprehensive is the Proceeds of Crime Act 2002, which creates the Assets Recovery Agency, whose task is to ensure that criminals do not benefit from their crimes. The powers of the court lie in the Crown Court jurisdiction, requiring either a conviction in the Crown Court or a committal to that court by the magistrates.

There are three issues which deserve some further consideration.

The first is the in/on distinction. This is firmly established up to the level of the Court of Appeal. *Parker* was followed in *Waverly Borough Council v Fletcher*[131]. The respondent, using his metal detector, found a mediaeval gold brooch buried some nine inches below the ground in a public park of which the claimant council were the freehold owners. He returned to dig up the brooch. The council's case succeeded, for two principal reasons: the first was the in/on distinction, that the council as owner and occupier of the land had possession of things found in their land; the second reason was that the respondent, in digging up the brooch, trespassed on the council's land.

However, some commentators regard the in/on distinction as arbitrary and unjustified.[132] The distinction evolved over time in the cases, but, in retrospect, can be seen to underpin the decisions in *Elwes v Brigg Gas Conpany*[133], *South Staffordshire Water Company v Sharman*[134], *City of London Corporation v Appleyard*[135] and *Waverly Borough Council v Fletcher*,[136] all of which decisions seem correct. The argument for a rethink is not established.

The second issue for further consideration is the case of a chattel found within a chattel, ie, container and contents. It seems sensible to regard a person who has possession of a container to have possession also of its contents. In *Moffatt v Kazana*[137], for example, it was assumed, and the judge held, that whoever had possession of the biscuit tin had also possession of its contents, the banknotes. Lower down the scale, it has never been doubted that the parcels containing notes found in *Bridges v Hawkesworth*[138] and *McDowell v Ulster Bank*[139] were to be treated as one item. However, there is a much cited case which appears to reach a contrary conclusion, *Merry v Green*.[140] The claimant bought a bureau at auction. He discovered a secret drawer in the bureau, in

---

[131] [1995] QB 334.
[132] See, in particular, Hickey, *op. cit.*, pp. 46-50, analysing the reasons for the distinction given by Donaldson LJ in *Parker* and by Auld LJ in *Fletcher*. See also Kohler [1992] Current Legal Problems, Part 1, p 69.
[133] (1886) LR 33 Ch D 562.
[134] [1896] 2 QB 44.
[135] [1963] 1 WLR 982.
[136] [1995] QB 334.
[137] [1969] 2 QB 152.
[138] (1851) 15 Jur 1079.
[139] (1899) 33 Irish Law Times 225.
[140] (1841) 7 M & W 623. The case is very much concerned with the law of larceny (theft) at that time, and may for that reason be no longer applicable; but see Hickey, *op. cit.*, pp. 21-25.

which was a purse of money. The judge held that the case turned on whether the bureau was sold "with contents", and there was insufficient evidence that such was the seller's, or the auctioneer's, intention. It is understandable that in a consensual transaction such as a sale the seller's intention should be paramount. It is arguably different where the finding takes place outside the context of a consensual transaction, where the finder's claim is based purely on the acquisition of possession. In those circumstances, the presumption that a container includes its contents seems very strong.[141]

The last issue for further consideration is the case where the land where the finding takes place is subject to a lease. If the finder cannot prove a manifest intention to exercise control, the occupier of the land will be deemed to have prior possession; but the question arises whether the lessor or the lessee has that prior possession. The question can be examined by referring again to *Elwes v Brigg Gas Company*[142] and *City of London Corporation v Appleyard*.[143] In *Elwes* the freeholder had prior possession because the prehistoric canoe had clearly been buried in the land before the lease was granted, and under the terms of the lease the freeholder's title did not pass to the lessee. In *Appleyard* the freeholder won because there was a clause in the building lease reserving "articles of value" to the freeholder. David Hoath[144] considered what the decision would have been in the absence of such a clause. His argument is premised on the importance of prior possession. He points out that all the banknotes which were found in the wall safe were issued in 1943 or 1944, some twenty years before the lease vested in Yorkwin. The freeholder therefore must have had prior possession and would have won even without the "articles of value" clause.

---

[141] The presumption was misapplied in *City of London Corporation v Appleyard*, [1963] 1 WLR 982, where the judge held that the wall safe was part of the land leased to Yorkwin; he could not then go on to decide that the contents of the safe (the wooden box containing banknotes) were also comprised in the lease. A transfer of land does not, unless the transferor intends it, include a transfer of chattels found on the land: see *Moffatt v Kazana* [1969] 2 QB 152.
[142] (1886) LR 33 Ch D 562.
[143] [1963] 1 WLR 983.
[144] [1990] Conv 348; cf. Kohler [1993] Current Legal Problems, Part 1, p 69.

APPENDIX 2

Treasure

There have for long been special rules relating to the finding of treasure. At common law this was governed by the law of treasure trove, but this had become generally regarded as archaic and inadequate. The common law has been replaced by entirely new provisions contained in the Treasure Act 1996. The Act contains a fairly broad definition of "treasure", as follows[145]:

(1) an object at least 300 years old when found which is not a coin but which has a metallic content of at least 10% by weight in gold or silver;

(2) an object which, when found, is at least 300 years old and is one of at least two coins in the same find, which contain at least 10% by weight in gold or silver;

(3) an object which, when found, is one of at least ten coins in the same find which are at least 300 years old;

(4) an object which would have been treasure trove under the old law;

(5) an object which, when found, is part of the same find as an object within (1) to (4), found at the same time or earlier;

(6) an object which would be within (1) to (4) if it had been found at the same time.

The Secretary of State may by order add to the definition by designating any class of object which is at least 200 years old and which he considers to be of outstanding historical, archaeological or cultural importance. The Secretary of State may also by order exclude any class of object from the definition.

Ownership of treasure vests, subject to prior interests and rights, in the Crown.[146] The finder of an object which he believes or has reasonable grounds for believing is treasure must notify the coroner of the district within fourteen days from the day after the find or the day on which the finder first

---

[145] Ss 1-3, Treasure Act 1996.
[146] S 4. Exceptionally, ownership will vest in the franchisee, such as the owner of the Duchy of Lancaster or the Duchy of Cornwall; ss 4 and 5. For the meaning of "prior interests and rights" see s 4(2).

believes or has reason to believe that the object is treasure. The coroner will decide whether the object is treasure.

Where treasure has vested in the Crown, the Secretary of State may direct that the treasure shall be transferred or otherwise disposed of. If he directs transfer to a museum, he must decide whether a reward is to be paid, the amount of the reward, and to whom the reward is to be paid.[147]

---

[147] S 10 and the Code of Practice made under s 11.

Chapter 4

THE CONTRIBUTION OF EQUITY

English law, and in particular English property law, has three constituent elements: common law, equity and statute. This chapter explores the contribution which equity has made to our law of property. The detailed history and development of equity need not concern us here.[148] Suffice it to say that the various rules and principles of equity were developed by successive Chancellors from around the 13th century. They were systematised by two great Chancellors, Lord Nottingham (who held office from 1675 to 1682) and Lord Eldon (1801 to 1806 and 1807 to 1827). Equity was until 1875 administered in a separate court, the Court of Chancery. The Judicature Acts of 1873 and 1875[149] abolished all the old separate courts and created one Supreme Court of Judicature, administering both common law and equity. It was provided that "Generally, in all matters… in which there is any conflict or variance between the rules of equity and the rules of common law with reference to the same matter, the rules of equity shall prevail."[150] The Supreme Court of Judicature has three levels: the High Court, the Court of Appeal, and the Supreme Court (previously the House of Lords). The High Court is the lowest level in this hierarchy. It has three divisions, the Queen's Bench Division, the Chancery Division and the Family Division. All the divisions exercise a concurrent jurisdiction in both common law and equity, but certain matters traditionally dealt with in the Court of Chancery are assigned to the Chancery Division: they include questions arising from land law, including mortgages; trusts; the administration of the estates of deceased persons; and various types of intellectual property, namely, patents, trademarks, registered designs and copyrights.[151]

In the evolution of equity it became clear that two notions are central to equity's modification of the common law: these are *conscience* and *notice*. By "conscience" is meant that actions having legal effect, such as a transfer of property, shall be carried out with a good conscience, or in good faith; or,

---

[148] There are good accounts in the standard textbooks: see, for example, Hanbury and Martin, *Modern Equity*, 19th ed, chapter 1; Megarry and Wade, *The Law of Real Property*, 7th ed, chapter 5.
[149] Supreme Court of Judicature Act 1873 and Supreme Court of Judicature Act 1875.
[150] S 25(11), Supreme Court of Judicature Act 1873; now s 49, Supreme Court Act 1981.
[151] S 61 and Sch 1, Supreme Court Act 1981.

putting the matter the other way round, unconscionable conduct will justify the intervention of equity. By "notice" is meant that, where one person has acted against another person unconscionably, or is threatening to do so, and a third party is also involved in the matter, equity will intervene against the third party if she knows, or has reasonable means of knowing, about that unconscionability. The third party will not be allowed to assist in the unconscionable conduct, or to derive an advantage from it.[152]

Many examples of the operation of these two notions will be seen in the following discussion of equity's contribution to the law of property.

In the modern law, seven distinctive contributions of equity can be discerned and are described in the next part of this chapter.

Trusts

A trust is the most significant and far-reaching contribution of equity to the law of property. In its simplest form, a trust involves the transfer of property to one person, Celia, with a direction that she shall hold the property for another person, David. Common law would not recognise the obligation against Celia, but equity would enforce it, regarding it as unconscionable for Celia to claim the property beneficially, as common law would have allowed. The device of a trust would be useful if, for example, David was a minor incapable of managing the property,[153] or if he was a person lacking full mental capacity. In the example, Celia will be compelled to manage the property for the sole benefit of David, and she will be precluded from obtaining any benefit for herself. Another situation where a trust would be a convenient method would be if the intended beneficiary is leaving the country for an extended period.[154] There are, in fact, very many contexts in which a trust might be employed. For example, there are many trusts for charitable purposes. The property legislation of 1925 uses trusts extensively, in

---

[152] On the central importance of "notice" see Lord Browne-Wilkinson in *Barclays Bank plc* v *O'Brien* [1994] AC 180 at 195A.
[153] In the case of land a minor cannot hold a legal estate: s 1(6), Law of Property Act 1925, and a conveyance which purports to convey a legal estate to a minor operates as a declaration that the land is held in trust for the minor: sch 1, para 1, Trusts of Land and Appointment of Trustees Act 1996.
[154] Legal historians think that a trust (then known as a use) was created by some of those embarking on a Crusade in the Holy Land.

particular in the law relating to concurrent interests (co-ownership) and consecutive interests in land.[155] A trust was always necessary in order to create consecutive interests in personal property.[156] Trusts are used in many commercial law contexts, including pension fund trusts. Equity also recognises secret trusts, taking effect on death.[157]

All types of property may be subjected to a trust, including an equitable interest under an existing trust (in this latter case, the transaction will create a sub-trust). More typically, the trust will comprise the legal ownership of the property, so that the trustee has legal ownership and the beneficiary has an equitable interest. [158]

There are two forms of trust which arise by operation of law, rather than by the declared intention of the person creating the trust (the settlor). The first form is a resulting trust, where the property is held for the transferor. An obvious case is where an express trust is created, but the designation of the beneficial interest is incomplete. If, for example, Celia transfers property to David on trust for Emma for life, but does not direct what is to happen on Emma's death, David will hold on a resulting trust for Celia on Emma's death (the beneficial interest reverts to Celia). However, there are more subtle situations which give rise to a resulting trust. One can give rise to co-ownership. If Celia buys land and has the legal estate transferred to her, but one or more other persons have also contributed to the purchase money, equity would regard it as unconscionable for Celia to claim that she held the entire legal estate beneficially, unless there is evidence that the contributors intended to make a gift to Celia. In the absence of such evidence, she will be compelled to hold the property on a resulting trust for herself and the other contributors in shares proportionate to their respective contributions.[159] At least, that is the position in relation to commercial transactions.[160] The House of Lords[161] and the Supreme Court[162] have held that the position in relation to

---

[155] For co-ownership see chapter 7. For consecutive interests, see ch 2. In both cases, the employment of a trust is closely connected with overreaching: see chapter 6.
[156] See ch 2.
[157] See ch 5, p 105.
[158] For the significance of this distinction see p 46 *et seq*.
[159] A resulting trust of land may be created without any written formality: s 53(2), Law of Property Act 1925. See further ch 5.
[160] *Malayan Credit Ltd* v *Jack Chia MPH Ltd* [1986] AC 549, reviewing many previous cases. See also the recent development in *Marr v Collie* [2017] UKPC 17 discussed in ch 8, "The Family Home".
[161] *Stack* v *Dowden* [2007] 2 AC 432.

family homes is different, and that they are governed by the law of constructive trusts.[163]

The second form of implied trust is a constructive trust. Such a trust arises where property is vested in one person in circumstances which make it unconscionable for that person to retain the property, or the entirety of that property, for herself; a constructive trust will be imposed by equity in order to remedy that unconscionability. There is a very wide variety of situations where a constructive trust will be imposed, and it is possible here to give only a few examples. A clear example is *Bannister v Bannister*[164], where a conveyance of two cottages was made by the seller to her brother-in-law who, in return for buying the land at well below its market value, orally promised the seller that she could live in one of the cottages rent-free for the rest of her life. The purchaser then sought in these proceedings to evict the seller from her home. The Court of Appeal decided that the purchaser held the legal estate on a constructive trust to give effect to the life interest which he had promised.[165]

Take another example, this time from a commercial context. *Banner Homes Group plc v Luff Developments Ltd*[166] concerned two property development companies which reached an understanding falling short of a concluded contract that Banner Homes would not compete against Luff Developments in bidding for some land, in order that the land could be acquired for a jointly owned venture company. Contrary to that understanding, and behind the back of Banner Developments, the land was in fact acquired by a company which was a wholly owned subsidiary of Luff Developments. The Court of Appeal imposed a constructive trust, under which shares of the subsidiary company should be divided equally between Banner Homes and Luff Developments.

A significant category of constructive trusts arises from the rule that a trustee cannot gain any unauthorised personal benefit from the trust, and must not put himself into a position where his personal interest conflicts with his duty

---

[162] *Jones v Kernott* [2012] 1 AC 776.
[163] For detailed discussion see ch 8, "The Family Home".
[164] [1948] 2 All ER 133.
[165] A constructive trust of land may be created without any written formality: s 53(2), Law of Property Act 1925. See further ch 5.
[166] [2000] Ch 372.

as trustee.[167] This rule has many ramifications. Two are relevant here. In *Keech v Sandford*[168] a trustee held a lease for an infant beneficiary. The landlord refused to grant a new lease for the infant, and the trustee then negotiated a new lease for himself. It was held that the trustee could not retain the benefit of the lease for himself, but that instead the infant beneficiary was entitled. That principle has been carried to considerable lengths. Perhaps the high-water mark was reached in *Boardman* v *Phipps*.[169] The appellant, Boardman, was the solicitor for trustees of the Phipps family trust. The trust had a substantial holding in a private company, Lester & Harris Ltd. The appellant on behalf of the trustees attended various company meetings and obtained information about the company's affairs. Eventually, the appellant bought for himself a significant quantity of the company's shares. Thereafter, the company was very successful, and substantial profits were made both for the Phipps family and the appellant. The appellant acted honestly throughout. The House of Lords, affirming the lower courts, held that the appellant could not keep the shares and the resulting profits for himself, but was entitled to be remunerated on a liberal scale for his work and skill in furthering the company's profitability. However, this should not be taken as tacit allowance for fiduciaries acting in breach of their fiduciary duty to be remunerated by the court for their hard work or skill in securing profit. In *Guinness v Saunders*[170] Lord Goff considered that the jurisdiction of the court to remunerate trustees outside those circumstances allowed by the specific trust deed "is restricted to those cases where it cannot have the effect of encouraging trustees in any way to put themselves in a position where their interests conflict with their duties as trustees"[171].

Secondly, it is clear that the rule prevents a trustee from retaining a bribe or a secret commission received from a third party.[172] However, there has been considerable debate, among the judiciary in the decided cases and between academics, as to whether the trustee is merely personally liable to account for the money or other property so received, or whether the money or property is

---

[167] This rule derives from *Keech* v *Sandford* (1726) Sel Cas Ch 61. It applies not only to trustees but also to other fiduciaries, including personal representatives and agents.
[168] (1726) Sel Cas Ch 61.
[169] [1967] 2 AC 46.
[170] [1990] 2 AC 663.
[171] Ibid at 701.
[172] See, for example, *Williams* v *Barton* [1927] 2 Ch 9.

held on a constructive trust for the beneficiary.[173] The difference can be very significant. A constructive trust creates a proprietary interest, so that, if the trustee who had acted improperly were to become insolvent, the beneficiary's claim would have priority over the trustee's unsecured creditors. It would also mean that the beneficiary could follow the money or other property into the hands of a third party (other than a purchaser for value taking without notice of the beneficiary's rights), could claim any increase in value of the money or other property, and could trace into any other money or property for which the original money or property had been exchanged. The Court of Appeal held in *Lister & Co v Stubbs*[174] that there was merely a personal liability to account. That decision was disapproved by the Privy Council in *Attorney General for Hong Kong v Reid*[175], but continued to be binding in English law.[176] However, seven justices of the Supreme Court have now held unanimously in *FHR European Ventures LLP v Cedar Capital Partners*[177] that there is a constructive trust, creating a full proprietary remedy. [178]

There is a group of cases where the courts have considered the effect where a purchaser of property has agreed with the seller to hold the property "subject to" a prior right of a third party which otherwise would not be binding on the purchaser. Suppose, for example, that the purchaser agrees to hold land subject to a contractual licence previously granted by the seller to a third party. The Court of Appeal in *Ashburn Anstalt v Arnold*[179] held that a contractual licence does not create a proprietary interest and therefore would ordinarily not be binding on the purchaser. Does the fact that the purchaser has agreed to take subject to the third party's rights make a difference? The position was analysed by Fox LJ in *Ashburn*.[180] He held that, contrary to the view of Lord Denning MR in *Binions v Evans*[181], the agreement to take "subject to" is not enough, in itself, to raise a constructive trust against the purchaser. What needs to be shown is that the purchaser intended to take on a new obligation

---

[173] See the references collected in the judgment of Lord Neuberger in *FHR European Ventures LLP v Cedar Capital Partners LLC* [2014] 3 WLR 535, at paras 10, 11, 13-29.
[174] (1890) 45 Ch D1.
[175] [1994] 1 AC 324.
[176] *Sinclair Investments Ltd v Versailles Trade Finance Ltd* [2012] Ch 453.
[177] [2014] 3 WLR 535.
[178] See also ch 1, n 13 and text thereto; ch 3, n 128 and text thereto.
[179] [1989] Ch 1.
[180] Ibid at 25-26. This approach was followed by the Court of Appeal in *Chaudhary v Yavuz* [2011] EWCA Civ 1314.
[181] [1972] Ch 359 at 368.

to honour the third party's rights in circumstances where it would be unconscionable for the purchaser then to go back on that agreement. There are various ways in which that crucial element of unconscionability may be shown. For example, it may be shown that the seller might not have disposed of the property at all if the purchaser had not so agreed; or if the purchaser paid a significantly reduced price, as a *quid pro quo*; that might very well prove unconscionability. Fox LJ approved the decision and the reasoning of Dillon J in *Lyus* v *Prowsa Developments Ltd*.[182] There a company's land was subject to a mortgage in favour of the National Westminster Bank. The company contracted to sell a house on the land to the claimants, Mr and Mrs Lyus. The company then became insolvent, and the bank decided to sell the land. The bank could have sold the land free from the claimant's contract, but in fact the bank wished to honour, and to take advantage, of the claimants' contract. The bank sold and transferred the house to the respondent company "subject to and with the benefit" of the claimants' contract; the respondent company assured the bank that the claimants' rights would be dealt with quickly and to the claimants' satisfaction. It was held that a constructive trust would be imposed on the respondent company obliging it to honour the claimants' contract.

As stated previously, the notion of a constructive trust applies in a wide variety of situations. Some have been dealt with in the above paragraph, but other applications will be met later in this book: see the discussion of *Midland Bank Trust Co Ltd* v *Green*[183], later in this chapter; chapter 5 ("Formalities for the Disposition of Property"), the sections on "Contracts for the sale or other disposition of property" (specifically enforceable contracts of sale), and on "Dispositions on death" (secret trusts and *donatio mortis causa*); and chapter 8 ("The Family Home").

Estate Contracts

Generally, a contract relating to property, such as a contract for the sale of that property, is enforceable only against the other contracting party, and the usual remedy for a breach of that contract is the common law remedy of damages,

---

[182] [1982] 1 WLR 1044.
[183] [1981] AC 513.

to compensate the innocent party for the loss caused by the breach. Equity, however, devised the remedy of specific performance, an order that the contract shall be carried out according to its terms. Specific performance will be awarded on a discretionary basis, where the remedy of damages would be inadequate. Specific performance will be routinely awarded in the case of a contract for the sale or other disposition of land; land is regarded as having unique value.[184] Further, and crucially for the law of property, it became established that specific performance could be awarded against a third party to whom, in breach of contract, the land had been conveyed. The position in equity is thus radically different from the position at common law. Even further, equity has for long adopted the maxim that "Equity regards as done that which ought to be done". If a contract is specifically enforceable, equity treats the parties as if the contract has already been performed, so that the purchaser of land has, from the date of the contract, an equitable interest in the land.[185] The same is true of a person who holds an option to purchase the land.[186] The Court of Appeal in *Pritchard* v *Briggs*[187] held that a right of preemption (a right of first refusal, "If I decide to sell my land I will first offer it to you") does not create an equitable interest, but for registered land that decision has been reversed by section 115 of the Land Registration Act 2002. The reasoning that applies to contracts to sell land applies also to contracts for other dispositions of land. Therefore, we have equitable leases, equitable mortgages, equitable easements, and so on: equitable analogues of common law transactions.

The leading case is *Walsh* v *Lonsdale*.[188] The owner of land contracted in writing to grant a lease for seven years, the rent to be payable in advance on demand. The tenant took possession of the land and paid a yearly rent in arrears. The rent became overdue, and the lessor demanded a year's rent in advance. It was not paid, and the lessor seized the tenant's goods to enforce

---

[184] Shares in a private company are also treated as having unique value: see *Oughtred* v *Inland Revenue Commissioners* [1960] AC 1; *Neville* v *Wilson* [1997] Ch 144. See ch 5, p 92.
[185] In the case of a sale, the seller is regarded as holding on a constructive trust for the buyer: *Lysaght* v *Edwards* (1876) 2 Ch D 499. However, the Supreme Court has held, surprisingly, that the buyer cannot confer a proprietary interest on another person, not even on the seller: *Scott* v *Southern Pacific Mortgages Ltd* [2014] UKSC 52.
[186] An option to purchase may be viewed, depending on the context, either as an irrevocable offer to sell or as a conditional contract to sell: see ch 5, p 81. An option to renew a lease is analogous.
[187] [1980] Ch 338.
[188] (1882) LR 21 Ch D 9.

payment (the remedy of distress).[189] The tenant claimed that the distress was illegal. He argued that he was merely a yearly tenant[190] and that the agreement to pay rent in advance on demand was inconsistent with a yearly tenancy. The tenant's argument was rejected by the Court of Appeal: in equity there was a seven year lease, including the obligation to pay rent in advance.[191]

Restrictive covenants affecting land

A covenant is a contractual promise made by deed. It may be positive, requiring the covenantor to do something, or it may be negative, requiring the covenantor not to do something. At common law either form of covenant is enforceable between the parties, in accordance with the normal rules of privity of contract. For a breach of covenant the common law remedy is damages. Equity, however, devised further remedies; as well as the decree of specific performance, mentioned above, equity devised the remedy of an injunction, an order of the court that something shall not be done, or some activity shall stop being done. A mandatory injunction is rather more unusual; such an order is in positive form, but to enforce a negative obligation. An example would be an order to reduce the height of a tree because it is interfering with a neighbour's right to light. Obviously, an injunction might be an appropriate remedy in the case of a breach, or a threatened breach, of a negative covenant. But equity took a critical step in the case of *Tulk* v *Moxhay*.[192] There was a covenant to maintain the garden in Leicester Square in London "in an open state uncovered with any buildings". Lord Cottenham LC held that the covenant would be enforced by an injunction against a purchaser of the land who bought with notice of the covenant.[193] Thus, there was created a new equitable interest in land; equity, as before, would not allow to be done that which ought not to be done.

---

[189] The remedy of distress has been partially abolished by the Tribunals, Courts and Enforcement Act 2007.
[190] For the implication of periodic tenancies, arising from the taking of possession and the payment of a periodic rent, see chapter 5, p 85.
[191] See also *Industrial Properties (Barton Hill) Ltd* v *Associated Electrical Industries Ltd* [1997] QB 580, where A agreed to sell land to B, who agreed to grant a lease to C; C was treated as an equitable lessee.
[192] (1848) 2 Ph 774.
[193] There were earlier intimations: *Whatman* v *Gibson* (1838) 9 Sim 196; *Mann* v *Stephens* (1846) 15 Sim 377.

The decision was based primarily on the fact that the purchaser had notice of the covenant, so that it would be unconscionable for the purchaser to act in breach of the covenant. However, subsequent decisions have established two limiting factors. The first is that *Tulk* v *Moxhay* applies only to restrictive covenants, not to positive covenants.[194] The burden of positive covenants does not run with freehold land.[195] The test is whether the covenant is in substance negative, and can be complied with by the covenantor by doing nothing. In *Tulk* v *Moxhay* itself the covenant was positive in form, but negative in substance. The second limiting factor is that the covenant will be enforced against a successor in title only if the covenant was made for the protection of other land owned by the covenantee.[196] As a corollary to the decision that the burden of a restrictive covenant could pass to successors in title of the original covenantor, equity developed its own principles for determining when the benefit of the covenant would pass to successors in title of the original covenantee.[197]

The burden of a restrictive covenant does not run with property other than land.[198]

---

[194] *Haywood* v *Brunswick Permanent Benefit Building Society* (1881) 8 QBD 403; *Austerberry* v *Corporation of Oldham* (1885) 29 Ch 750; *Rhone* v *Stephens* [1994] 2 AC 310. There have been several proposals, none yet implemented, to allow the burden of a positive covenant to run with freehold land: see the Report of the Committee on Positive Covenants Affecting Land (1965) Cmnd 2719; The Law of Positive and Restrictive Covenants (1984) Law Com No 127; Commonhold: A Consultation Paper (1990) Cm 127. There are various statutory exceptions, for example, s 106 Town and Country Planning Act 1990 (as amended). Such a planning agreement is registrable as a local land charge.

[195] Positive covenants between lessor and lessee, affecting the land comprised in the lease, are treated quite differently. In the case of covenants made before 1996, the fundamental principle is that the benefit and burden of covenants which touch and concern the land will run with the lease and the reversion. In the case of covenants made after 1995, the fundamental principle is that the benefit and burden of all covenants comprised in the lease will run with the lease and the reversion, except covenants which are expressed to be personal: Landlord and Tenant (Covenants) Act 1995. For detailed accounts see Megarry & Wade, *The Law of Real Property*, 7th ed, ch 20; Gray & Gray, *Elements of Land Law*, 5th ed, ch 4.5.

[196] *Formby* v *Barker* [1903] 2 Ch 539; *LCC* v *Allen* [1914] 3 KB 642.

[197] The benefit can pass by express assignment along with the benefited land, by annexation to the benefited land, or under a building or development scheme. The details are beyond the scope of this book.

[198] *Port Line Ltd* v *Ben Line Steamers* [1958] 2 QB 146, not following *Lord Strathcona SS Co* v *Dominion Coal Co* [1926] AC 108 (Canada). There may, however, be other methods of attaching burdens to personal property; see *De Mattos* v *Gibson* (1859) De G & J 276 (best explained on the basis of the tort of knowing interference with contractual rights), and *Swiss Bank Corp* v *Lloyds Bank Ltd* [1979] Ch 548 (constructive trust). See also *Oughtred* v *Inland Revenue Commissioners* [1960] AC 206, and *Neville* v *Wilson* [1997] Ch 144 (specifically enforceable contract for sale of shares creates a constructive trust); see ch 4.

The equity of redemption

The concept of an equity of redemption arises in the law of mortgages. A mortgage may be created over any kind of property, tangible or intangible, in order to secure the performance of some obligation, most commonly the payment of a debt. If a debtor becomes insolvent (unable to pay all her debts in full), her unsecured creditors will have to suffer a shortfall. If, however, a debt is secured by a mortgage over specified property, the creditor will have various rights directly over that property, including the right to take possession of tangible property[199] and the power to sell the property and to pay off the debt from the proceeds of sale.[200] To the extent of the value of the mortgaged property, a secured creditor therefore has priority over the unsecured creditors. A mortgage is created by the transfer of the property to the mortgagee.[201] The contract creating the loan and the mortgage will stipulate when the loan is to be repaid and what interest the loan will carry. The debtor will have a contractual right to redeem the mortgaged property by repaying the loan together with the accrued interest. But what if the debtor fails to repay in time and the value of the mortgaged property exceeds the amount owing? The common law would allow the creditor to seize the mortgaged property and thus extinguish the contractual right to redeem. This is known as foreclosure. Foreclosure should be carefully distinguished from sale. In a sale, any surplus in the proceeds of sale, after payment of the expenses of the sale and all other amounts owing, are held on trust for the debtor, whose rights are overreached by the sale.[202] Foreclosure, on the other hand, completely destroys the debtor's right of redemption.

---

[199] Where the mortgaged property consists of or includes a dwelling house, the right to take possession is regulated: ss 36-39, Administration of Justice Act 1970; s 8, Administration of Justice Act 1973.
[200] Where a mortgage is created by deed, a power of sale is implied by s 101, Law of Property Act 1925.
[201] In the case of a legal mortgage of land, the mortgage of an estate in fee simple takes effect as a lease for three thousand years; the mortgage of a lease takes effect as a sub-lease less at least one day shorter than the lease. S 85(2), Law of Property Act 1925 proscribed the creation of a mortgage by transfer of the fee simple to the mortgagee which had traditionally been the mechanism for giving security for the loan prior to 1926. Alternatively, a legal mortgage of land can be created by "a charge by deed expressed to take effect by way of legal mortgage" (a legal charge): ss 85, 86, Law of Property Act 1925. Where the title to the land is registered, a legal mortgage *must* take effect by way of a legal charge: ss 85(3), 86(3), Law of Property Act 1925 (as amended); ss 23, 51, Land Registration Act 2002.
[202] S 105, Law of Property Act 1925. For overreaching, see chapter 6.

Equity, from at least the early part of the seventeenth century,[203] took a radically different view. The strict contractual approach of the common law could amount to forfeiture by the mortgagee, allowing the mortgagee to make a windfall profit. Equity would allow the debtor to redeem the mortgaged property after the contractual date by paying the principal of the loan, interest and costs. Thus was created an equitable right to redeem. It came to be realised that this intervention of equity meant that the mortgage was never more than security for the loan; the maxim was, "Once a mortgage, always a mortgage, and nothing but a mortgage". The mortgagor (the borrower) remained the true owner of the property, subject only to the removable incumbrance, the mortgage. This conclusion is summarised by saying that the borrower has an equity of redemption, the sum total of her residual rights over the property. The value of the equity of redemption is the market value of the property less the total amounts outstanding. If the property has a market value of £30,000, and there is £10,000 outstanding, the equity of redemption is worth £20,000. Estate agents speak of the "equity" in the property, or the "equity value" of the property.[204] It follows that foreclosure requires an order of the court, destroying both the contractual and the equitable right to redeem; the court is likely to order sale rather than foreclosure if the equity of redemption has significant value[205].

An equitable charge

A charge arises when a particular item of property is made liable for the discharge of an obligation, usually a debt or some other payment of money, without any transfer of the property to the chargee. The common law did not recognise such a transaction, but equity gave effect to it. Since there is no transfer, a chargee cannot take possession or foreclosure, but otherwise a chargee has the same remedies as a mortgagee.

An equitable charge is implied when property is transferred on sale, but the whole or part of the purchase money remains unpaid. The charge is security for the unpaid money.

---

[203] Lord Nottingham as Chancellor was particularly important in this development.
[204] Consider also the term "negative equity", the dire situation which arises when the amount outstanding on the mortgage exceeds the total market value of the property.
[205] See s 91(2), Law of Property Act 1925.

Another use of the equitable charge is to provide a proprietary remedy to a beneficiary against a trustee who, in breach of trust, has mixed trust money with her own money in a bank account.[206]

The express creation of an equitable charge must be in writing, signed by the person creating the charge or by her agent acting under written authority.[207] If the charge is contractual, it presumably requires a written contract signed by all the parties.[208]

Equity also recognises the concept of a floating charge, which will be described here only very briefly. A floating charge "is one which hovers over a designated class of assets in which the debtor has or will in the future acquire an interest, the debtor having a liberty to deal with any of the assets free from the charge so long as it remains floating. The chargee's interest is thus in a changing fund of assets, not in any asset *in specie*, but when an event occurs which causes the charge to crystallize, it attaches as a fixed security to all the assets then comprised in the fund and to any assets of the specified description subsequently acquired by the debtor".[209] The crystallizing event, or events, may be defined in the charge, but under the general law will include a company going into administration or liquidation.[210] A floating charge created by a company is registrable under section 860 of the Companies Act 2006, and failure to register will render the charge void against the liquidator or administrator and any creditor of the company.[211]

Rights of entry or re-entry

A right of entry or re-entry is often used as a forfeiture clause, seeking to compel the performance of contractual obligations. For example, a lease will commonly contain a forfeiture clause, exercisable on non-payment of rent or breach of any other of the tenant's obligations. A right of entry exercisable

---

[206] *Re Hallett's Estate* (1880) 13 Ch D 66.
[207] S 53(1)(a), Law of Property Act 1925; *Murray* v *Guinness*, unreported, Lightman J, 29th May 1998. This citation is taken from Megarry & Wade, *The Law of Real Property*, 7th ed, para 15-015, n 115.
[208] S 2, Law of Property (Miscellaneous Provisions) Act 1989. The point was left open by the Court of Appeal in *Kinane* v *Mackie-Conteh* [2005] EWCA Civ 45 at [18]
[209] Goode, *Commercial Law*, 3rd ed, p 587. For a fuller description see ch 25 of the same work.
[210] *National Westminster Bank plc* v *Jones* [2002] 1 BCLC 55.
[211] S 860(1), Companies Act 2006.

over or in respect of a legal lease is a legal interest in land.[212] All other rights of entry or re-entry are equitable interests only. Such a right may, for example, be used to provide an indirect method of enforcing a positive covenant, affecting freehold land, against successors in title of the original covenantor.[213]

An equitable right of entry can also be employed in a slightly more complicated situation. If Celia owns a factory and hires machinery from David, and the machinery is firmly attached to the floor of the factory, the machinery will become a fixture (part of Celia's land), so that if Celia subsequently mortgages the factory to Ella, the machinery is part of the mortgaged property, so that David will be unable to reclaim the machinery from Ella.[214] However, if the agreement between Celia and David includes a right for David to reclaim the machinery on default by Celia, that will create an equitable right of entry binding on Ella.[215]

Proprietary estoppel

This is a contribution of equity to the law of property with very wide significance.[216] The essential idea is that, if one person, Celia, the estate owner of some land, by her words or conduct encourages another person, David, to believe that he has or will be granted some rights over Celia's land, and David acts to his detriment in reliance on that belief, if it would be unconscionable for Celia to go back on the belief that she has induced, she will not be allowed to deny (will be estopped from denying) that David is entitled to a remedy against her. The nature of that remedy is a matter for the court's discretion; it could be a personal remedy of monetary compensation, ranging all the way up to a transfer of the fee simple. Unlike the contractual doctrine of promissory estoppel which can be used only as a shield and not as a sword,[217]

---

[212] S 1(2)(e), Law of Property Act 1925.
[213] See *Shiloh Spinners Ltd* v *Harding* [1973] AC 691.
[214] *Hobson* v *Gorringe* [1897] 1 Ch 182; *Reynolds* v *Ashby & Son* [1904] AC 466.
[215] *Re Samuel Allen & Sons Ltd* [1907] 1 Ch 575; *Re Morrison, Jones & Taylor Ltd* [1914] 1 Ch 50. A tenant's right to remove tenants' fixtures (agricultural, ornamental and trade fixtures) at the end of the lease is also an equitable interest: *Poster* v *Slough Estates Ltd* [1969] 1 Ch 495.
[216] Although the origins of equitable estoppel can be traced to an earlier time, the main foundations were laid in the 19th century by *Ramsden* v *Dyson* (1866) LR 1 HL 129, especially the dissenting judgment of Lord Kingsdown; *Dillwyn* v *Llewelyn* (1862) 4 De GF & J 517; and *Plimmer* v *Wellington Corp* (1883-84) LR 9 App Cas 699. These cases are still often cited today.
[217] *Combe* v *Combe* [1951] 2 KB 215.

proprietary estoppel can be used as a sword, ie, it can be used to found a cause of action. Take, for example, *Crabb v Arun District Council*,[218] one of the leading modern cases. The claimant owned land to which he had access via a right of way over the council's adjoining land. He wished to sell part of his land which contained the access point. A representative of the council assured the claimant that, if he sold the intended land, the council would grant him a new right of way to his retained land. The claimant, in reliance on that assurance, then sold the intended land without reserving a right of way to his retained land. The council then refused to grant him a new right of way. The claimant could not argue that he was entitled on a contractual basis, because the terms of any contract had not been concluded, and in any event the council's representative did not have authority to enter into a contract on behalf of the council. The claimant was therefore compelled to rely on equitable estoppel. He did so successfully. The Court of Appeal held that it would be unconscionable for the council to renege on the assurance which had been given to the claimant. He was entitled to a right of way in equity, on terms to be agreed or otherwise settled by the court.[219]

It has been stated in the Court of Appeal that proprietary estoppel applies only to land.[220] However, there is no obvious justification for such a restriction, and there are indications in some cases that the concept can apply more widely. In *Re Basham*[221] the claimant was awarded the entire estate of the deceased.[222] In *Thorner v Major*[223] the claimant was awarded a farm together with the assets comprising the farming business, which included live and dead stock and money standing in a current account.

---

[218] [1976] Ch 179.
[219] The court decided that, in view of the high-handed conduct of the council, which had resulted in the claimant's land being sterilised for a considerable period of time, the claimant should not now be obliged to make any payment for the right of way.
[220] *Western Fish Products Ltd v Penwith District Council* [1981] 2 All ER 204 at 218, per Megaw LJ.
[221] [1986] 1 WLR 1498.
[222] The decision has been criticised by some on the basis, inter alia, that a right arising by equitable estoppel must relate to specific assets: see, for example, Hayton [1987] CLJ 215. However, the decision has been approved more than once by the Court of Appeal: see Robert Walker LJ in *Jennings v Rice* [2003] 1 P & CR 100, para 46.
[223] [2009] 1 WLR. It would have been extremely artificial, and contrary to the common understanding of the owner and the claimant, to distinguish between the land and the other assets of the farm.

There is a very wide range of circumstances in which a proprietary estoppel may arise.[224] The following examples will show some of this range. Perhaps the most common scenario is the improvement of the owner's land. In *Inwards v Baker*[225] Mr Baker, the father of Jack, in 1931 encouraged Jack to build a bungalow on his father's land. The bungalow was built largely at Jack's expense, and Jack had lived there with his family ever since. The father did not during his lifetime or at his death in 1951 by his will give any interest in the land to Jack. In 1963 the trustees of the father's will sought an order for possession against Jack. The Court of Appeal held that Jack had a defence based on proprietary estoppel: he could remain in the bungalow "as long as he desires as his home".[226]

In *Pascoe v Turner*[227] the claimant, Mr Pascoe had lived with the respondent, Mrs Turner, from 1964 in houses owned by Mr Pascoe. In 1973 he began an affair with another woman and lived elsewhere. Mrs Turner stayed on in Mr Pascoe's house. On several occasions he said to Mrs Turner, "The house is yours and everything in it". In reliance on those declarations Mrs Turner spent some £230 (about a quarter of her capital) on repairs and improvements. There was no formal grant to her of any interest in the house. In April 1976 Mr Pascoe's solicitors gave Mrs Turner two months' notice to determine her licence to occupy, and in August Mr Pascoe commenced these proceedings for possession. The Court of Appeal held that there was an effective gift of the contents of the house.[228] With regard to the house itself, it was held that Mrs Turner had an equity arising by estoppel, and that, in all of the circumstances, she was entitled to the fee simple. Mr Pascoe was ordered to execute a conveyance forthwith at his expense transferring the fee simple to Mrs Turner.

Another fairly common scenario is where the owner of land promises to leave an interest in that land by will. There are several cases where such a promise has been made to a person looking after the landowner or members of her family, or who has worked for the landowner for a significant period of time

---

[224] The most detailed classification is in Gray & Gray, *Elements of Land Law*, 5th ed, paras 9.2.18 *et seq*. For the use of proprietary estoppel in alleviating problems caused by the requirement that a contract for the disposition of land shall be in writing, see ch 5.
[225] [1965] 2 QB 29.
[226] [1965] 2 QB 29 at 37G, per Lord Denning MR.
[227] [1979] 1 WLR 531.
[228] Applying *Re Stoneham* [1919] 1 Ch 149; see see ch 5, "Formalities for the Disposition of Property".

for no payment, or at low market wages. In *Greasley* v *Cooke*[229] the respondent, Doris Cooke, at the age of 16, in 1938 went to work as a maidservant at the house of Arthur Greasley. He had three sons and a daughter, who were then teenagers. Arthur Greasley died in 1948. Doris Cooke stayed on, looking after various members of the Greasley family for nearly forty years until 1975. She was on various occasions assured by two of the sons, Kenneth and Hedley, that she could regard the property as her home for the rest of her life, and she did not receive any payment for her services after the death of Arthur. By an action started in 1978, the owners of the house sought possession against Doris Cooke. She counterclaimed for a declaration that she was entitled to occupy the house rent free for the rest of her life. The Court of Appeal declared that she was entitled to occupy the house rent free for so long as she wished to stay there.

In *Gillett* v *Holt*[230] the respondent, Mr Kenneth Holt, was a prosperous farmer owning various properties in Lincolnshire. The claimant, Mr Geoffrey Gillett, had worked for Mr Holt on the main farm, The Limes, from 1957, when the claimant was aged 16. The claimant and Mr Holt became good friends, and over the years they attended various social functions together. The claimant married in 1964, and Mrs Gillett was absorbed into the friendly relationship. The claimant became, in effect, Mr Holt's business manager. On various occasions Mr Holt assured the claimant that he would by his will leave The Limes to the claimant. However, from 1992 rifts began to appear in the relationship between the claimant and Mr Holt; in 1995 Mr and Mrs Gillett were summarily dismissed, and Mr Holt threatened to change his will so as to exclude them. The Court of Appeal held that, although the claimant had clearly benefited in various ways from the relationship (socially and financially), he had also acted to his detriment in reliance on the repeated assurances from Mr Holt; he had given up educational opportunities when he first went to work for Mr Holt, and he had worked loyally for some forty years at The Limes, at below market wages, forgoing other employment opportunities. It would therefore now be unconscionable for Mr Holt to go back on those assurances. The result was that the claimant was entitled to the freehold estate in The Limes free from a mortgage, together with £100,000 to

---

[229] [1980] 1 WLR 1306.
[230] [2001] Ch 210.

compensate the claimant for his not gaining an interest in any of the other farming business owned by Mr Holt.

A limit to the availability of proprietary estoppel was confirmed in *Yeoman's Row Management Ltd v Cobbe*.[231] The parties, both experienced in the field of property development, made an incomplete oral contract, envisaging that in due course it would be replaced by a comprehensive written contract. The general nature of the oral contract was that the claimant would, at his own expense, seek to obtain planning permission for the residential development of land owned by the respondent, and that, if and when planning permission was granted, the respondent would sell the land to the claimant. The claimant spent a considerable amount of time and money in obtaining the desired planning permission. The respondent then withdrew from the oral contract. The House of Lords, reversing the High Court and the Court of Appeal, held that the respondent's conduct, though unattractive, was not unconscionable. The claimant "ran a commercial risk, with his eyes open, and the outcome has proved unfortunate for him".[232] The claimant was entitled only to a quantum meruit to recompense him for his services in applying for and obtaining the planning permission. This judgment appeared to severely restrict the availability of proprietary estoppel, but shortly afterwards the House of Lords clarified in *Thorner v Major*[233] that this restriction applies to purely commercial cases and that proprietary estoppel is still available in more domestic circumstances.

The appellant, David Thorner, was a farmer who for nearly thirty years did a substantial amount of work without pay on Steart Farm, the farm owned by his father's cousin, Peter Thorner. From 1990 until his death in 2005, Peter Thorner, in various ways, some of them rather indirect, encouraged David to believe that he would inherit the farm. Over those years the farm changed in some respects, as Peter sold some land and bought other land. In 1997 Peter, unknown to David, made a will by which he appointed David his executor, gave various pecuniary legacies to different people, and left the whole of his residuary estate to David. That will was not found on Peter's death, and the trial judge inferred that it had been destroyed (and therefore revoked). Peter never made a new will; he therefore died intestate and the respondents to the

---
[231] [2008] UKHL 55
[232] Ibid, per Lord Walker of Gestingthorpe at para 91.
[233] [2009] 1 WLR 776.

appeal were his personal representatives. The House of Lords held that David had reasonably believed that he would inherit the farm (the land and its assets), and he had acted to his detriment by continuing to work there unpaid, forgoing other work opportunities. There was no uncertainty in defining the farm, although it changed its identity over the years; Peter and David had a common understanding that what was meant was the farm as it stood at Peter's death. These circumstances meant that David had an equitable right arising by propriety estoppel, and the equity was satisfied by holding that David was entitled to the land and buildings constituting Steart Farm, together with the live and dead stock and other assets of Peter's farming business, including about £24,000 in the farm's current account.

The courts' methodology, in approaching a case of proprietary estoppel, is to proceed in two stages. At the first stage the court considers whether there have been representations made by the owner of the property, on which the claimant has relied to her detriment. If the court is satisfied on those two elements an equity arises. Then, at the second stage, the court considers what remedy is appropriate, and will choose the minimum remedy which is sufficient to satisfy the equity.[234] At the conclusion of the first stage, the claimant's rights are said to be inchoate (incomplete or undefined). What if, at that stage, the land is transferred to a new owner? In unregistered land that point has not been firmly decided, although the better argument seems to be that the claimant's rights are sufficiently proprietary to be capable of binding the new owner.[235] In registered land the point has been put beyond doubt by section 116 of the Land Registration Act 2002, which provides: "It is hereby declared for the avoidance of doubt that, in relation to registered land...an equity by estoppel...has effect from the time the equity arises as an interest in land capable of binding successors in title..." At the second stage, the court can choose from a wide range of remedies. In many cases the court will seek to put the claimant in the position which she had been led to expect. In *Crabb v Arun District Council*[236] the claimant was led to expect the grant of a right of way, and his land was sterilised without such a right; the court ordered that a right of way should be granted. In many of the cases the claimant had been

---

[234] *Crabb v Arun District Council* [1976] Ch 179 at 198, per Scarman LJ.
[235] See *Ahmad Yar Khan v Secretary of State for India* (1901) LR 28 1A 211 at 218, per Lord Macnaghten; *JT Developments Ltd v Quinn* (1990) 62 P & CR 33l; *Voyce v Voyce* (1991) 62 P & CR 290; *Lloyd v Dugdale* [2002] 2 P & CR 13.
[236] [1976] Ch 179.

led to expect a right of occupation. However, there are several different ways in which such a right can be created: by a licence, or by a life interest, or by a lease, or by the transfer of the fee simple. In *Inwards* v *Baker*[237] the court decided that the claimant was entitled to live in the bungalow which he had built on his father's land "as long as he desired as his home".[238] That could be construed either as an irrevocable licence or as a life interest. There was case law authority at the time which held that a contractual licence to occupy created an irrevocable proprietary interest,[239] and it was reasonable to suppose that a similar licence arising by equitable estoppel was similarly proprietary in nature. That would have protected Jack Baker for as long as he lived in the bungalow, but would apparently have left him in limbo if he had wished to move house. However, in *Ashburn Anstalt* v *Arnold*[240] the Court of Appeal reversed that previous line of authority, holding that a contractual licence to occupy was merely personal, incapable of binding the licensor's successors in title; it is difficult to see how a licence arising by proprietary estoppel could have any wider effect.[241] After *Ashburn* it would seem that the courts should abandon reliance on an estoppel licence and choose instead the obvious alternative, a life estate. The Court of Appeal, however, seems to have continued to believe in the proprietary status of an estoppel licence.[242]

Returning to *Inwards* v *Baker*, the court's declaration in favour of Jack could alternatively be interpreted as a life interest; indeed, that was the interpretation adopted by the Court of Appeal in *Dodsworth* v *Dodsworth*.[243] The problem, however, is that the conferment on Jack of a life interest would, as the law then stood, attract the very cumbersome machinery of the Settled Land Act 1925. Suffice it to say that the Act would necessitate the execution of a vesting instrument to vest the legal estate in Jack, and the appointment of at least two trustees to receive any capital money arising from the exercise by Jack of his statutory powers of disposition. That machinery, cumbersome as it

---

[237] [1965] 2 QB 29.
[238] A similar declaration was made in *Greasley* v *Cooke* [1980] 1 WLR 1306; [1980] 3 All ER 710.
[239] The leading case was *Errington* v *Errington and Woods* [1952] 1 KB 290.
[240] [1989] Ch 1. This ruling was strictly obiter, but has been widely followed: *Kewal Investment Ltd* v *Arthur Maiden Ltd* [1990] 1 EGLR 193; *Canadian Imperial Bank of Commerce* v *Bello* (1991) 64 P & CR 48; *IDC Group Ltd* v *Clark* [1992] 1 EGLR 187; *Camden LBC* v *Shortlife Community Housing Ltd* (1992) 90 LGR 358; *Nationwide Anglia Building Society* v *Ahmed* (1995) 70 P & CR 381.
[241] The argument is elaborated in *"Contractual and Estoppel Licences as Proprietary Interests in Land"* [1991] Conv 39 (GB).
[242] *Matharu* v *Matharu* (1994) 68 P & CR 93.
[243] (1973) 228 EG 1115.

was, would have the great advantage of enabling Jack to move house: he could sell the house and direct the trustees to invest the proceeds in a new house for him and his family to occupy. The Settled Land Act 1925 has now been repealed and replaced by provisions in the Trusts of Land and Appointment of Trustees Act 1996; steps would now be taken to vest the legal estate in trustees of land, who have the dispositive powers of an absolute owner[244] and the power to acquire land for occupation by a beneficiary.[245]

Nevertheless, some people might consider even the modern position under the Trusts of Land and Appointment of Trustees Act 1996 as too complicated for the position arising from *Inwards* v *Baker*. The Court of Appeal in *Griffiths* v *Williams*[246] showed that a simpler solution would be to confer on a successful claimant a lease at a nominal rent; the lease could, for example, be granted for the life of the claimant, which under section 149(6) of the Law of Property Act 1925 would be converted into a lease for ninety years determinable after the death of the tenant.

The remaining method of providing a right of occupation is for the owner's entire estate to be transferred to the claimant. There are clearly cases where such an outcome is entirely appropriate: *Gillett* v *Holt*[247] and *Thorner* v *Major*,[248] for example. But consider again *Pascoe* v *Turner*.[249] Mrs Turner had relied to her detriment on assurances given by Mr Pascoe that the house where she lived, and which she had previously shared with Mr Pascoe, would be hers. The detriment was that she had spent £230 (about a quarter of her capital) on repairs and improvements to the house. In considering what remedy to award Mrs Turner, the Court of Appeal said:[250] "We are satisfied that the problem of remedy on the facts resolves itself into a choice between two alternatives: should the equity be satisfied by a licence to the defendant to occupy the house for her lifetime or should there be a transfer to her of the fee simple?". The court then held that a licence would not give her sufficient protection (even though it was assumed that a licence created a proprietary interest), and that "the equity to which the facts in this case gives rise can only

---

[244] S 6(1), Trusts of Land and Appointment of Trustees Act 1996.
[245] S 8(1), Trustee Act 2000.
[246] (1977) 248 EG 947.
[247] [2001] Ch 210.
[248] [2009] 1 WLR 776.
[249] [1979] 1 WLR 431.
[250] Ibid at 438H-439A.

be satisfied by compelling the plaintiff to give effect to his promise and her expectations. He has so acted that he must now perfect the gift." That statement shows a remarkable poverty of imagination. Why did the court not consider a life interest or some form of lease, in particular a lease for life? The transfer of the fee simple is arguably disproportionate to the amount of Mrs Turner's contribution, greatly exceeding her reasonable expectation.

In cases where improvements have been made, it will sometimes be more appropriate to fashion a remedy which seeks to compensate the claimant in money, rather than conferring a right of occupation. In the Australian case of *Commonwealth of Australia* v *Verwayen*[251] Deane J put forward the hypothetical example of a claimant who is induced to spend $100 in erecting a shed on a plot of land worth $1,000,000.[252] Here it would seem wholly disproportionate for the claimant to be awarded the fee simple, or indeed any right of occupation. The likely outcome is that the claimant would be reimbursed the "wasted" expenditure of $100.

An alternative measure of compensation would be to assess the rise in value of the improved property. There is a New Zealand case where that measure was adopted, partly because the improvements were not up to workmanlike standards.[253]

In *Dodsworth* v *Dodsworth*[254] the respondent persuaded her brother and his wife (the claimants) to live with her in her bungalow, promising the claimants that they, and the survivor of them, could live in the bungalow rent free for their lives. In reliance on that promise the claimants spent over £700 on improvements to the bungalow. Later, the respondent wished to sell the bungalow and buy a smaller and less expensive property for herself. In these proceedings the respondent sought possession against the claimants. It was conceded that an equity had arisen in favour of the claimants; the question for the Court of Appeal was how that equity should be satisfied. It was held that a right of occupation would be disproportionate and unfair to the plaintiff; the claimants were entitled to be reimbursed their expenditure, and they could remain in occupation until the reimbursement was complete. That right of

---

[251] (1990) 170 CLR 394.
[252] Ibid at 441.
[253] *Lepel* v *Huthnance* (1979) NZ Recent Law 269; cited by Gray & Gray, *Elements of Land Law*, 5th ed, para 9.2.116 n 1.
[254] (1973) 228 EG 115.

occupation acted as a kind of security to ensure that the reimbursement was made. In other cases, an equitable charge has been imposed as security for any money ordered to be repaid.[255]

Some form of monetary compensation may also be appropriate in a case where services have been rendered gratuitously in the expectation of some interest in a property. Such a case is *Jennings* v *Rice*.[256] The claimant, who was a full time bricklayer, had worked part time for Mrs Royle, a widow, since 1970. He started as a gardener, being paid 30p per hour. As time went on, the work expanded to include running errands for Mrs Royle, taking her shopping and doing minor maintenance work around the house. In the 1980s she stopped paying him, though she did give him £2,000 towards the purchase of his own house. In the early 1990s Mrs Royle, then in her eighties, became increasingly infirm. From 1994 the claimant stayed overnight at Mrs Royle's house, in order to help with her care and to provide security. The claimant's wife also helped with care for Mrs Royle. On various occasions Mrs Royle said to the claimant that he would be all right financially, and stated, "This will all be yours one day", or words to that effect. She died in 1997, intestate, and the respondent was her personal representative. Her estate was valued at £1.2 million, and the house and furniture at £435,000. The Court of Appeal held that it would be disproportionate to award the claimant the house, with a value of £420,000. A suitable house for the claimant and his family would cost £150,000. £420,000 would far exceed what he could reasonably have expected as remuneration for his work. He was awarded £200,000, based partly on an estimate of the nursing home costs which Mrs Royle might have incurred if the claimant, and his wife, had not provided care. It can be inferred that the court thought it unnecessary to impose a charge to secure payment of that sum; the estate was already in administration and there were adequate assets to meet the claimant's entitlement.

---

[255] See, for example, *Unity Joint Stock Banking Association* v *King* (1853) 25 Beav 72.
[256] [2003] 1 P & CR 100. See also the similar case of *Campbell* v *Griffin* [2001] WTLR 981.

The distinction between law and equity

It remains to be considered whether it is still necessary to distinguish in this way the contribution that equity has made to the law of property. After all, it might be argued, the two systems of land and equity were fused in 1875. The traditional view is that only the administration of law and equity was fused; from 1875 both law and equity would be administered in the same court, with equity prevailing in the event of conflict.[257] Lord Denning consistently took the opposite view; he argued that there was fusion of substance of the two systems.[258] He embodied that view into his law reform agenda. It is as if he were saying, "All law is equity, and equity prevails". Put in that way, the argument is obviously fallacious; it had few supporters, in either the judiciary or the academic community. However, in the last 40 years or so senior members of the judiciary, in both the United Kingdom and other Commonwealth jurisdictions[259], have begun to argue for a more restrained conception of fusion in substance: that the combination of law and equity produces a single coherent body of law.[260] This view is epitomised by the statement of Lord Browne-Wilkinson in *Tinsley* v *Milligan*[261]: "...English law has one single law of property made up of legal and equitable interests. Although for historical reasons legal estates and equitable estates have differing incidents, the person owning either type of estate has a right of property, a right in rem not merely a right in personam". That seems correct, but it means that it is still necessary to make the distinction between law and equity. There are many situations where equity will differ from the common law: different but not necessarily in conflict.[262] In the context of the law of property the most important difference is the distinction between a legal estate and an equitable interest. In all seven of the areas where equity has

---

[257] The most celebrated statement of that view is by Ashburner, *Principles of Equity*, 1st ed, p 23: "...the two streams of jurisdiction, though they run in the same channel, run side by side, and do not mingle their waters".

[258] See, for example, *Errington & Errington* v *Woods* [1952] 1 KB 290 at 298; *Boyer* v *Warbey* [1953] 1 QB 234 at 245-46.

[259] See, for example, *United Scientific Holdings Ltd* v *Burnley Borough Council* [1978] AC 904, at 924H-925B, per Lord Diplock, at 944E-F, per Lord Simon (UK); *Aquaculture Corpn* v *New Zealand Green Mussel Co Ltd* [1990] 3 NZLR 299 (New Zealand); *Catt* v *Marac Australia Ltd* (1986) NSWLR 659 (Australia); *Le Mesurier* v *Andrus* (1986) 54 OR (2d) 1 (Canada).

[260] This phrase is taken from Pearce & Stevens, op cit, p 14.

[261] [1993] 3 All ER 65 at 86. See also Lord Goff in *Lord Napier and Ettrick* v *Hunter* [1993] 1 All ER 385 at 401.

[262] There are full, wide ranging accounts in Hanbury & Martin, *Modern Equity*, 19th ed, paras 1-020 *et seq*; Pearce & Stevens, *The Law of Trusts and Equitable Obligations*, 4th ed, pp 11 *et seq*.

made a significant contribution, the successful claimant will acquire an equitable interest in the property.

The classical distinction, before the enactment of any statutory reforms relating to land, was that legal estates bind the whole world, whereas equitable interests bind everyone except a purchaser for value in good faith of a legal estate who takes without notice of the equitable interest (equity's darling). If Celia owns the legal fee simple in a piece of land, or a legal lease, or owns a chattel, there is literally no one in the world who can successfully deny her ownership. An equitable interest is slightly weaker. If, for example, Celia is a beneficiary under a trust, and the trust property is sold by the trustee, Celia's equitable interest will bind the transferee unless the transferee can prove all the elements of the defence of equity's darling,[263] ie, that she was (1) a purchaser for value,[264] (2) of the legal estate or legal title, (3) who bought in good faith, and (4) who took without notice of Celia's equitable interest. The only element which requires elaboration is that of notice. Notice comes in three forms: (a) actual notice, ie, actual knowledge; (b) imputed notice, ie, notice acquired by the purchaser's agent acting in that transaction; and (c) constructive notice, ie, knowledge which the purchase would have acquired if she had made all reasonable inquiries about the title to the property being bought.[265] In relation to reasonable inquiries, there is a distinction between land and other property. In general, it is impossible to make inquiries about the title to property other than land. There is usually no kind of documentary title to chattels, and therefore the purchaser cannot be expected to make any inquiries.[266] The position in relation to land is very different. In the case of unregistered land there is normally a documentary title (title deeds), and the purchaser can require the production of title deeds back to a good root of title[267] which is at least 15 years old at the date of the contract of sale.[268] Thus,

---

[263] The defence of equity's darling is one composite plea: *Pilcher* v *Rawlins* (1872) 7 Ch App 259.
[264] A person who acquires title by adverse possession is not a purchaser and will therefore take subject to all equitable interests: *Re Nisbet and Potts' Contract* [1906] 1 Ch 386.
[265] See s 199(1)(ii), Law of Property Act 1925.
[266] *Manchester Trust* v *Furness* [1895] 2 QB 539. The log book of a car (officially the "registration document") is not a document of title: *Central Newbury Car Auctions Ltd* v *Unity Finance Ltd* [1957] 1 QB 371; *Stadium Finance Ltd* v *Robbins* [1962] 2 QB 664.
[267] A good root of title "is a document which describes the land sufficiently to identify it, which shows a disposition of the whole legal and equitable interest contracted to be sold, and which contains nothing to throw any doubt on the title": Megarry & Wade, *The Law of Real Property*, 7th ed, para 15-078, n 540, quoting Williams, *Vendor and Purchaser*, p 124.
[268] S 44(1), Law of Property Act 1925.

if Celia is selling the fee simple in unregistered land in 2014, she must produce title deeds starting with a disposition of the property dated not later than 1999. The purchaser is deemed to have constructive notice of any equitable interests disclosed by those title deeds. However, under a contract to grant or assign a lease or a sub-lease, the intended lessee or assignee is not entitled to call for the title to the reversion,[269] and in such a case the lessee or assignee will not have notice of any equitable interests binding the reversion.[270]

Further, a prudent purchaser of land is expected to make a physical inspection of the land and will have constructive notice of any equitable interest which a physical inspection would have revealed. As part of that principle, if someone other than the vendor is present on the property, the purchaser will have constructive notice of any equitable interest owned by that person. This is the rule in *Hunt* v *Luck*.[271] But what if the vendor is in occupation, but some other person is also in occupation? That question has arisen in a series of cases concerned with a matrimonial, or family, home. In *Caunce* v *Caunce*[272] the legal estate in the matrimonial home was vested in the husband, but the wife had made a financial contribution to its purchase, and it was not in dispute that the wife had an equitable interest in the property. They were living together in the house when the husband entered into various legal mortgages. The mortgagees made no inquiries of the wife. The husband was subsequently declared bankrupt, and the question arose whether the wife's equitable interest was binding on the mortgagees. It was held that there was no duty to make inquiries of the wife, and that the mortgagees therefore took free from her interest. Stamp J reasoned as follows:[273] "...where the vendor or mortgagor is himself in possession and occupation of the property, the purchaser or the mortgagee is not affected with notice of the equitable interests of any other person who may be resident there, and whose presence is wholly consistent with the title offered. If you buy with vacant possession on completion and you know, or find out, that the vendor is himself in possession and occupation of the property, you are, in my judgment, by reason of your failure to make further inquiries on the premises, no more

---

[269] S 44(2) – (4), Law of Property Act 1925.
[270] S 44(5), Law of Property Act 1925. There is an exception where the grant of a lease or sub-lease will trigger first registration under s 4(1), Land Registration Act 2002 (mainly a lease or sub-lease for more than seven years).
[271] [1902] 1 Ch 428.
[272] [1969] 1 WLR 286.
[273] Ibid at 295H-296A.

fixed with notice of the equitable interest of the vendor's wife who is living there with him than you would be affected with notice of the equitable interest of any other person who might also be resident on the premises, e.g. the vendor's father, his "Uncle Harry" or his "Aunt Matilda", any of whom, be it observed, might have contributed towards the purchase of the property. The reason is that the vendor being in possession, the presence of his wife or guest or lodger implies nothing to negative the title offered. It is otherwise if the vendor is not in occupation and you find another party whose presence demands an explanation and whose presence you ignore at your peril."

If a purchaser takes free from an equitable interest because of the absence of notice, not only does that first purchaser take free but so also do her successors in title (the principle is, once defeated, always defeated). The equitable interest will not revive as against a subsequent purchaser who has notice, nor as a donee.[274] Were that not so, the first purchaser would be greatly inhibited as to the dispositions which she could make. There is one exception, which is where a trustee sells the property to a purchaser without notice but later re-acquires the property; the trusts will revive.[275]

The doctrine of notice does not apply to registered land, where the fundamental principle is that all interests in land should be entered on the register (the mirror principle). There is, however, a major exception in the recognition of overriding interests, ie, those unregistered interests which override a disposition of registered land.[276] Here is to be found an echo of the rule in *Hunt v Luck*: the definition of overriding interests includes[277] "An interest belonging at the time of the disposition to a person in actual occupation, so far as relating to land of which he is in actual occupation, except for-... (b) an interest of a person of whom inquiry was made before the disposition was made and who failed to disclose the right when he could reasonably have been expected to do so; (c) an interest – (i) which belongs to a person whose occupation would not have been obvious on a reasonably

---

[274] *Wilkes* v *Spooner* [1911] 2 KB 473. This is a principle of general application, even in a statutory context. When, for example, s 4(6), Land Charge Act 1972, provides that an interest shall be void against a purchaser for non-registration (see p 77, *post*), it is obvious that successors in title of the purchaser, whoever they may be, will be in the same position. See the comments on *Midland Bank Trust Co Ltd* v *Green* [1981] AC 513, n 312, *post*.
[275] *Re Stapleford Colliery Co* (1980) Ch D 432.
[276] Defined in sch 3, Land Registration Act 2002.
[277] Ibid, para 2; formerly, s 70(1)(g), Land Registration Act 1925.

careful inspection of the land at the time of the disposition, and (ii) of which the person to whom the disposition was made does not have actual knowledge at that time." In *Williams & Glyn's Bank Ltd* v *Boland*[278] Mr Boland held the matrimonial home on trust for himself and his wife. They were living there together when the husband mortgaged the registered legal estate to the bank. The bank made no inquiries of Mrs Boland. The House of Lords held that Mrs Boland had an overriding interest binding on the bank. *Caunce* v *Caunce*, being an unregistered land case, was not directly relevant, but Lord Wilberforce criticised[279] the "easy-going practice of dispensing with enquiries as to occupation beyond that of the vendor."

That kind of scenario came under scrutiny again in the unregistered land case of *Kingsnorth Finance Co Ltd* v *Tizard*.[280] The wife had an interest by contribution in the matrimonial home, but she and her husband had separated and the wife lived elsewhere. However, she came back to the house every day to look after the children, and occasionally stayed overnight when the husband was away. She also kept some clothes in the house. The judge held that the finance company was put on notice of her interest; and he also held that, if the husband's title had been registered, the wife would have been in actual occupation and therefore would have an overriding interest. The decision in *Tizard* certainly puts the duty of inquiry at a very high level, too high in the opinion of some commentators.[281] Under the Land Registration Act 2002 the occupation must be "obvious on a reasonably careful inspection of the land"; was Mrs Tizard's occupation "obvious"? It must certainly be correct to say that a person can be in actual occupation who is not physically present at the relevant time, away for a few days visiting a relative, for example. In *Chokar* v *Chokar*[282] the wife was in hospital giving birth to her second child. While she was away the husband transferred the house to a purchaser, who changed the locks. The wife was held to be in actual occupation. In *Link Lending Ltd* v *Bustard*[283] the person concerned had been in residential care for more than a year, but was intending to return home when her mental health improved. She was held to be in actual occupation.

---

[278] [1981] AC 487.
[279] Ibid at 508. There was also earlier criticism by Russell LJ in *Hodgson* v *Marks* [1971] Ch 892 at 934-935.
[280] [1986] 1 WLR 783.
[281] See Clarke, All ER Rev 1986, 181-184; Thompson [1986] Conv 283.
[282] [1984] FLR 313.
[283] [2010] EWCA Civ 424.

What if a child under the age of majority is living in the property? It is possible for such a child to have an interest by contribution.[284] Should a purchaser make inquiries? Under the now repealed Land Registration Act 1925, in *Hypo-Mortgage Services Ltd* v *Robinson*[285] the Court of Appeal held that there is no duty of inquiry, since such a child does not have an independent right of occupation and instead occupied as a 'shadow' of their parent(s). This reasoning has been somewhat overturned by the Land Registration Act 2002. Schedule 3 para 2(b) allows a person to claim an overriding interest based on their actual occupation if they do not fail to disclose their interest when they might reasonably be expected to do so. In the absence of a statutory provision as to the age of maturity in a particular context, the law regards an adolescent child as gradually achieving maturity, as he or she approaches the age of majority (18). The question, in any given context, is whether a particular child has achieved a sufficient level of competence, understanding and independence to be capable of taking a decision in that context.[286] A child who has reached that point of development is known as a *Gillick*-competent child. That is a difficult test to apply in the context of the disposition of a family home, but it is not easy to see how it can be avoided.[287]

After the decisions in *Tizard* and *Boland*, an occupying beneficiary appeared to be fairly well protected. However, subsequent developments have considerably weakened that protection. Firstly, it was always clear that a beneficiary who was in equity a co-owner of land had an interest potentially capable of being overreached under the Trusts of Land and Appointment of Trustees Act 1996;[288] the interests of Mrs Boland and Mrs Tizard were not overreached because at least two trustees are required to give a valid receipt for capital money.[289] In *City of London Building Society* v *Flegg*[290] the two trustees who held the legal estate in a house entered into a mortgage with the building society. The House of Lords held that the mortgage overreached the

---

[284] A child under the age of majority cannot hold a legal estate in land: s 1(6), Law of Property Act 1925, but can be a beneficiary under a trust.
[285] [1972] 2 FLR 71.
[286] *Hewer* v *Bryant* [1970] 1 QB 357; *Gillick* v *West Norfolk and Wisbech Area Health Authority* [1986] AC 112.
[287] Where a consent is required for the exercise by trustees of land of any of their powers, a child under the age of majority cannot consent and the consent of a parent or guardian is required instead: s 10(3), Trusts of Land and Appointment of Trustees Act 1996.
[288] For overreaching see ch 6.
[289] S 27(2), Law of Property Act 1925.
[290] [1988] AC 54; followed by *Nationwide Anglia Building Society* v *Ahmed* (1995) 70 P&CR 381, and *Scott* v *Southern Pacific Mortgages Ltd* [2014] UKSC 52.

interests of the occupying beneficiaries, who were not consulted and of whom no inquiries had been made. The building society therefore had priority.

Secondly, the House of Lords held in *Abbey National Building Society* v *Cann*[291] that, where, as is commonly the case, a mortgage is used to fund the original purchase of the property, the purchase and the mortgage are to be treated as one simultaneous transaction, so that a beneficiary who goes into occupation on the completion of the transaction does not have priority.

Thirdly, where a beneficiary knows that a mortgage is required in order to finance the purchase of a property, she cannot claim that her interest is binding on the mortgagee. This is a species of estoppel, or it could be said that she has authorised the creation of the mortgage. This point was first decided by the Court of Appeal in the unregistered land case of *Bristol and West Building Society* v *Henning*.[292] It was soon applied to registered land in *Paddington Building Society* v *Mendelsohn*.[293] The principle was adopted and extended by the House of Lords in *Abbey National Building Society* v *Cann*,[294] where Mrs Cann was making a financial contribution, but she knew that her son needed to borrow £4,000 to finance the purchase. In fact he borrowed £25,000. It was held that the building society had priority for the entire loan. Finally, it has been held that, where the original mortgage is replaced by a new mortgage, the new mortgage has the same priority, up to the amount secured by the original mortgage.[295] This is best explained as the application of the principle of subrogation, whereby the second mortgagee steps into the shoes of the first mortgagee.

One response of the financial institutions to the decision in *Boland* was to seek the consent of any persons who were, or were likely to be, in occupation of the property which was proposed to be mortgaged. Suppose, for example, that a husband and wife have beneficial interests in the matrimonial home, but the legal estate is vested in the husband alone. Suppose, then, that the husband decides to raise money by mortgaging the property. If the wife is in actual occupation, the decision in *Boland* puts the financial institution at risk. The lender may well respond by asking the husband to obtain his wife's written

---

[291] [1991] 1 AC 56. For a fuller account of this case see ch 6, "Protection of the Purchaser".
[292] [1985] 1 WLR 778.
[293] (1985) 50 P & CR 244.
[294] [1991] 1 AC 56.
[295] *Equity & Law Home Loans Ltd* v *Prestidge* [1992] 1 WLR 137.

consent to the proposed mortgage. The courts have recognised that there is a real danger that the husband will by misrepresentation or undue influence induce the wife's consent, and they have sought means of guarding against that possibility. In *Barclay's Bank plc* v *O'Brien*[296] the House of Lords held that, if the lender has actual or constructive notice of any misrepresentation or undue influence, the wife may claim to have the transaction set aside.[297] The lender is therefore required to make appropriate inquiries and to ensure that the wife receives independent advice. In *Royal Bank of Scotland* v *Etridge (No 2)*[298] the House of Lords gave detailed guidance as to how lenders should act. The guidance reads virtually as if it were a statute, and it needs to be followed to the letter.

The classical distinction as to the priority between legal estates and equitable interests – that legal estates bind the whole world, but equitable interests bind all except equity's darling – was significantly affected in relation to land by the reforms of 1925. Firstly, in relation to unregistered land, which was the almost universal norm at that time, the Land Charges Act 1925, updated and re-enacted by the Land Charges Act 1972, introduced a system of registration of incumbrances. The system is designed to improve on the uncertainties created by constructive notice (what inquiries are reasonably to be expected?). The fundamental principles of land charges registration are that registration constitutes actual notice,[299] and that failure to register will make the interest void against a purchaser.[300] The Act contains a list of those interests which are registrable: the most notable are, in summary, estate contracts,[301] second legal

---

[296] [1994] 1 AC 180.
[297] It should be observed that the concept of notice is being used here in a different way, not so as to determine priority between two transactions (that concept of notice does not apply to registered land), but so as to enable the wife to raise a defence against the bank.
[298] [2002] 2 AC 773, especially the speech of Lord Nicholls. The cases cited were concerned with mortgages and guarantees, but it can be assumed that the notice principle which they embody can be applied to the situation considered in the text, the waiver by consent of an equitable interest.
[299] S 198, Law of Property Act 1925. Even a lessee who has no right to investigate the title to the reversion will have notice: *White* v *Bijou Mansions Ltd* [1937] Ch 610, affirmed [1938] Ch 351. Compare the position with regard to unregistrable equitable interests, governed by the old doctrine of notice: s 44(5), Law of Property Act 1925.
[300] S 4(6), Land Charges Act 1972. There are two categories of purchaser who will defeat an interest for non-registration: a class C(iv) charge and a charge of class D will be defeated by a purchaser of a legal estate for money or money's worth; other charges will be defeated by a purchaser for value of any interest. Even a purchaser with actual knowledge will take free from an unregistered interest: *Midland Bank Trust Co Ltd* v *Green* [1981] AC 513. Unlike the position in registered land, there is no protection for the owner of the interest who is in actual occupation: *Lloyds Bank plc* v *Carrick* [1996] 4 All ER 630.
[301] S 2(4), Land Charges Act 1972; "estate contract" includes an option to purchase and a right of pre-emption. This is a class C(iv) land charge.

mortgages and equitable changes,[302] restrictive covenants,[303] equitable easements,[304] and statutory rights to occupy the family home.[305] The list does not include all equitable interests. The most notable omission is an equitable interest arising under a trust of land, which continues to be governed by the doctrine of notice.[306]

The second reform of 1925 was the introduction of a system of full title registration by the Land Registration Act 1925. The governing statute is now the Land Registration Act 2002. The fundamental principle here is that all interests in a piece of land shall be entered on the register (the mirror principle). The effect is to erode substantially the distinction between legal estates and equitable interests. The purchaser's task is to search the register, and the purchaser will be bound by those estates and interests (whether legal or equitable) which are on the register. As already seen, there is a major exception in the case of overriding interests, but there also the distinction between legal estates and equitable interests plays little part.

In order to pave the way for the new system of registration of land and also the 'temporary' system of land charges for unregistered land some fundamental changes to the infra structure of land ownership were required. Section 1 of the Law of Property Act 1925 reduced the number of permissible legal estates in land to two[307] (freehold and leasehold)[308] and the number of legal interests to five[309]. All other interests in land, if valid, would subsequently take effect in equity[310]. The effect of these reforms was to reduce the possibility that legal interests would be automatically binding on the

---

[302] S 2(4), Land Charges Act 1972. This is a class C(i) or C(iii) land charge.
[303] S 2(5), Land Charges Act 1972. This is a class D(ii) land charge. A restrictive covenant made between a lessor and a lessee is excluded, even if the covenant affects land not comprised in the lease: *Dartstone Ltd* v *Cleveland Petroleum Co Ltd* [1969] 3 All ER 668, an unfortunate result.
[304] S 2(5), Land Charges Act 1972. This is a class D(iii) land charge.
[305] S 2(7), Land Charges Act 1972. This is a class F land charge.
[306] Hence the cases of *Caunce* v *Caunce* [1969] 1 WLR 286, and *Kingsnorth Finance Co Ltd* v *Tizard* [1969] 1 WLR 783, discussed earlier. There are other non-registrable equitable interests, particularly rights of entry: *Shiloh Spinners Ltd* v *Harding* [1973] AC 691; *Poster* v *Slough Estates Ltd* [1969] 1 Ch 495.
[307] S 1(1) Law of Property Act 1925.
[308] The statutory phrases in s1(1) are;
    (a) a fee simple absolute in possession (ie, not in reversion or remainder) – 'possession' under s205(1)(xix) includes the receipt of rents and profits or the right to receive the same if any, and
    (b) a term of years absolute (note the definition in s205(1)(xxvii) – 'absolute' is virtually deprived of all meaning).
[309] S 1(2) Law of Property Act 1925.
[310] S 1(3) Law of Property Act 1925.

purchaser of unregistered land[311] and that the Land Charges regime would be used to give purchasers of unregistered land knowledge of equitable interests (except for beneficial interests under a trust as discussed above). Although the registered land system was not as sensitive as to whether interests were legal or equitable these reforms made the first registration of land more efficient.

The effect of non-registration of land charges was given a severe test in M*idland Bank Trust Co Ltd* v *Green*.[312] Walter Green was the freehold owner of Gravel Hill Farm, some 300 acres of unregistered land. His son, Geoffrey, farmed the land under a lease from his father. In 1961 Walter granted to Geoffrey an option to purchase the freehold at the very favourable price of £75 per acre (valuing the land, therefore, at about £22,500). The option was registrable as a class C(iv) land charge under the Land Charges Act 1925 (subsequently the Land Charges Act 1972), but the option was not registered. In 1967 Walter, after a family disagreement, decided that he wished to defeat Geoffrey's option and, on legal advice, he conveyed the freehold to his wife, Evelyne, for a consideration of £500. Evelyne had actual knowledge of the option. The land was then worth about £40,000. In 1967 Geoffrey, having learned of the conveyance to his mother, registered the option and then gave notice exercising the option. In 1968 Evelyne died, and by her will she left all her property to Walter for life, and then in equal shares to her five children, one of whom was Geoffrey. In 1970 Geoffrey started proceedings against his father and his mother's executors, claiming specific performance of the option and damages for the tort of conspiracy. Walter died in 1972, and his executrix was substituted as a respondent. Geoffrey died in 1973 and his executors carried on the action on behalf of the estate. The action first came before the courts in 1977, by which time the value of the land had risen to some £400,000.

The Court of Appeal, reversing Oliver J, found in favour of Geoffrey's estate.[313] Lord Denning MR held that Evelyne was not protected by the Act, because she was guilty of fraud, in the sense of "dishonest dealing done so as to deprive unwary innocents of their rightful dues". Also, she was not a purchaser for money or money's worth, because she had not given "fair and

---

[311] See *Wilkes v Spooner* [1911] 2 KB 473.
[312] [1981] AC 513.
[313] [1980] Ch 590.

reasonable value".[314] Eveleigh LJ held that the conveyance to Evelyne was in reality a gift, the consideration of £500 being a sham (even though it was actually paid).

The House of Lords unanimously allowed the appeal.[315] Lord Wilberforce delivered the only substantial speech. He held that the statutory provisions (now mainly contained in section 4(6) of the Land Charges Act 1972) were too clear to be evaded. Evelyne had paid money for the land, and there was no requirement that she should pay the full value (or any particular value). There is no requirement in the Act that the purchaser be in good faith; the definition of "purchaser" in what is now section 17(1) of the Act omits that phrase, differing (presumably intentionally) from the definition in section 205 of the Law of Property Act 1925 (and in other parts of the 1925 legislation). It is not fraud to rely on legal rights conferred by an Act of Parliament.[316]

The decision has never been doubted; it is certainly a correct interpretation and application of the statutory provisions. However, it is instructive to consider whether the decision would have been the same if Walter's title to the land had been registered. There are two reasons for thinking that the decision would then have been in favour of Geoffrey's estate: (1) Geoffrey was as lessee in actual occupation of the land at the time of its sale to Evelyne, and therefore would have had an overriding interest under section 70(1)(g) of the Land Registration Act 1925, now schedule 3 to the Land Registration Act 2002;[317] (2) the definition of "purchaser" in section 3(xxi) of the Land Registration Act 1925 did include a requirement of good faith, and, even on a narrow definition of good faith (buying honestly and without an improper motive),[318] it is strongly arguable that Evelyne did not satisfy that requirement.

Various academic commentators, after the decision in *Midland Bank* v *Green*, proposed that a purchaser, whether of registered or unregistered land, who took with actual knowledge of an unregistered interest should not be

---

[314] Ibid at 624-625.
[315] [1981] AC 513.
[316] It is to be observed that the decision embodies the wider application of *Wilkes* v *Spooner* [1911] 2 KB 473, advocated in n 274, ante: the option was void against Evelyne, and therefore void against her personal representative, and therefore void against the beneficiaries under her will.
[317] See also *Midland Bank plc* v *Carrick* [1996] 4 All ER 630, for the lack of such protection in unregistered land.
[318] *Smith* v *Morrison* [1974] 1 WLR 659.

protected.[319] The Law Commission rejected that argument,[320] and section 29 of the Land Registration Act 2002 omits any requirement of good faith.

Thus the modern legislation omits any ethical element in determining whether a purchaser should be protected in these circumstances. However, the law of torts can produce a result which is in substance the opposite of that in land law. Oliver J held that Walter's estate was liable in damages for the tort of conspiracy, and the Court of Appeal affirmed the decision that husband and wife could together commit the tort of conspiracy.[321] Evelyne's estate escaped liability only because the action was out of time. Walter's estate had few assets, so that its liability in damages, for both breach of contract and conspiracy, had little value. In the end, some kind of justice was provided for Geoffrey's estate, because it was successful in an action in negligence against the solicitors who failed to advise registration of the option.[322] Lord Wilberforce stated that the action was settled for a considerable sum.[323]

Consider again the decision in *Lyus* v *Prowsa Developments Limited*,[324] which was discussed earlier.[325] That was a registered land case, and the decision depended in part on the requirement that the purchaser be in good faith, a requirement which has now been eliminated by the Land Registration Act 2002. Would that decision now be the same? The reasoning of Dillon J was based largely on the non-statutory element of unconscionability as giving rise to a constructive trust; the reasoning was approved by the Court of Appeal in *Ashburn Anstalt* v *Arnold*[326] and should still be followed.

---

[319] Howell, *Notice: A Broad and a Narrow View* [1996] Conv 34; Smith, *Land Registration: Reform at Last* in Jackson and Wilde, *The Reform of Property Law* (1997), 129 at 136; *Informal Transactions in Land, Estoppel and Registration* (1995) 58 MLR 637 at 655 (GB).
[320] *Land Registration for the Twenty-First Century: A Consultative Document*, Law Com No 254, paras 3.45 and 3.46.
[321] *Midland Bank Trust Co Ltd* v *Green (No 3)* [1982] Ch 529.
[322] *Midland Bank Trust Co Ltd* v *Hett, Stubbs & Kemp* [1979] Ch 384.
[323] [1981] AC 513 at 526. That conclusion might be fortuitous, because the decision that the action was brought within the limitation period might have been incorrect: see *Bell* v *Peter Browne & Co* [1990] 2 QB 495.
[324] [1982] 1 WLR 1044.
[325] P 51, *ante*.
[326] [1989] Ch 1.

Test the issue further by supposing the following hypothetical situation. If Evelyne Green, having bought the land for £500 from Walter, had immediately given the land back to Walter, would Walter step into Evelyne's shoes and take the land free from Geoffrey's option? It is easy to discern unconscionable conduct on the part of both parents and it may very well be that a constructive trust would be imposed.[327]

Consider also another possible scenario.[328] Suppose that the solicitor acting for Geoffrey, and therefore owing him a fiduciary duty to give him competent advice, had failed to register the option, and had then bought the land himself at an advantageous price. This situation seems clearly to fall within equity's rule that a fiduciary must not put himself into a position where his personal interest conflicts with his fiduciary duty.[329] A constructive trust should therefore be imposed.

---

[327] Compare *Re Stapleford Colliery Co* (1880) Ch D 432, cited in n 121, *ante*. On the actual facts of *Green*, Evelyne's will gave a life interest in the land to Walter, who outlived her for a short time. There appears to have been no challenge to that gift.
[328] This scenario is based on the facts of *Battison v Hobson* [1896] 2 Ch 403.
[329] See the discussion at p 50, *ante*.

Chapter 5

FORMALITIES FOR THE DISPOSITION OF PROPERTY

There are different kinds of property and there are various kinds of dispositions which may be made. The law needs to decide on the formalities, if any, required to make effective dispositions. They vary from a complete absence of formality to the most formal documentation. In many cases some form of written documentation is needed; that is conducive to certainty and the avoidance of fraud. This chapter considers a range of different formalities concerned with the transfer of tangible property. There is a broad division between chattels and land.

Contracts for the sale or other disposition of property

A contract for the sale of goods is governed by the Sale of Goods Act 1979. The Act contains no formal requirements for the entry into a contract for the sale of goods. Therefore, a contract may be made orally, whatever the nature or value of the goods. How, and when, is the transfer of ownership effected? One might think that the answer would be, by the seller delivering the goods to the buyer; but the Sale of Goods Act provides differently. Section 17(1) states that "Where there is a contract for the sale of specific or ascertained goods the property in them [ie, the seller's title to the goods, whatever it may be] is transferred to the buyer at such time as the parties to the contract intend it to be transferred." That general provision is supplemented by section 18, which sets out five "rules for ascertaining intention." The most striking is Rule 1, which reads as follows: "Where there is an unconditional contract for the sale of goods in a deliverable state the property in the goods passes to the buyer when the contract is made, and it is immaterial whether the time of payment or the time of delivery, or both, be postponed." Where this rule applies, the contract for the sale and the transfer of ownership are collapsed into one, and the whole transaction may be effected without any formality.

By contrast, consumer hire-purchase (and credit sale) agreements will be "regulated agreements" within section 8 of the Consumer Credit Act 1974, and are required by section 61(1) of the Act to be in writing signed by both parties. The rationale is consumer protection.

Contracts concerning land also require a high degree of formality. They are governed by section 2 of the Law of Property (Miscellaneous Provisions) Act 1989. The requirement is that a contract for the sale or other disposition of an interest in land shall be in writing, incorporating all the terms which the parties have expressly agreed, and signed by or on behalf of both parties to the contract.[330]

It needs to be observed that the Act marks a watershed from the previous law. Previously, the law required written evidence of the contract, failing which the contract would be unenforceable, but not void.[331] If either party had partly performed the contract, that party (it might be both) could enforce the contract. So, for example, the deposit of title deeds relating to a particular piece of land (or the land certificate), unaccompanied by any written evidence, would constitute an equitable mortgage.[332] After the Act that is no longer the case; if the contract is not in writing signed by both parties it is void, and there is no room for the doctrine of part performance.[333]

It is clear that section 2 applies to the disposition, or the creation, of all interests in land.[334] It applies, for example, to the creation of a mortgage, however short term or temporary the mortgage is intended to be.[335] It also applies to the creation of an option to purchase (or to renew a lease). The generally accepted view was that an option comprised a standing offer to sell (or renew) which could be accepted by the unilateral exercise of the option by the option holder according to its terms.[336] However, on that view, the exercise of the option would give rise to a new contract for sale (or renewal), requiring a new contract signed by both parties. That would be an extremely inconvenient result, which was avoided by Hoffmann J in *Spiro* v *Glencrown Properties Ltd*[337], by holding that, in this context, the option could be regarded as a conditional contract, so that the exercise of the option removed the condition, rather than created a new contract.

---

[330] It would seem that the signature may be in electronic form, for example by e mail: see *Golden Ocean Group Ltd* v *Salgaocar Mining Industries PVT Ltd* [2012] EWCA Civ 265.
[331] S 40, Law of Property Act 1925.
[332] *Russel* v *Russel* (1783) 1 Bro CC 269.
[333] *Firstpost Homes Ltd* v *Johnson* [1995] 1 WLR 1567; *United Bank of Kuwait plc* v *Sahib* [1997] Ch 107.
[334] "Disposition" is defined as in s 205 (1) (ii), Law of Property Act 1925; "Interest in land" means any estate, interest or charge in or over land: s 2(6), Law of Property (Miscellaneous Provisions) Act 1989.
[335] *United Bank of Kuwait plc* v *Sahib* [1997] Ch 107.
[336] *Helby* v *Matthews* [1895] AC 471; *Beesly* v *Hallwood Estates Ltd* [1960] 1 WLR 549.
[337] [1991] Ch 537.

The statutory requirements apply to a variation of the original contract. If the variation is not in writing signed by both parties, the original contract remains valid.[338]

The Court of Appeal has held[339] that section 2 does not apply to a boundary agreement, ie, an agreement between neighbours fixing the line of the boundary between their two properties, even if the agreement involves the transfer of a trivial amount of land.

There are exceptions to section 2. These include a contract to grant short leases, defined by section 54(2) of the Law of Property Act 1925,[340] a contract made in the course of a public auction, and "nothing in this section affects the creation or operation of resulting, implied or constructive trusts."[341]

The courts have recognised that the exception for constructive trusts has to be limited in its scope. As Neuberger LJ has said,[342] it is necessary to "avoid regarding [section 2(5)] as an automatically available escape route from the rigours of section 2(1)."

The exception was applied by the Court of Appeal in *Yaxley* v *Gotts*.[343] In that case the claimant was a builder who made an oral agreement with Mr. Brownie Gotts in relation to a house which, at that stage, Mr. Gotts was planning to buy. The house, on three floors, was already converted into flats, but was in need of refurbishment. The agreement was that the claimant would work on the refurbishment of the whole property, in return for which he would be granted a lease of the ground floor, which he would convert into two flats. Later it emerged that the buyer of the house was Alan, the son of Mr. Brownie Gotts. The claimant spent considerable time and money on the refurbishment of the whole house, encouraged by continuing representations from the Gotts that the claimant would become entitled to the ground floor. The work was completed and all the flats were let. The court held that, despite the absence of writing, the claimant could rely on proprietary estoppel. The claimant had proved that, in view of the Gotts' actions and words, it would now be unconscionable for them to deny that the claimant was entitled to a

---

[338] *McCausland* v *Duncan Lawrie Ltd* [1997] 1 WLR 38.
[339] *Joyce* v *Rigolli* [2004] 1 P & CR DG22 at para D56, following *Neilson* v *Poole* (1969) 20 P & CR 909.
[340] See below under "Deeds."
[341] S 2(5).
[342] *Kinane* v *Mackie-Conteh* [2005] 2 P&CR DG3 at [40].
[343] [2000] Ch 162.

beneficial interest in the house. On the facts, the appropriate way of giving effect to the estoppel was to impose a constructive trust on the Gotts, within the section 2(5) exception, with the result that the claimant was entitled to a 99 year lease of the ground floor, with an account of the rents paid in the interim to Mr. Alan Gotts.[344]

The judgment of Robert Walker LJ contains a detailed explanation as to why estoppel can be used to overcome section 2.[345] The essence is that he considers that to grant relief by way of estoppel is not so offensive to the public policy, or mischief, underlying section 2 as to frustrate the will of Parliament. So also Beldam LJ: "I do not think it inherent in a social policy of simplifying conveyancing by requiring the certainty of a written document that unconscionable conduct or equitable fraud should be allowed to prevail."[346]

Deeds

A deed, along with a will, represents the highest degree of documentary formality provided, or required, by English law. A deed can be used for two quite different purposes. The first is to make a formal contract, obviating the need for consideration.[347] The second is for the disposition of all types of tangible property, chattels and land, and for the disposition of various types of intangible property. A deed is required for the transfer or creation of any legal estate or legal interest in land. Section 52(1) of the Law of Property Act 1925 provides as follows: "All conveyances of land or of any interest therein are void for the purpose of conveying or creating a legal estate unless made

---

[344] Compare this with *Yeoman's Row Management Ltd* v *Cobbe* [2008] UKHL 55 discussed above at p 62.
[345] [2000] Ch 162 at 180 D-E.
[346] Ibid at 193 C. See also Pill LJ in *Shah* v *Shah* [2002] QB 35 at paras 19-33, in the context of the execution of deeds. Compare Lord Scott of Foscote, with the concurrence of Lord Hoffmann, Lord Brown of Eaton - Under-Heywood and Lord Mance, in *Yeoman's Row Management Ltd* v *Cobbe* [2008] UKHL 55 at para 29: "The proposition that an owner of land can be estopped from asserting that an agreement is void for want of compliance with section 2 is, in my opinion, unacceptable. The assertion is no more than the statute provides. Equity can surely not contradict the statute."
[347] See, for example, *Shah* v *Shah* [2002] QB 35, below. A deed is also required for the creation of a power of attorney, ie, a formal delegation of authority to an agent: s 1, Powers of Attorney Act 1971. For example, a trustee's powers may be delegated by a power of attorney: s 25, Trustee Act 1925; s 9, Trusts of Land and Appointment of Trustees Act 1996; Trustee Delegation Act 1999. A power of attorney is also useful for an advance delegation of the power of decision-making in relation to an individual's property or person, where that individual might lose the power of such decision-making: see Part 1 of the Mental Capacity Act 2005.

by deed."[348] "Conveyance" is widely defined so as to include a mortgage, charge, lease, and the creation of any other interest in land.[349] For example, the creation of a legal easement, such as a right of way or a right of light, will fall within section 52(1). The requirement for a deed applies also to registered land, by virtue of the prescribed forms of transfer set out in schedule 1 to the Land Registration Rules 2003.[350]

There are various exceptions to section 52(1). They include assents by personal representatives and certain short leases.[351] A personal representative, ie, an executor or administrator of a deceased person's estate, may transfer a legal estate by a document in writing signed by the personal representative and naming the person in whose favour it is given; this is known as an assent. It need not be in the form of a deed.[352] The excepted short leases are defined in section 54(2) of the Law of Property Act 1925, which reads as follows: "Nothing in the foregoing provisions of this Part of this Act shall affect the creation by parol of leases taking effect in possession for a term not exceeding three years (whether or not the lessee is given power to extend the term) at the best rent which can be reasonably obtained without taking a fine." The phrase "by parol" means that such leases can be created orally, without any kind of writing; "fine" is an old-fashioned word meaning a premium in more modern terminology, that is, a capital payment, unusual in the case of such short leases.

The standard periodic tenancies (weekly, monthly, quarterly and yearly tenancies) are within the exception, and therefore they can be created orally. Indeed, they can be created by implication, without any explicit agreement at all. If Brian allows Celia to take possession of his land, and Celia starts to pay rent calculated on a periodic basis, Celia will acquire a tenancy commensurate with that period.

---

[348] By contrast, the creation or disposition of an equitable interest in land requires only a written instrument signed by the person creating or disposing of the interest, or by that person's agent authorised in writing: s 53(1)(a), Law of Property Act 1925.
[349] S 205(1)(ii), Law of Property Act 1925.
[350] See the specimen form of transfer set out in Megarry & Wade, *The Law of Real Property* 7th ed, para 7-149.
[351] S 52(2), Law of Property 1925.
[352] S 36(4), Administration of Estates Act 1925.

It will be noticed that the exception applies only to the creation of a short lease and does not extend to the transfer (assignment) of such a lease, which still therefore requires a deed.[353]

What, then, is a deed? It used to be said that a deed needed to be "signed, sealed and delivered." That was changed for human beings by section 1 of the Law of Property (Miscellaneous Provisions) Act 1989;[354] "signed, witnessed and delivered" summarises the present requirements. These requirements are set out in section 1(2), (2A) and (3), as follows:

"(2) An instrument shall not be a deed unless-

(a) it makes it clear on its face that it is intended to be a deed by the person making it or, as the case may be, by the parties to it (whether describing itself as a deed or expressing itself to be executed or signed as a deed or otherwise); and

(b) it is validly executed as a deed-

(i) by that person or a person authorised to execute it in the name or on behalf of that person; or

(ii) by one or more of those parties or a person authorised to execute it in the name or on behalf of one or more of those parties.

(2A) For the purposes of subsection (2)(a) above, an instrument shall not be taken to make it clear on its face that it is intended to be a deed merely because it is executed under seal.

(3) An instrument is validly executed as a deed by an individual if, and only if-

(a) it is signed-

(i) by him in the presence of a witness who attests the signature; or

(ii) at his direction and in his presence and the presence of two witnesses who each attest the signature; and

(b) it is delivered as a deed..."

---

[353] *Crago* v *Julian* [1992] 1 WLR 372.
[354] S 1(1)(b). A seal is still required for execution by a corporation of any kind.

86

The clearest way for an instrument to make it clear on its face that it is intended to be a deed is to adopt the traditional form of drafting:

"THIS DEED is made the – day of - 2017....", and ending with an attestation clause:

" Signed as a deed by – in the presence of -."

Presumably, a document commencing with the words "THIS CONVEYANCE", or "THIS TRANSFER", or "THIS LEASE", and continuing as above to an attestation clause, would show the necessary intention that it is to be a deed, relying on the words "or otherwise" at the end of section 1(2)(b).

The requirement that the signature be witnessed was new in 1989, although attestation was common before the Act. What if the person incurring an obligation under the deed subsequently proves that the witness was not in fact present when she signed the document? That was the situation in *Shah v Shah*.[355] The respondents had undertaken to pay to the claimant the sum of £1.5 million, together with interest amounting to some £170,302. They signed a document which started with the words "THIS DEED" and which finished with an attestation clause, stating that they had both signed in the presence of a witness, whose signature appeared alongside theirs. It was subsequently established that the witness was not present at the time, but added his signature a short time later. The claimant had no knowledge of the defect. The defendants argued that the document was invalid as a deed.[356] The Court of Appeal held that the defendants had represented to the claimant that the document was valid as a deed, the claimant had relied on that representation to his detriment, and the defendants were estopped from asserting that the document was invalid as a deed.

The last requirement for a document to be valid as a deed is that it be delivered. In the modern law, this does *not* mean that the document be handed over to the person intended to benefit. It means only that the person executing the document intends to be bound by it as a deed. That will usually be clear from the wording of the document and from the fact that it is signed

---

[355] [2002] QB 35.
[356] It could not be valid as a contract because there was no consideration for the defendants' promise.

and witnessed. However, the document can be delivered in escrow, ie, subject to a condition. Unless and until the condition occurs, the effect of the deed is suspended, though it cannot be revoked. The deed ceases to have effect if the condition does not occur. An everyday example is the execution of a deed of conveyance or transfer a few days before the agreed date for completion of a transaction, for example the sale of a house There is an implied condition that the effect of the deed is suspended until the purchase money is paid.

Finally, it needs to be observed that, at some time in the future, both contracts for the disposition of land and conveyances or transfers will be carried out by paperless (ie, electronic) transactions. The way has been prepared by two statutes, the Electronic Communications Act 2000 and the Land Registration Act 2002. This is a brief summary of what is envisaged.

Firstly, the Electronic Communications Act provides, in section 8, that electronic forms of contracting may be applied to contracts for the sale or other disposition of land, whether registered or unregistered. In 2001 a draft order was issued for consultation, which proposed the addition of section 2A of the Law of Property (Miscellaneous Provisions) Act 1989.[357] A further draft order was published by the Land Registry in 2007. The idea is that, if all the terms of the contract are incorporated, the date and time of the contract are defined, and the electronic signatures of the authenticating persons are certified, that will satisfy the writing requirements of the 1989 Act.

Secondly, section 91 of the Land Registration 2002 provides, in relation to registered land, an electronic alternative to the conventional conveyancing methods of written instruments and deeds. The section applies to a disposition of a registered estate or charge, a disposition of an interest protected by a notice on the register, and a disposition which triggers first registration.[358] The conditions for compliance are similar to those prescribed by the Electronic Communications Act, summarised above.[359] Where the section applies, a document is to be regarded as in writing and signed as necessary, or, as the case may be, as a deed.[360] If the document is authenticated by an agent, the agent is deemed to have the written authority

---
[357] The draft Law of Property (Electronic Communications) Order 2001, art 4.
[358] S 91(2), Land Registration Act 2002.
[359] S 91(3).
[360] S 91 (4) and (5).

of the principal.[361] Access to the registry for these purposes will be provided under a "Land registry network"[362], which will be available to persons who enter into a "network access agreement" with the registrar.[363] In order to facilitate do-it-yourself conveyancing, the registrar will be obliged to provide assistance to those who are not parties to a network access agreement.[364] It is implicit that the entry of a document on the register will actually effect the intended transaction. So, for example, where agreement is reached for the sale of land, the contract will become effective only on being entered electronically on the register; without such entry there will be no contract.

Thirdly, section 93 of the Land Registration Act 2002 will, when implemented, require, not merely permit, the use of electronic methods. This will apply to contracts as well as dispositions, so that, at that stage, the position under the Electronic Communications Act will, in relation to registered land, be superseded. The exact scope of section 93 will be defined in due course by rules to be made by the Lord Chancellor.[365] We can suppose, for example, that it will not apply to various kinds of informally created interests, such as short leases or interests arising under constructive or resulting trusts. The idea was that compulsory electronic conveyancing would be introduced gradually, and to that end the Land Registration (Electronic Conveyancing) Rules 2008 apply section 93 to stand alone registered charges. However, the planned application of section 93 to electronic transfers[366] has now been put on indefinite hold (as at July 2011).

The Law Commission has provided a useful illustration of the way in which electronic conveyancing might operate.[367]

Trusts and dispositions of an equitable interest

A trust may be created over all kinds of property, tangible or intangible, including an existing equitable interest under a trust. The essential idea is

---

[361] S 91(6).
[362] S 92.
[363] Sch 5.
[364] Sch 5, para 7.
[365] S 93.
[366] See the draft Land Registration (Electronic Conveyancing) Rules 2011.
[367] See their report, "Land Registration for the Twenty-First Century. A Conveyancing Revolution" (Law Com No 271), paras 2.52 *et seq*.

that the property shall be held for the benefit of another person, the beneficiary. No special form of words is necessary to create the trust; in particular, it is not necessary to use the word "trust". All that is needed is a clear intention that the property shall be held for the beneficiary (or beneficiaries). A striking example is the decision of the Court of Appeal in *Paul* v *Constance*.[368] Mr. Constance received a cheque. With the agreement of the claimant, with whom he had been living for some six years, he paid it into a bank account in his sole name. He said to the claimant at the time, and on various subsequent occasions, "The money is as much yours as mine". Mr. Constance died intestate, and the money was claimed by his wife from whom he had separated. The decision was that he had created a trust under which he held the money on trust for himself and the claimant in equal shares, so that his wife was entitled to only one half.

On the other side of the line is *Jones* v *Lock*.[369] A father wished to make a gift of money to his baby son. He produced a £900 cheque, payable to himself, and said, "Look you here, I give this to baby; it is for himself." He gave the cheque to the baby but then retrieved it and put it in a safe. The cheque was found when the father died, and the question for the court was whether the cheque belonged to the father's estate. Clearly there was no direct gift, since that would require the father to endorse the cheque, so as to transfer the legal title. However, it was argued that the father, through his words and actions, had declared a trust of the cheque. That argument was rejected, the court holding that the father had intended a direct gift, not to incur the obligations of a trustee. The cheque, therefore, belonged to the father's estate.

In the case of land, section 53 of the Law of Property Act 1925 provides as follows:

"(1)(b) A declaration of trust respecting any land or any interest therein must be manifested and proved by some writing signed by some person who is able to declare such trust or by his will.

(c).....

(2) This section does not affect the creation or operation of resulting, implied or constructive trusts."

---

[368] [1977] 1 WLR 527.
[369] (1865) LR 1 Ch App 25.

Three points should be noted. Firstly, the section applies, of course, only to express trusts. Secondly, the requirement is that the declaration of trust be "manifested and proved by some writing", not that the declaration should actually be in writing. The written evidence may, for example, be in the form of a letter recording the terms of the trust.[370] Thirdly, the written document must be signed by the person who is able to create the trust, that is the beneficial owner of the property to be subjected to the trust. If that property is itself an equitable interest under a trust, the signature required is that of the beneficiary, not the trustee.[371]

The requirement of written evidence is clearly designed to create certainty and to prevent fraud. Indeed, section 53(1)(b) is the modern version of section 8 of the Statute of Frauds 1677. However, it is well established that a court of equity will not allow a statute designed to prevent fraud to be used as an instrument of fraud. So, for example, if Celia transfers land to David, subject to an oral undertaking by David that he will hold the land for the benefit of Edward, David will not be permitted to deny the trust and claim the land for himself.[372] It would be sufficient, in order to prevent fraud, to impose on David a resulting trust back to Celia, but it would seem that the intended trust in favour of Edward will be enforced.[373]

The disposition of an existing equitable interest is governed by a different, and more rigorous, formal requirement. Section 53(1)(c) of the Law of Property Act 1925 provides as follows:

"A disposition of an equitable interest or trust subsisting at the time of the disposition must be in writing signed by the person disposing of the same, or by his agent thereunto lawfully authorised in writing or by will." However, as we have seen, section 53(2) qualifies that by providing that "This section does not affect the creation or operation of resulting, implied or constructive trusts."

---

[370] *Morton* v *Tewart* (1842) 2 Y & C Ch 67; *Childers v Childers* (1857) 1 De G & J 482.
[371] *Tierney* v *Wood* (1854) 19 Beav 330; *Kronheim v Johnson* (1877) 7 Ch D 60.
[372] *Rochefoucauld* v *Boustead* [1897] 1 Ch 196. See also *Bannister v Bannister* [1948] 2 ALL ER 133.
[373] See *Taylor* v *Salmon* (1838) 4 My & Cr 134; *Binions v Evans* [1972] Ch 359; *Neale v Willis* (1968) 19 P & CR 839. See also the discussion of secret trusts in the section "Dispositions on death", *post*, p.105.

The following points should be noted. The requirement is that the disposition shall be in writing, not merely evidenced in writing. The signature may be that of the person making the disposition or of an agent authorised in writing. The purpose of this requirement is to prevent hidden oral transactions in equitable interests, and to ensure that a trustee can ascertain the identity of the beneficiary.[374] The requirement is not limited to land; it applies to all kinds of property.[375] It applies to all kinds of trusts, not merely to express trusts.

These seemingly innocuous provisions have given rise to a line of very complex court decisions. The following is a simplified account.[376] The first point is, what is covered by the word "disposition"? It is obvious that a direct transfer of the equitable interest by the original beneficiary to a new beneficiary is a disposition. But the same effect can be achieved, indirectly, if the original beneficiary directs the trustee to hold for a new beneficiary. The House of Lords held in *Grey v Inland Revenue Commissioners*[377] that such a transaction is a disposition and is therefore required to be in writing. If, however, the trustee on the direction of the beneficiary transfers the legal title to the trust property to a new beneficiary, a separate disposition of the equitable interest is not required.[378] Where the original beneficiary contracts to transfer the equitable interest to a new beneficiary, with the consent of the beneficiary, and the contract is specifically enforceable, the contract creates a constructive trust, which, by virtue of section 53(2) of the Law of Property Act 1925, is exempt from the requirement of writing.[379] If the original beneficiary declares a trust of the equitable interest in favour of a new beneficiary, that is not a disposition within section 53(1)(c), but is rather a declaration of trust (creating a sub-trust) and is governed by section 53(1)(b).[380]

---

[374] Per Lord Upjohn in *Vandervell v Inland Revenue Commissioners* [1967] 2 AC 291 at 311. It is to be observed, however, that there is no obligation to notify the trustee about the disposition.

[375] The leading cases are *Grey v Inland Revenue Commissioners* [1960] AC 1, *Oughtred v Inland Revenue Commissioners* [1960] AC 206, and *Vandervell v Inland Revenue Commissioners* [1967] 2 AC 291 (all relate to company shares).

[376] As Smith remarks in *Property Law*, 8th ed, p 129, "These issue take us deep into difficult equity theory: rather too difficult for a general book on property!"

[377] [1960] AC 1.

[378] *Vandervell v Inland Revenue Commissioners* [1967] 2 AC 291. The best explanation of this result is that the original beneficiary's interest is destroyed by the transfer of the legal title to the new beneficiary: see Spencer, "Of Concurring Beneficiaries and Transferring Trustees" (1967) 31 Conv (NS) 175.

[379] *Oughtred v Inland Revenue Commissioners* [1960] AC 206; *Re Holt's Settlement* [1969] 1 Ch 100; *Neville v Wilson* [1997] Ch 144. Of course, if the contract is for the transfer of an interest in land, the contract itself must be in writing: s 2, Law of Property (Miscellaneous Provisions) Act 1989.

[380] See *Nelson v Greening & Sykes (Builders) Ltd* [2008] 1 EGLR 59.

So much for the statutory formalities. The courts of equity have worked out the methods of creating a trust. One is by the owner of the property declaring that she holds the property on trust for a specified beneficiary. The other is for the owner to transfer the property to another person to hold on trust for the specified beneficiary. If the second (transfer) method is employed, it had long been regarded as essential that the correct method should be employed to transfer the property to the trustee. If, for example, the property was a legal estate in land, a deed was required. Failing that, the trust would be regarded as incompletely constituted and ineffective. The definitive case embodying this proposition is *Milroy* v *Lord*.[381] Turner LJ stated the law as follows:[382] "I take the law of this Court to be well settled, that, in order to make a voluntary settlement valid and effectual, the settlor must have done everything which, according to the nature of the property comprised in the settlement, was necessary to be done in order to transfer the property and render the settlement binding upon him. He may, of course, do this by actually transferring the property to the persons for whom he intends to provide, and provision will then be effectual, and it will be equally effectual if he transfers the property to a trustee for the purposes of the settlement, or declares that he himself holds it in trust for those purposes;....but, in order to render the settlement binding, one or other of these modes must, as I understand the law of this court, be resorted to, for there is no equity in this court to perfect an imperfect gift. The cases, I think, go further to this extent, that if the settlement is intended to be effectuated by one of the modes to which I have referred, the Court will not give effect to it by applying another of those modes. If it is intended to take effect by transfer, the court will not hold the intended transfer to operate as a declaration of trust, for then every imperfect instrument would be made effectual by being converted into a perfect trust."

The two methods of creating a trust may be combined as, for example, if Celia transfers property to herself and David to hold on trust for Edward. The legal result in such a case is that the trust is effective as against Celia, and she is obliged to complete the trust as intended by transferring the property into the name also of David.[383]

---

[381] (1862) 4 De GF&J 264.
[382] Ibid at 274-275.
[383] *Choithram (T) International SA v Pagarani* [2001] 1 WLR 1.

There is an important qualification to the "either/or" rule in *Milroy v Lord*. If the donor has done everything required to be done by her to transfer the property to a trustee, but something remains to be done by a third party to complete the transfer, equity will compel the donor to hold the property on trust for the intended beneficiary. The leading case is *Re Rose*.[384] The donor executed a deed in order to transfer shares to a trustee. However, the transfer was not registered in the company's books until two months later, by which time the donor had died. The Court of Appeal held that, although registration in the company's books was required to transfer the legal title to the shares, the donor had during his lifetime done all that was necessary to transfer the legal title, and that his estate held the shares on trust for the intended beneficiary. This was applied to the analogous case of registered land in *Mascall v Mascall*.[385] That case concerned an intended direct gift, but the same principle applies. The donor decided to give some land to his son. He executed a transfer in the son's favour, and handed over the transfer and the land certificate to his son. However, the father changed his mind and recovered possession of the documents before any application was made for registration. The Court of Appeal decided that the father held the land on trust for his son.

There is one clear exception to the principle of *Milroy v Lord*, and that is proprietary estoppel. If the donor, by her words or deeds, has led the donee to act in reliance on the proposed gift, especially if the reliance is detrimental to the done, the court may regard it as unconscionable for the donor to deny that the gift is effective. In such a case, the court might remedy the injustice by imposing a trust on the donor.[386]

The strict "either/or" rule in *Milroy v Lord* was re-examined and softened by the decision of the Court of Appeal in *Pennington v Waine*.[387] The donor executed a transfer of shares in a private company to her nephew, intending him to become a director of the company, a position open only to shareholders. The transfer form was not delivered to the nephew; it was sent

---

[384] [1952] Ch 499. See also Lord Wilberforce in *Vandervell v Inland Revenue Commissioners* [1967] 2 AC 291 at 330. Cf *Re Fry* [1946] Ch 312, where, as the donor was domiciled abroad, the transfer required Treasury consent, and the application for consent was incomplete.
[385] (1984) 50 P & CR 119.
[386] See, for example, *Dillwyn v Llewelyn* (1862) 4 De GF & J 517 (trust); *Pascoe v Turner* [1979] 1 WLR 431 (transfer of legal fee simple).
[387] [2002] 1 WLR 2075.

to the donor's agent, who told the nephew that he need not take any further steps to implement the transfer. The nephew agreed to become a director and was so appointed. The donor died a few weeks later. It was held that the process of transferring the shares had gone so far that it would be unconscionable for the donor, and her personal representative after her death, to withdraw from the transaction, so that the estate held the shares on trust for the nephew. The decision is surprising and very controversial. It is surprising, because it goes against a long-standing line of authority.[388] It is controversial, because it introduces a greater degree of uncertainty into this branch of the law.[389] Even if it be accepted that unconscionability is a relevant concept, it is difficult to see that the donor's behaviour was in fact so reprehensible.

The effect of *Pennington v Waine* on the future development of the law remains unpredictable but the courts have moved back towards the principle laid down in *Re Rose* in more recent cases. In *Zeitel v Kaye*[390] the Court of Appeal dutifully cited *Pennington v Waine*, but then proceeded to reason on pure *Re Rose* principles, without even a nod in favour of the softer approach in *Pennington v Waine*. The following year in *Curtis v Pulbrook*[391], Briggs J reasoned that a man intending to transfer some shares to his wife and daughter had not done everything necessary for him to effect transfer of the shares and so the principle from *Re Rose* did not apply on the facts of the case. Briggs J considered that *Choithram* and *Pennington* did not follow or establish any clear principle[392]: "I reach that conclusion without any great comfort that the existing rules about the circumstances when equity will and will not perfect an apparently imperfect gift of shares do not serve any clearly identifiable or rational policy objective". From this evidence it would appear that the *Re Rose* principle has been re-established.

---

[388] Halliwell, [2005] Conv 192, states that the decision is "completely irreconcilable with all the earlier authorities". Other commentators have been equally critical: see, for example, Tijo and Yeo, [2002] LMCLQ 296; Ladds, (2003) 17 *Trust Law International* 35; Doggett, [2003] CLJ 263.
[389] In various contexts, not least for tax purposes, it may be important to determine as precisely as possible when a transfer takes effect.
[390] [2010] EWCA Civ 159.
[391] [2011] EWHC 167 (Ch).
[392] Ibid at para 47.

Gifts of chattels

We are all surely familiar with the idea of giving presents to friends or relatives, birthday presents, wedding presents, or whatever. How do we do it? Obviously, by handing over the gift item to the donee with the intention, explicit or implicit, of transferring ownership. In other words, what is required is intention plus delivery. A deed may also be used, but is unlikely, for obvious reasons.

The necessity of delivery, the physical handing over of possession, is well established, the foundation case being *Cochrane* v *Moore*.[393] The rule works well enough with gifts of small, portable objects, but runs into difficulties with heavy or bulky objects, or collections of objects. How, for example, would one make a gift of a grand piano, or of a set of dining chairs? In *Re Cole*[394] the donor, then a very rich man, wanted to give the entire contents of his new house to his wife. He took her to the house and showed her around it. On the ground floor she handled certain of the items. He said to her, "It's all yours". Some years later Mr. Cole became insolvent and was declared bankrupt. Mrs. Cole claimed that her husband had given to her the contents of the house, but her claim was resisted by Mr. Cole's trustee in bankruptcy on behalf of the creditors. The Court of Appeal held that there were sufficient words of gift to prove the donor's intention, but that there was no delivery, and therefore no effective gift.

The case appears to be correctly decided on the basis of case law authority, but in such circumstances the requirement of delivery seems to be extremely technical and virtually impossible to satisfy. Are there any means by which Mr. Cole could have made an effective gift to his wife? He could, of course, have executed a deed of gift, but that seems unlikely. He could have sold the property to her for a nominal price; as has been seen,[395] no delivery is required in a sale of goods. He could have declared himself a trustee for his wife, where, except in the case of a trust of land, all that is required is that the

---

[393] (1890) 25 QBD 57.
[394] [1964] Ch 175.
[395] See p 81, *ante*.

intention should be clear.[396] All of these modes of disposition would be effective, but they all seem highly artificial.[397]

The need for delivery is relaxed or modified in certain situations. If the donee is already in possession of the property, for example as a bailee, there is no need for the property to be returned to the donor then redelivered to the donee: words of gift are sufficient to change the possession from that of bailee to that of donee.[398] In the case of a collection of objects, such as a quantity of furniture, there may be delivery of the whole by handing over a representative object, such as a chair.[399] A church organ may be delivered by the donor putting her hand on the organ in the presence of the donee and speaking words of gift.[400] The law has also recognised the possibility of delivery by the handing over of a key, as for example where the object is contained in a locked box, provided that the donee has access to the box and that the donor is excluded from access.[401]

It is sufficient if the donee acquires possession after the words of gift are spoken, provided that the intention to make a gift is continuing. In *Thomas* v *The Times Book Co Ltd*[402] the poet Dylan Thomas was commissioned by the BBC to write a verse play for radio, *Under Milk Wood*. The project was under the direction of the BBC producer Douglas Cleverdon, who worked very closely with Dylan Thomas. In 1953 Thomas lost the manuscript, but Cleverdon supplied him with copies. That was important, because Thomas was about to fly to America to give some poetry readings, and he planned to read from *Under Milk Wood*. Before leaving, Thomas said to Cleverdon that if he (Cleverdon) could find the manuscript he could keep it. Thomas gave the

---

[396] See p 90, *ante*, and *Jones* v *Lock* (1865) LR 1 Ch App 25, there cited. Counsel for Mrs. Cole did not attempt to argue that there was a trust. Such an argument was at the time precluded by *Milroy* v *Lord* (1861) 4 De G F & J 264. Even under the softer approach of *Pennington* v *Waine* [2002] 1 WLR 2075, it seems difficult to argue that the claim of the trustee in bankruptcy was unconscionable.

[397] Even a completed gift can be reopened and set aside in the event of a subsequent bankruptcy. If the transfer was at a significant undervalue and was made in order to defeat or prejudice creditors, it can be reopened at any time: s 423, Insolvency Act 1986. Further, a transfer at a significant undervalue can be reopened if made within two years of the bankruptcy, or within five years if the transferor was insolvent at the date of the transfer: s 339, Insolvency Act 1986.

[398] *Winter* v *Winter* (1861) 4 LT 639; *Re Stoneham* [1919] 1 Ch 149; *Pascoe* v *Turner* [1979] 1 WLR 431.

[399] *Lock* v *Heath* (1892) 8 TLR 295. Mrs. Cole's handling of certain items seems to have been considered as her merely inspecting them.

[400] *Rawlinson* v *Mort* (1905) 93 LT 555.

[401] *Re Wasserberg* [1915] 1 Ch 195. There will be no delivery if the donor has a duplicate key: *Re Craven's Estate* [1937] Ch 423 at 428.

[402] [1966] 1 WLR 911.

names of various pubs where he might have left the manuscript, or in the alternative suggested that he might have left it in a taxi. Cleverdon found the manuscript a few days later in one of the pubs named by Thomas. Thomas died in New York about three weeks later.

Under Milk Wood was first performed on the BBC in 1954, to great acclaim. The Times Book Company bought the manuscript in 1961 for £2,000. The claimant, Mrs. Caitlin Thomas, was the widow of Dylan Thomas and his sole personal representative. Plowman J dismissed the claim; the gift was completed when Douglas Cleverdon found the manuscript and took it into his possession with the consent of Dylan Thomas. At that point the two essential elements of intention and delivery coincided. The Times Book Company had a good title derived from Cleverdon.

It would have been different, of course, if Dylan Thomas had died before Douglas Cleverdon had found the manuscript, for then the death would terminate the consent and the manuscript would then belong to the deceased's estate.[403]

Finally, there is a significant exception to the requirement of delivery. If the intended donee subsequently acquires ownership of the chattel, and the donor has a continuing intention to make the gift, that acquisition of ownership completes the gift.[404] A particular application of the principle is the rule in *Strong v Bird*,[405] which applies when the intended donee becomes the personal representative[406] of the donor on her death. The vesting of the legal title in the personal representative completes the gift, so that the donee/personal representative becomes entitled to the chattel instead of the persons claiming under the deceased's will or on intestacy. It has been held that the general principle applies no matter by what route the ownership of the chattel becomes vested in the intended donee.[407]

---

[403] For a similar analysis where a cheque was not processed by the paying bank before the death of the drawer, see *Re Swinburne* [1926] Ch 38; and see *Re Beaumont* [1902] 1 Ch 886; *Re Owen* [1949] 1 All ER 901; s 75, Bills of Exchange Act 1882.
[404] *Re Bowden* [1936] Ch 71.
[405] (1874) LR 18 Eq 315.
[406] For the meaning and function of "personal representative", see the next section, "Dispositions on death".
[407] *Re Ralli's Will Trusts* [1964] Ch 288; see especially per Buckley J at 301 (the claimant was a trustee of the deceased's will and a trustee of a pre-existing settlement; the property came to him in his former capacity, but the vesting of the legal title in him was sufficient to complete the constitution of the trust under the

Dispositions on death

English law provides for the inheritance of property on death. It therefore needs to provide mechanisms for deciding who shall inherit the property on the death of its present owner, and by what means the property shall be transferred to the new owner. The present owner of property, if of full age and capacity, may make a will, directing who shall inherit her property after her death. In the absence of a will, the deceased will die intestate, and the law will determine who will inherit from among the next of kin. If there is a will which fails to deal with the whole of the deceased's estate, there will be a partial intestacy. The next of kin on intestacy are defined by statute, principally the Administration of Estates Act 1925 and the Intestates' Estates Act 1952. The next of kin comprise: the surviving spouse or civil partner[408]; issue, ie, children or remoter descendants; parents; brothers and sisters of the whole blood; brothers and sisters of the half blood; grandparents; uncles and aunts of the whole blood; uncles and aunts of the half blood. Surviving issue of a deceased child take the share of the deceased child, and deceased brothers, sisters, uncles and aunts are represented by their surviving descendants (ie, nephews, nieces and cousins). If there are no next of kin, the intestate's estate passes to the Crown (or the Duchy of Lancaster or the Duchy of Cornwall) as *bona vacantia*.[409]

The fundamental rule relating to wills is that the testatrix may leave her property to whomsoever she chooses: freedom of testation. However, that freedom is restricted by the Inheritance (Provision for Family and Dependants) Act 1975, which provides that defined categories of the deceased's family and dependants may apply to the court for reasonable financial provision to be made to the applicant out of the deceased's estate. The defined categories are: the surviving spouse or civil partner of the deceased; a former spouse or civil partner who has not formed a subsequent marriage or civil partnership; a person who during the whole of the period of two years immediately before the death was living in the same household as the deceased as the husband, wife or civil partner of the deceased; a child of the deceased; a person who

---

settlement). However, that point seems to conflict with *Re Brooks' Settlement Trusts* [1939] 1 Ch 993, which was not cited in *Re Ralli*.

[408] Not, as yet, including the survivor of a cohabitation relationship. However, such a person may apply to the court under the Inheritance (Provision for Families and Dependants) Act 1975; see the next paragraph.

[409] See the table in s 46, Administration of Estates Act 1952, as substituted by s 1, Inheritance and Trustees' Powers Act 2014.

was treated as a child of the deceased's family; and any other person who immediately before the death was being maintained, wholly or partly, by the deceased.[410] The Court must be satisfied that the effect of the deceased's will or the law relating to intestacy is not such as to make reasonable financial provision for the applicant.[411] When so satisfied, the court has power to make a wide range of orders so as to ensure that the applicant receives reasonable financial provision.[412] There is a wide range of factors which the court must take into account, including the financial resources and financial needs of the applicant.[413] Such resources will obviously include any financial provision made for the applicant by the deceased during her lifetime. The Act confers on the court a very wide- ranging discretion, to be moulded to the particular circumstances, with the result that the decision on a particular application may be difficult to predict.

What are the formal requirements for the making of a valid will? Section 9 of the Wills Act 1837[414] provides as follows:

> "No will shall be valid unless-
>
> (a) it is in writing, and signed by the testator, or by some other person in his   presence and by his direction; and
>
> (b) it appears that the testator intended by his signature to give effect to the will;
>
> (c) the signature is made or acknowledged by the testator in the presence of two or more witnesses present at the same time; and
>
> (d) each witness either-
>
>> (i)   attests and signs the will; or

---

[410] S 1, Inheritance (Provision for Families and Dependants) Act 1975, amended by sch 2, Inheritance and Trustees' Powers Act 2014.
[411] Ibid, s 1(1).
[412] Ibid, s 2.
[413] Ibid, s 3.
[414] As amended and re-enacted by s 17, Administration of Justice Act 1982.

> (ii) acknowledges his signature in the presence of the testator (but not necessarily in the presence of any other witness), but no form of attestation shall be necessary."[415]

The need for formalities is obvious: the possibility of fraud is at its highest, since the person most likely to be aware of any fraud is dead.

The will must be signed. As originally enacted, section 9 required a signature "at the foot or end" of the will. That requirement was abolished by section 17 of the Administration of Justice Act 1982; the signature may be in any position, provided that "it appears that the testator intended by his signature to give effect to the will". What if the signature is at the beginning of the document? In *Wood* v *Smith*, [416] the testator started by writing, "My Will by Percy Winterborne of 150, High Street, Margate", followed by dispositions to various beneficiaries. The Court of Appeal held that, since the writing and signing were one operation, the signature was valid.[417]

Clerical errors in a will can be rectified to express the testator's true intention[418]. By a generous interpretation, the Supreme Court has held that the term "clerical error" includes a mistake in signing the will. In *Marley* v *Rawlings*[419] Mr and Mrs Rawlings instructed their solicitor to prepare wills for them both. They each left their estate to the other, but if the survivor should die within a period of one month then the entire estate was left to the appellant, Terry Michael Marley. By an oversight, the solicitor gave each spouse the other's draft will for signature, and nobody noticed the mistake. Mrs Rawlings died in 2003, Mr. Rawlings died in 2006, and only then was the mistake discovered. The two sons of Mr and Mrs Rawlings challenged the validity of the will; if it was invalid, Mr Rawlings had died intestate, and the sons would inherit his estate. It was held that that Mr Rawlings' will should

---

[415] Exceptionally, an informal (even oral) will can be made by a soldier or airman on active service, by a mariner or seaman at sea, and by a member of the navy or marine forces: s 11, Wills Act 1837; Wills (Soldiers and Sailors) Act 1918.
[416] [1993] Ch 90.
[417] See also *Weatherhill* v *Pearce* [1995] 1 WLR 592, where the handwritten attestation clause read, "Signed by the said testator Doris Weatherhill"; held to be a valid signature.
[418] S 20, Administration of Justice Act 1982.
[419] [2014] 2 WLR 213.

be rectified, by substituting the relevant parts of the will that his wife had signed. On that basis, the will was valid, and the appellant was successful.[420]

English law is stricter than many jurisdictions in requiring that the will be signed in the presence of two or more witnesses present at the same time. The signing ceremony can easily go wrong, as *Re Groffman (deceased)*[421] vividly illustrates. Mr Groffman had earlier prepared and signed his will. He asked two friends, Mr Block and Mr Leigh, to act as witnesses. They were all together in the house of Mr and Mrs Block. In the lounge Mr Groffman pointed to his will, which was folded and in the inside pocket of his jacket. There was no convenient space in that room for the witnesses to sign the will, so Mr Groffman and Mr Block went into the adjoining dining room, where Mr Groffman took the will from his pocket and unfolded it. His signature was then visible, and Mr Block signed the will as a witness. Mr Block then returned to the lounge, and Mr Leigh went into the dining room. He also signed the will as a witness. The will was held invalid. Mr Groffman had not acknowledged his signature in the lounge when both witnesses were present, because his signature was not visible to them. He had acknowledged his signature in the dining room, but in the presence of each witness separately, and that was insufficient.

The decision is legally correct, but it raises the question whether English law is too strict in requiring at least two witnesses present at the same time. As the judge in *Re Groffman* stated, there was no doubt that the document represented Mr Groffman's testamentary intentions. The problem arises from the two witness rule. Would one witness not be enough to guard against fraud? In the case of a deed, only one witness is required if the person making the deed signs it himself. If the deed is signed by someone else at his direction and in his presence, two witnesses are needed, but there is no requirement that the witnesses be present at the same time.[422] There is another major difference between deeds and wills, and that is, that, in the case of a will, a beneficial gift to a witness, or to the spouse or civil partner of a

---

[420] If the appellant had been unsuccessful, it seems clear that he could claim compensation from the solicitor under the tort of negligence: *White* v *Jones* [1995] 2 AC 207.
[421] [1969] 1 WLR 733.
[422] S 1(3), Law of Property (Miscellaneous Provisions) Act 1989. See p 86, *ante*.

witness, is void.[423] There is no such provision in the case of a deed. This draconian rule is clearly designed to ensure that a witness is independent. Would one independent witness not be enough to guard against fraud?

Various overseas jurisdictions recognise a holographic will as valid without witnesses. A holographic will is a will written entirely in the testator's own handwriting. Such a will is valid, for example, in various Canadian provinces and some of the states of the USA. It was also valid in Scotland until the Requirements of Writing (Scotland) Act 1995.[424]

Would English law be improved by a provision recognising a holographic will? It is doubtful; in these days of digital word processing, the notion seems rather old fashioned, and Scots law has moved in the opposite direction.

It needs to be observed that neither a will nor the rules of intestacy make a disposition directly to a beneficiary. Rather, there is a two stage process. The property of the deceased person first vests, by operation of law, in the deceased's personal representative.[425] The personal representative is a person appointed as executor be the deceased's will (and who is able and willing to act), or otherwise an administrator appointed by the court (usually one of the next of kin). An executor must first "prove" the will by obtaining a grant of probate. He does this by producing a will valid on its face (ie, containing the necessary three signatures) and the testator's death certificate. An administrator has a grant of letters of administration. In either case, the personal representative's task is to collect together all the deceased's assets, and out of the resulting fund to pay all the deceased's debts, taxes, funeral and testamentary expenses, and other liabilities. When the residue is ascertained, the personal representative must then transfer the various assets to the beneficiaries entitled under the will or on intestacy. While the estate is being administered the beneficiaries are not regarded as having an interest in any of the assets; they have only a right to compel the personal representative, in a fiduciary capacity, to administer the estate in accordance with the law.[426]

---

[423] S 15, Wills Act 1837, as amended. The rule does not apply if there are more than two witnesses and there are at least two independent witnesses: s 1, Wills Act 1968. It also does not apply when no witnesses at all are required, as in those situations where an informal will is recognised as valid: see n 415, *ante*.
[424] S 1(2)(c).
[425] S 1, Administration of Estates Act 1925. There are exceptions, which need not concern us here: see ss 1(1) and 3, Administration of Estates Act 1925.
[426] *Commissioner of Stamp Duties (Queensland) v Livingston* [1965] AC 694; *Eastbourne Mutual Building Society v Hastings Corporation* [1965] 1 WLR 861; *Lall v Lall* [1965] 1 WLR 1249.

That right is a chose in action which can be assigned, and it will form part of the beneficiary's estate should the beneficiary die while the process of administration is incomplete.[427] When that process is completed, the personal representative becomes a trustee for the beneficiaries, who from that point have an equitable interest.[428] The final task of the personal representative is to transfer the legal title to the various assets to the beneficiaries. This can be done by means of an assent. In the case of property other than land the assent may be oral, and may be inferred from the conduct of the personal representative.[429] Chattels may, of course, be handed over (delivered) to the beneficiaries. However, an assent to the vesting of a legal estate in land "shall be in writing, signed by the personal representatives, and shall name the person in whose favour it is given and shall operate to vest in that person the legal estate to which it relates; and an assent not in writing or not in favour of a named person shall not be effectual to pass a legal estate..."[430] The assent must be in writing, but need not be in the form of a deed.[431] The purpose, clearly, is to make the assent a link in the documentary title to a legal estate in land; the will itself does not form part of the documentary title.[432] Such an assent in relation to unregistered land is now one of the triggers for first registration of title.[433] Where the title is already registered, the personal representative, on producing the grant of probate or letters of administration, may, but need not, become the registered proprietor in place of the deceased proprietor.[434] The personal representative may also, without first becoming the registered proprietor, apply to register a transfer to the beneficiary or to a purchaser.[435]

Finally, there are three other ways by which dispositions of property may become effective on death.

---

[427] See, for example, *Re Leigh's Will Trusts* [1970] Ch 277, where a widow had a claim to her husband's unadministered estate, which contained certain company shares. By her will, she bequeathed "all the shares which I hold and any other interest or assets which I may have" in the company. It was held that the language of her bequest was wide enough to include her claim to her husband's shares.
[428] *Attenborough* v *Solomon* [1913] AC 76; *Harvell* v *Foster* [1954] 2 QB 367.
[429] There may be registration requirements, for example in the case of company shares.
[430] S 36(4), Administration of Estates Act 1925.
[431] S 52(2)(a), Law of Property Act 1925. See also p 85, *ante*.
[432] On a sale, the rights of the beneficiaries under the will or on intestacy will be overreached.
[433] S 4(1)(a), Land Registration Act 2002.
[434] Rule 163, Land Registration Rules 2003.
[435] Rule 162, Land Registration Rules 2003.

The first is by proprietary estoppel. If the claimant has been promised, or has been led to believe that she will become entitled to some land on the death of the owner, and she has acted in reliance on that promise or understanding, the claimant may be awarded such remedy as the court thinks fit. This could result in a transfer of an interest in the land to the claimant.[436]

Secondly, there is the principle of secret trusts. There may be reasons why a testator will wish to avoid publicity about a gift taking effect on his death. Where a will is admitted to probate, any member of the public may obtain a copy of the will on payment of a fee. That publicity can be avoided by the creation of a secret trust. If by the will a gift is made to David, and David agrees with the testator, orally or in writing, to hold the property for Ella, it would be fraud for David, after the testator's death, to deny the trust and claim the property beneficially. It is well established that a court of equity will compel David to hold on trust for Ella. The trust is valid despite not complying with section 9 of the Wills Act 1837 and, in the case of land, despite also not complying with section 53(1)(b) of the Law of Property Act 1925.[437] That is a fully secret trust, where the will contains no mention at all of the trust. What if the will creates a trust binding on David, but fails to state who the beneficiary shall be? If it is proved that David had agreed with the testator that he would hold the property for Ella, equity will again enforce the trust. That is a half secret trust (half in the will and half outside the will), but the validity of a half secret trust was not finally established until the decision of the House of Lords in 1929 in *Blackwell* v *Blackwell*.[438]

There is authority for two distinctions between fully and half secret trusts. In the case of fully secret trusts it makes no difference whether the promise to hold on trust for a third party is made before or after the date of the will.[439] However, in the case of a half secret trust the Court of Appeal held in *Re Keen*[440] that communication of the terms of the trust after the date of the will is invalid. There is no logic in the distinction; it has been criticised by many

---

[436] The leading cases are *Gillett* v *Holt* [2001] Ch 210, and *Thorner* v *Major* [2009] 1 WLR 776. See also *Jennings* v *Rice* [2003] 1 P & CR 8. See further ch 4, "The Contribution of Equity".
[437] The leading case is *McCormick* v *Grogan* (1869) LR 4 HL 82. The result is the same if a beneficiary on intestacy has promised to hold the property for a third party, and the deceased beneficiary failed to make a will in reliance on that promise: *Strickland* v *Aldridge* (1804) 9 Ves Jr 516.
[438] [1929] AC 318.
[439] *Moss* v *Cooper* (1861) 1 J & H 352.
[440] [1937] Ch 236, followed in *Re Bateman's Will Trusts* [1970] 1 WLR 1463. See also per Lord Sumner in *Blackwell* v *Blackwell* [1929] AC 318 at 339.

commentators and has not been followed in other jurisdictions.[441] Another suggested distinction is that, in the case of a fully secret trust of land, an oral promise is sufficient, but in the case of a half secret trust the promise must be evidenced in writing.[442] Again, there is no logic in the distinction, and section 53(1)(b) of the Law of Property Act 1925 should in both cases be avoided by applying the principle in *Rochefoucauld* v *Boustead*.[443]

The third route for creating a disposition taking effect on death is the donatio mortis causa (a gift made in contemplation of death). As the Latin phrase suggests, the idea is imported from Roman law. The essential elements were defined by Lord Russell CJ in *Cain* v *Moon*:[444] (a) the gift must have been made in contemplation, but not necessarily in the expectation, of death; (b) the property must have been delivered to the donee; and (c) the gift must have been made in such circumstances as to show that the property should revert to the donor if she should recover. The need for delivery requires a little explanation. In the case of chattels, this requirement is similar to that in the case of an immediate lifetime gift, but there are indications in the case law that the rules may be slightly less stringent. It is sufficient if the donor hands over the means of gaining control over the chattel, such as a key to the box or place where the property is situated.[445] However, a donatio mortis causa can also be made of a chose in action such as a debt or the credit in a bank account. Here the requirement of delivery is modified to make it sufficient for the donor to hand over such documents as constitute "the essential indicia or evidence of title, possession or production of which entitles the possessor to the money or property to be given".[446] So, for example, the delivery of a bank deposit pass-book is sufficient.[447] For a long time, relying on dicta of Lord Eldon in *Duffield* v *Elwes*,[448] it was thought that there could not be a donatio mortis causa of land. However, that view was decisively rejected by the Court of Appeal in *Sen* v *Headley*.[449] The deceased, when terminally ill in

---
[441] For details see the standard textbooks on wills and trusts.
[442] *Re Baillie* (1886) 2 TLR 660 at 661.
[443] [1897] 1 Ch 196; see text to n 372, *ante*.
[444] [1896] 2 QB 283.
[445] *Re Lillingston* [1952] 2 All ER 184. See also *Woodward* v *Woodward* [1995] 3 All ER 980, where the possibility that the donor had retained a second set of car keys, when he was too ill to drive, was held insignificant.
[446] *Birch* v *Treasury Solicitor* [1951] Ch 298 at 311.
[447] *Birch* v *Treasury Solicitor*, supra.
[448] (1827) 1 Bli (NS) 497.
[449] [1991] Ch 425.

hospital, said to the claimant: "The house is yours, Margaret. You have the keys. They are in your bag. The deeds are in the steel box." After the deceased's death, the claimant found the box in a cupboard in the house and took possession of the deeds. It was held that she was entitled to the house by virtue of a donatio mortis causa. She had the essential indicia of title in the form of the title deeds[450], and the intention to make a gift conditional on death was clear. The Court reasoned that the whole doctrine of a donatio mortis causa was an anomalous exception to the Wills Act, but to exclude land from the doctrine would be to add a further anomaly. The gift was therefore completed by imposing a constructive trust on the deceased's personal representative. Nourse LJ re-articulated Lord Russell's three part test: A must make a gift to B in contemplation of impending death; the gift is conditional on death and may be revoked at any time prior to the death of A and will revert to A if A survives; there must be delivery of the subject matter of the gift.

In *King v Chiltern Dog Rescue*[451] the Court of Appeal clarified that the first of these criteria will be closely scrutinised and the donor must both anticipate death in the near future and that death must be from a known cause (with frailty or old age being insufficient). Patten LJ indicated that the survival period of the donor in a successful donation mortis causa claim would be measured in a matter of days rather than in any longer period. This reversed the decision at first instance in *King v Dubrey*[452] and overruled the decision in *Vallee v Birchwood*[453] where months had elapsed before the donor's death. This restriction on the availability of donatio mortis causa, to situations where the donor faced impending death and realistically did not have time to execute a valid will or codicil to their existing will, is practically necessary to constrain a doctrine that is open to abuse. Jackson LJ drew on Nourse LJ's observation in *Sen v Hedley* that donatio mortis causa is an anomaly in that it is immune to the Statute of Frauds 1677 and the Wills Act 1837, and an exception to the maxim that there is no equity to perfect an imperfect gift.

---

[450] Presumably the result would have been the same if the title to the land had been registered and the deceased had delivered the land certificate. The same result would be much less easy to achieve now, with paperless, electronic, land certificates.
[451] [2015] EWCA Civ 581.
[452] [2014] EWHC 2083 (Ch).
[453] [2013] EWHC 1449 (Ch).

Chapter 6

PROTECTION OF THE PURCHASER

One of the central problems of the law of property is the conflict between the purchaser of an item of property and other people who have a claim over that item. Probably the most striking example is in the case of the sale of stolen property. Suppose that a thief steals a rare book from Celia and sells it for £500 to David, who buys it in good faith and without any knowledge of the theft. In a contest between Celia and David, it is obvious that they cannot both win. Whoever loses may claim compensation from the thief: Celia's claim will lie in the tort of conversion, and David's claim will be based on section 12 of the Sale of Goods Act 1979.[454] However, in many cases the thief may disappear or may not be worth suing. Celia may be able to claim under an insurance policy, providing cover for lost or stolen property, but David is unlikely to have insurance cover against his loss.

A fundamental principle of the law of property is enshrined in the Latin maxim *nemo dat quod non habet* (often abbreviated as *nemo dat*): a person cannot give what she does not have. This principle is embodied in section 21(1) of the Sale of Goods Act 1979: "where goods are sold by a person who is not their owner, and who does not sell them under the authority or with the consent of the owner, the buyer acquires no better title than the seller had." In the above example of the sale of a stolen book this principle applies, so that Celia's claim against David will succeed. The only protection which the law affords to David is under the Limitation Act 1980, which lays down time limits for claims to recover property. Section 4 provides that there is no time limit on an action against the thief, but there is a time limit on an action against an innocent buyer from the thief, which is six years from the date of the sale.

The *nemo dat* rule applies throughout the law of property, to all species of property, including land. However, in the case of land its effect is mitigated or obviated by conveyancing systems designed to allow the buyer to investigate fully the title to the land.[455] Where the title to land is registered, registration vests the legal title in the registered proprietor, leaving no room

---

[454] On s 12 see ch 1.
[455] See further ch 6.

for the operation of the *nemo dat* rule.[456] The Court of Appeal has now held, dispelling earlier doubts, that this principle (that registration has a vesting effect) applies even where the registration is procured by virtue of a forged disposition.[457]

However, in the case of chattels (tangible personal property), there are significant exceptions to the *nemo dat* rule, mainly contained in the Sale of Goods Act 1979. Three of those exceptions will be considered here, together with one contained in Part III of the Hire-Purchase Act 1964. First, the sale of goods exceptions. These are: (1) sale by a seller with a voidable title (section 23 of the Sale of Goods Act); (2) sale by a seller in possession (section 24); (3) sale by a buyer in possession (section 25(1)).

Section 23 of the Act provides as follows: "When the seller of goods has a voidable title to them, but his title has not been avoided at the time of the sale, the buyer acquires a good title to the goods, provided he buys them in good faith and without notice of the seller's defect of title." This is a statutory embodiment of the principle established in equity that, where the contract is affected by behaviour of which equity disapproves (misrepresentation, undue influence and economic duress), the contract may be rescinded by the seller, but not against a second buyer who has no notice of the improper behaviour.

For example, if Celia is induced by David's fraud to sell goods to him, she is entitled to rescind the contract; but if, before that right is exercised, David re-sells the goods to Edward, an innocent buyer, the right of rescission is lost.[458]

Section 24 provides as follows: "Where a person having sold goods continues or is in possession of the goods, the delivery or transfer by that person .... of the goods....under any sale, pledge or other disposition thereof, to any person receiving the same in good faith and without notice of the previous sale, has the same effect as if the person making the delivery or transfer were expressly authorised by the owner of the goods to make the same."

---

[456] S 58(1), Land Registration 2002.
[457] *Swift 1st Ltd* v *The Chief Land Registrar* [2015] EWCA Civ 330, disapproving *Malory Enterprise Ltd* v *Cheshire Homes (UK) Ltd* [2002] Ch 216 (which was regarded as decided *per incuriam*). See also *Argyle Building Society* v *Hammond* (1984) P & CR 148.
[458] Compare the position where the original sale is void for mistaken identity. There, the *nemo dat* rule applies to the second sale, and the second buyer does not acquire any title: see *Cunday* v *Lindsay* (1878) 3 App Cas 459; *Ingram* v *Little* [1961] 1 QB 1; *Shogun Finance Ltd* v *Hudson* [2004] 1 AC 919.

The effect can be simply illustrated. If Alan sells a table to Brian for £1,000, but remains in possession of it, a subsequent sale by him for £1,500 to Celia, who takes in good faith and without notice of the previous sale, confers a good title on Celia. Alan has committed a breach of his contract with Brian, but has also committed a conversion (he has sold a table belonging to Brian). Brian may make a proprietary claim against the £1,500 paid by Celia. If, meanwhile, Alan had used that money to buy new property, Brian will be able to trace his claim into the new property, will be able to claim any profits accruing to the new property, and will have priority over unsecured creditors if Alan were to be declared bankrupt.[459]

Section 25(1) provides as follows: "Where a person having bought or agreed to buy goods obtains, with the consent of the seller, possession of the goods...., the delivery or transfer by that person....of the goods, under any sale, pledge, or other disposition thereof to any person receiving the same in good faith and without notice of any .... right of the original seller in respect of the goods, has the same effect as if the person making the delivery or transfer were a mercantile agent in possession of the goods....with the consent of the owner."

Again, the effect can be simply illustrated. If Alan agrees to sell a table to Brian, and allows Brian to have possession, a subsequent sale of the table by him to Celia, who takes in good faith and without notice of any rights retained by Alan, confers a good title on Celia. The reference to "a mercantile agent" is a reference to a person who is authorised to sell the table on behalf of Alan. The contractual and proprietary consequences mirror those arising from section 24, as stated above.

It will be noticed that both section 24 and section 25(1) deem the subsequent sale to be made with the consent or authority of the "owner." Suppose that Alan, in both situations, had only a limited title; for example he was a finder or a thief of the item sold. Does the deemed consent or authority of the "owner" mean that Celia will obtain a good title free from the rights of the true owner? That issue arose in *National Employers Mutual General Insurance Association Ltd* v *Jones*.[460] A car was stolen from Miss Hopkin. The car was then sold onwards to four buyers and ultimately to the appellant, Mr. Jones,

---

[459] See *Trustee of the Property of F. C. Jones (a firm)* v *Jones* [1997] Ch 159; *Foskett* v *McKeown* [2001] 1 AC 102 at 128, per Lord Millett.
[460] [1990] 1 AC 24.

who bought in good faith. The respondents were Miss Hopkin's insurers, who bought out her interest in the car after the theft. The House of Lords, affirming the Court of Appeal, held that the "owner" referred to in section 25(1) was the person who set in train the series of sales down to the appellant, ie, the thieves, and therefore the appellant acquired only the limited title that the thieves had. The same reasoning must apply to section 24. It will also influence the meaning of the phrase "a good title" in section 23.

Following that decision, suppose that Mr. Parker in *Parker* v *British Airways Board*[461] had sold the bracelet which he found at Heathrow. A buyer in good faith would acquire only the finder's title to the bracelet, and would be vulnerable, within the six year time limit, to a claim from the person who lost the bracelet. Relative title is the key to understanding.

It is hardly necessary to stress the importance of possession in sections 24 and 25(1). The rationale for these provisions is that an innocent purchaser is misled into thinking that the person with possession is entitled to sell the property.

The last exception to the *nemo dat* rule to be considered here is contained in Part III of the Hire-Purchase Act 1964, as amended. The key provisions are section 27(1) and (2). They read as follows:

(1) "This section applies where a motor vehicle has been bailed ....under a hire-purchase agreement,..and, before the property in the vehicle has become vested in the debtor, he disposes of the vehicle to another person.

(2) Where the disposition referred to in subsection (1) above is to a private purchaser, and he is a purchaser of the motor vehicle in good faith without notice of the hire-purchase....agreement....that disposition shall have effect as if the creditor's title to the vehicle had been vested in the debtor immediately before that disposition."[462]

The effect can be simply illustrated. Suppose that the Crookesmoor Motor Company sells a car to Brian on hire-purchase terms. During the currency of that agreement Brian sells the car to Celia, who buys in good faith and without notice of the hire-purchase agreement. Crookesmoor's title (whatever

---
[461] [1982] 1 QB 1004. See ch 3, Appendix 1, for the *Parker* case   It would be wise for a finder who sells to disclose the source of his title and to limit his liability under s 12, Sale of Goods Act 1979.
[462] Note the direct and clear drafting, avoiding ambiguous expressions such as "owner" and "good title."

it was: they might have bought from a thief) vests in Celia. The contractual and proprietary consequences are similar to those considered above.

Overreaching is the other main technique used by the law to protect purchasers. Overreaching occurs when a person with a limited interest in an item of property exercises a power (a legal authority) to transfer that property. Such a transfer will enable the purchaser to take free of the rights of other claimants to that property. Probably the easiest case to understand is the sale by a mortgagee. Suppose that Brian, the fee simple owner of Blackacre, borrows money from the Citadel Building Society, secured by a legal mortgage of Blackacre to the building society.[463] Suppose that Brian defaults on the loan and the building society despairs of recovering its money. At a certain point,[464] the building society may exercise a power of sale. Suppose that the building society exercises its power of sale by selling Blackacre to David. David will acquire a title free from the rights of Brian. Brian's rights will be shifted to the proceeds of the sale paid to the building society, and if there is any surplus (the proceeds of the sale less the loan and the costs of the sale), that surplus will be held on trust for Brian.[465] Brian's interest in Blackacre is overreached.

A similar result would follow if Brian were to pledge his gold watch in order to secure a loan. If Brian were then to default on the loan, the pledgee would be entitled to sell the watch to a buyer, who would take free from Brian's right to take back the watch by paying off the loan (his right of redemption). Any surplus in the hands of the pledgee will be held for Brian. Brian's rights will be overreached.

A different form of overreaching, in the context of mortgages of land, is the statutory power conferred on a mortgagor or mortgagee in possession of the land to grant leases which will be binding on both mortgagor and mortgagee. The lease shall be granted for not more than 50 years for agricultural or occupation purposes or 999 years for building.[466] The effect is to give the lease a priority which it would not have without the statutory power.

---

[463] In registered land the legal mortgage will be a registered charge: s 51, Land Registration Act 2002.
[464] S 104, Law of Property Act 1925.
[465] S 105, Law of Property Act 1925.
[466] S 99(1)-(3), Law of Property Act 1925. The powers can be excluded or modified: s 99(13). They are usually excluded by standard form domestic mortgages.

The next example of overreaching is where trustees vary the investments which they are holding in a fund. Suppose, for example, that Alan and Brian are trustees holding on trust for Celia for life and then for David absolutely. At the outset the trust property comprised £1,500 in stocks and shares and a further £1,500 in stocks and shares. The first group of stocks and shares were producing an income of 4% but the second group was not earning any interest. Alan and Brian decided to invest the money from the second group in further income-producing stocks and shares. It is obvious that the trust in favour of the beneficiaries, Celia and David, attaches automatically to the new investments, and will continue to do so each time the investments are varied. The buyer of the original stocks and shares will take free from the trust. That is a form of overreaching.

A final example is overreaching under a trust of land, illustrated by the vivid case of *City of London Building Society* v *Flegg*.[467] In 1977 Mr. and Mrs. Maxwell-Brown bought a house (aptly named Bleak House) with the aid of a substantial financial contribution made by Mr. and Mrs. Flegg, who were the parents of Mrs. Maxwell-Brown. The legal estate was vested in Mr. and Mrs. Maxwell-Brown jointly, and they were registered as the joint proprietors. It was not in dispute that the Maxwell-Browns held the legal estate as trustees holding for themselves and the Fleggs. The four occupied Bleak House as their home. Later, the Maxwell-Browns, without the knowledge or consent of the Fleggs, borrowed money from the appellant building society, secured by a legal mortgage of Bleak House. The money was used to pay off earlier debts. The Maxwell-Browns defaulted on the repayments and were now bankrupt. The building society sought possession of the property. The House of Lords, reversing the Court of Appeal, held that the mortgage overreached the Fleggs' interest under the trust; their interest shifted from the land to the equity of redemption and the money borrowed from the building society. The case shows graphically that, in this form of overreaching, the beneficiaries are

---

[467] [1988] AC 54. The case would now be governed by the Trusts of Land and Appointment of Trustees 1996, and the trustees' powers would be conferred by s 6 of the Act. The result would be the same. For further consideration of the 1996 Act see chapter 7, *Co-ownership*. For further reading see Harpum, *Overreaching, Trustees' Powers and the Reform of the 1925 Legislation* [1990] CLJ 277; Ferris and Battersby, *The General Principles of Overreaching and the Reforms of 1925* (2002) LQR 270.

completely dependent on the integrity of the trustees. The Maxwell-Browns grossly betrayed their trust and the Fleggs were their victims.[468]

---

[468] See also *State Bank of India* v *Sood* [1997] Ch 276, where the mortgage was to provide security for existing debts, and therefore no money was paid. Overreaching still took effect. Where capital money is paid, it must be received by not fewer than two trustees, with a maximum of four: ss 27(2) and 34(2), Law of Property Act 1925; s 34(2), Trustee Act 1925.

Chapter 7

CO-OWNERSHIP

It is possible for many different kinds of property to be owned by two or more people at the same time. For example, a married couple may jointly own their family home and its contents, or their family car; they may well have a joint bank account. A group of students may jointly rent a house for a year in their degree course. Partners in a firm may jointly hold a lease of their commercial premises and may jointly own their business equipment. Two or more scientists or engineers may together own a patent for their invention. Two or more authors may together own the copyright in their work. The examples could be multiplied. The common thread is that the ownership is shared between the two or more people involved; they have concurrent interests. One may say that in such a situation ownership is fragmented horizontally, as opposed to the vertical fragmentation where interests in an item of property are held consecutively. [469]

Let us consider in slightly more detail the example of the students jointly renting a house for a year. The effect is that they jointly own the entire house for that year, and each of them, unless the lease provides otherwise, will be liable for the entire rent.[470] They may well agree between themselves to apportion the rent, presumably one quarter each, but that agreement would not affect the lessor. They will no doubt agree between themselves on the allocation of the bedrooms. They may draw up a timetable for their use of the kitchen and bathroom. However, they remain joint lessees of the entire house. Similarly, in the example of the married couple, they together own the entire house, not a half of the house each. During their life together they would need to agree on how they would use the parts of the co-owned house. Suppose then that their relationship founders and that they agree to separate. They could agree to live separate lives in the same house, one on the ground floor and the other on the upper floor. That arrangement would not affect the original co-ownership; they remain together entitled to the whole house, albeit occupying separate parts of it.

---

[469] For consecutive interests see ch 2. The two forms of fragmentation can be combined in one disposition; for example, a gift of land to Celia for life and then to David and Emma in fee simple.
[470] *Mikeover Ltd* v *Brady* [1989] 3 All ER 616.

The two forms of co-ownership

English law recognises two distinct forms of co-ownership, namely, joint tenancy and tenancy in common. The main significance of the distinction is seen when one of the co-owners dies. If the co-owners were joint tenants, the interest of the deceased joint tenant comes to an end at the moment of their death leaving the surviving joint tenant or joint tenants. This is the right of survivorship, or jus accrescendi. Thus, if there were two joint tenants and one died, the survivor would take the entire property and co-ownership would come to an end.[471] If there were three joint tenants and one died, the two survivors would take the entire property and the joint tenancy would continue between them. If, on the other hand, the co-owners were tenants in common, each of them is regarded as owning a share in the property, and that will pass to the deceased's estate, to be dealt with under the deceased's will or under the law of intestacy. Thus, if there were three tenants in common holding equal shares, and one died, that person's one third share would pass to the deceased's estate.[472] The right of survivorship is such an intrinsic element of a joint tenancy that, at common law, it was held that there could not be a joint tenancy between a human being and a corporate body, such as a limited company, because a corporate body does not suffer death. That was logical but inconvenient; it meant, inter alia, that a company, such as a bank, could not be appointed a trustee with a human being.[473] The law was changed by the Bodies Corporate (Joint Tenancy) Act 1899, which provides that a corporation can acquire and hold any property in joint tenancy in the same manner as if it were an individual.[474]

What if there are two joint tenants, and they die together at the same time, as for example in a car crash? It is likely that there will be no evidence to establish which of them was the survivor. The problem is solved in English law by section 184 of the Law of Property Act 1925, which establishes a presumption that the elder died first. That is obviously an arbitrary rule, but

---

[471] For the conveyancing problem created by this situation see below.
[472] In the 1925 property legislation the very apt expression "undivided share" is consistently used instead of tenancy in common: see, for example, ss 1(6) and 34, Law of Property Act 1925, and s 36(4), Settled Land Act 1925.
[473] Trustees are always made joint tenants because of the convenience that the right of survivorship provides when one trustee dies. In the case of land, a legal estate cannot be vested in tenants in common: s 1(6), Law of Property Act 1925.
[474] The corporation will cease to have an interest if it is dissolved: s 1(2), Bodies Corporate (Joint Tenancy) Act 1899.

it does solve the problem. However, it can produce unhappy results. Suppose, for example, that the two joint tenants are husband and wife, and that the husband is older than his wife. Suppose that this is the husband's second marriage and that the couple had living with them children of the husband's first marriage. Suppose finally that the wife died intestate. Section 184 would ensure that the entire property would pass to the wife's next of kin, to the exclusion of the husband's children from his first marriage. A much more satisfactory solution, adopted in some states of the United States of America, would be to treat the simultaneous deaths as bringing about a severance of the joint tenancy, converting it into a tenancy in common in equal share, so that a half share would devolve as part of the estate of each of the deceased persons.[475]

Creating the two forms of co-ownership

For a joint tenancy to exist the four unities must be satisfied: the unities of possession, interest, title and time.[476] The unity of possession means that the co-owners are together entitled to possession or enjoyment of the property, at present or in the future. This requirement is also true, of course, in the case of tenancy in common. The unity of interest means that the co-owners have the same interest in the property. There cannot, for example, be a joint tenancy where one person holds a life interest in a piece of land and another person holds the fee simple, or a lease. However, this requirement is satisfied if two people hold the same interest, but one of them also holds another interest. For example, if land is given to Celia and David as joint tenants for life, with remainder in fee simple to David, the unity of interest is satisfied. There is no unity of interest if the co-owners are given unequal shares, for example, two thirds to Celia and one third to David; they have to be tenants in common. The unit of title means that the co-owners derive their title from the same transaction, for example under the same deed or the same will. The rationale for this requirement is unclear, but it seems to be well established. The final unity is the unity of time, which means that the interests of the co-owners

---

[475] For example California. See *Re Estate of Meade* (1964) 39 Cal Rpts 282. Thank you to Gray & Gray, *Elements of Land Law*, 5th ed, para 7.4.12, n 3, for this authority.
[476] This requirement can be traced back at least to Coke. For modern authority see *A G Securities* v *Vaughan* [1990] 1 AC 417.

must vest at the same time.[477] So, for example, a gift to the heirs of Celia and the heirs of David would make the respective heirs tenants in common, if Celia and David died at different times. However, a gift by Celia's will to all her children at the age of 21 makes them joint tenants, even though the children's interests will vest at different times. This requirement never applied to trusts or wills, and since, as we shall see later in this chapter, all co-ownership of land now takes effect behind a trust, the unity of time has become rather weak.

Where the four unities are satisfied the common law presumes that a joint tenancy is created. If, therefore, the desire is to create a tenancy in common, that presumption must be rebutted by language sufficient to show a contrary intention. The clearest way is to vest the property in the co-owners "as tenants in common", but other words or phrases may also have that effect. These are known as "words of severance". The modern tendency is to construe the transaction as a whole, especially where the disposition is created by a document, such as a deed or a will; but, as examples, the following words or phrases have been held to create a tenancy in common: "in equal shares", "equally", "share and share alike", "to be distributed amongst them in joint and equal proportions", "amongst", and "respectively".

Equity takes a different view from the common law in three categories of cases (equity's special cases). The first is where two or more persons together purchase a property but provide the purchase money in unequal shares. Equity presumes that the parties intended to acquire shares in the property proportionate to their respective contributions.[478]

These presumptions of equity are rebuttable by proof of a contrary intention, which, in the case of a purchase of land, will be most clearly demonstrated by a declaration in the transfer that the purchasers are to hold in equal shares. Such a declaration, unless the transfer is rectified because of mistake, or is vitiated by fraud or mistake, is conclusive.[479]

---

[477] For the meaning of "vest" see ch 2.
[478] This presumption can be traced back at least to *Lake* v *Jackson* (1729) 1 Eq Ca Abr 290 at 291
[479] *Goodman* v *Gallant* [1986] Fam 186. For an example of a mistake leading to rectification of the declaration of trust, see *Wilson* v *Wilson* [1969] 1 WLR 1470.

For reasons which are at best obscure, four members of the House of Lords seem to have held in *Stack* v *Dowden*[480] that this presumption does not apply to the family home, because, they hold, the quantification of interests in the family home depends entirely on establishing the parties' common intention. This appears to establish a debatable distinction between domestic and commercial cases.[481]

The second of equity's special cases is where two or more people advance money for a loan secured by a mortgage, whether in equal or unequal shares. It is presumed that they each advanced their own and intended to take back their own, and the right of survivorship is inappropriate.[482] It became customary for conveyancers to insert in the mortgage deed a joint account clause, ie, a clause entitling the survivor to give a valid receipt. This simplifies the discharge of the mortgage on repayment of the loan. Such a clause is now impliedly incorporated by section 111 of the Law of Property Act 1925. Such a clause does not affect the presumption of a tenancy in common.[483]

The third of equity's special cases is where land is purchased by commercial partners for partnership purposes. Again, equity presumes that survivorship was not intended to apply. This presumption was extended in *Malayan Credit Ltd* v *Jack Chia-MPH Ltd*[484] to other kinds of business premises, where the parties, not being partners, were granted a five-year lease of the seventh floor of an office block. The parties agreed that one of them would occupy 62% of the floor space and the other party 38%, and their liability for rent and service charges was similarly apportioned. The Privy Council held that the parties took in unequal shares, 62% and 38%.

---

[480] [2007] 2 AC 432. The four Law Lords so holding are Baroness Hale of Richmond, with whom Lord Walker of Gestingthorpe, Lord Hoffmann and Lord Hope of Craighe agreed. Compare the minority opinion of Lord Neuberger of Abbotsbury, applying the presumption in a sophisticated manner. *Stack* v *Dowden* and subsequent cases are examined in more detail in ch 8, "The Family Home."

[481] This point is somewhat moot following *Marr v Collie* [2017] UKPC 17, see ch 8, "The Family Home".

[482] *Steeds* v *Steeds* (1889) 22 QBD 537.

[483] *Re Jackson* (1887) 34 Ch D 732. Similarly, the insertion of such a clause into the transfer in issue in *Stack* v *Dowden*, supra, was not conclusive as to the beneficial interests. It is worth remarking that, while it is certainly true that the insertion of a joint account clause in a mortgage deed is advantageous to the mortgagor/borrower, it creates the risk that the end position could be that the last survivor of the joint mortgagees/lenders holds the money used to repay the loan as a single trustee, thus exposing the other beneficial owner (or owners) to the possibility of being the victims of a breach of trust. Compare the two trustee rule imposed in statutory overreaching; see below.

[484] [1986] AC 549.

An express declaration of a joint tenancy is conclusive unless any vitiating factors apply.[485]

Transactions affecting property held by joint tenants

The general rule is that any transaction affecting property held by joint tenants must be effected by all the joint tenants acting together.[486] This rule applies, for example, to the surrender of a lease[487] or the exercise of a break clause in a lease.[488] However, there is a statutory exception in the case of personal representatives: one of two or more personal representatives may deal with property other than land.[489] The two highest courts have also held that the general rule does not apply to a notice to quit given by one joint tenant to terminate a periodic tenancy held by two or more persons as joint tenants. One joint lessor or joint lessee may give a valid notice to quit. The House of Lords so decided, in the case of joint lessees, in *Hammersmith & Fulham London Borough Council* v *Monk*.[490] The essential reason is that a periodic tenancy will be renewed only if all the parties agree, and the service of a notice to quit clearly demonstrates that the person serving that notice does not agree. The facts of *Monk* show graphically how harsh the result may be. A cohabiting couple obtained jointly a periodic tenancy of a council flat. That was a secure tenancy under the Housing Act 1985, which meant that the council could not terminate the tenancy except on proof of one of the grounds defined by the Act.[491] After a domestic dispute the female member of the couple served a notice to quit on the council, which was granted a possession order against her former partner. He was therefore rendered homeless. That decision provoked vigorous academic criticism, typified by the statement of Cretney:[492] "One moment you have an apparently secure tenancy; the next minute it has disappeared by the unilateral (and secret) action of your former

---

[485] *Barton* v *Morris* [1985] 1 WLR 1257.
[486] *Leek & Moorlands Building Society* v *Clark and Ellison* [1952] 2 QB 788.
[487] Ibid.
[488] *Hounslow London Borough Council* v *Pilling* [1993] 1 WLR 1242. A disclaimer must also be made by all the intended joint tenants, but once the joint tenancy is created, one joint tenant can release her interest to the other joint tenant: see s 36(3), Law of Property Act 1925; *Re Schar, deceased* [1951] Ch 280.
[489] S 2(2), Administration of Estates Act 1925.
[490] [1992] 1 AC 478. There are dicta stating that the same principle applies to a notice to quit served by one of two joint lessors, and that must be correct.
[491] See sch 2 to the Act.
[492] [1998] Fam Law 590.

partner of which you know nothing." Nevertheless, *Monk* has been approved by a panel of seven Justices of the Supreme Court in *Sims* v *Dacorum Borough Council*,[493] where the facts were almost identical to those in *Monk*, without any consideration of the academic criticism; a very disappointing outcome.

Severance of a joint tenancy

One joint tenant may convert her interest into a share as a tenant in common by a process known as severance. If there are two joint tenants and one severs, the result will be a tenancy in common between the two co-owners. For example, if Celia and David were joint tenants and David severs by transferring his interest to his daughter Emma, that will create a tenancy in common between Celia and Emma. If there were three joint tenants and one severs, there would then be a tenancy in common as to the severed one third share, leaving the other two joint tenants as joint tenants of the remaining two thirds share. What if there were three joint tenants, Celia, David and Emma, and Celia transferred her interest to David? That act of Celia does not sever the joint tenancy between David and Emma, so that David and Emma remain joint tenants of two thirds, and David has a one third share in addition.[494]

A joint tenancy may be severed in the following ways. The classic statement is in *Williams* v *Hensman*.[495] Page-Wood V-C stated as follows: "A joint tenancy may be severed in three ways: in the first place, an act of one of the persons interested operating upon his own share may create a severance as to that share. The right of each joint tenant is a right by survivorship only in the event of no severance having taken place of the share which is claimed under the jus accrescendi. Each one is at liberty to dispose of his own interest in such manner as to sever it from the joint fund. Secondly, a joint tenancy may be severed by mutual agreement. And in the third place, there may be a severance by any course of dealing sufficient to intimate that the interests of

---

[493] [2014] UKSC 63. The Court also held that there was no infringement of the appellant's human rights under article 8 of the European Convention on Human Rights, or under article 1 of the first protocol to the Convention. The Convention was incorporated into English law by the Human Rights Act 1998. The previous Government had embarked on a long promised review of the operation of the Act. The forthcoming Brexit means that this has stalled but the review, if it happens, is unlikely to benefit persons in the same position as Mr Sims!
[494] *Wright* v *Gibson* (1949) 78 CLR 313 at 350.
[495] (1861) 1 J & H 546.

all were to be treated as constituting a tenancy in common." Section 36(2) of the Law of Property Act 1925 adds a fourth method, severance by notice. Section 36(2) provides as follows: "...where a legal estate...is vested in joint tenants beneficially, and any tenant desires to sever the joint tenancy in equity, he shall give to the other joint tenants a notice in writing of such desire or do such other acts or things as would, in the case of personal estate, have been effectual to sever the tenancy in equity...". The opening words quoted, "where a legal estate ...is vested in joint tenants beneficially", if read literally, would limit all modes of severance to the situation where the same persons are joint tenants both in law and in equity. It is obvious that Parliament could not have intended that result, and the courts have consistently ignored the problem.

Let us examine in more detail severance by notice in writing. There is no requirement as to the form of the notice, except that it must be signed by at least one of the joint tenants and must specify the date of severance. The notice must show an intention to sever immediately. In *Re Draper's Conveyance*[496] it was held that a court summons requesting a sale and division of the proceeds was a sufficient notice. On the other hand, it was held in *Harris* v *Goddard*[497] that a request in divorce proceedings that the court should exercise its powers to make a property adjustment order did not effect a severance. Two reasons were given: firstly, the request was to make such an order at some time in the future, and secondly, the order ultimately made by the divorce court would not necessarily effect a severance. In similar vein is the decision in *Gore and Snell* v *Carpenter*[498], where, following the breakdown of a marriage, the parties entered into lengthy correspondence concerning the future of two houses which they owned as joint tenants. The correspondence contained a suggestion that there should be a severance, and that suggestion was embodied in a draft agreement. It was held that there was no severance by written notice. There is no requirement that the notice should be brought to the attention of the other joint tenant. Section 196(3) of the Law of Property Act 1925 provides that any notice under the Act is sufficiently served "if it is left at the last-known place of abode or business in the United Kingdom", and any notice sent by registered mail, or recorded or special delivery, is deemed

---

[496] [1969] 1 Ch 486, approved by the Court of Appeal in *Harris* v *Goddard* [1983] 1 WLR 1203. See also *Quigley* v *Masterson* [2012] 1 All ER 1224 (severance by application to Court of Protection).
[497] [1983] 1 WLR 1203.
[498] (1990) 60 P & CR 456.

by subsection (4) to have been delivered, unless returned, at the time that the letter in the ordinary course would be delivered. These provisions were applied in *Re 88, Berkeley Road*[499], where a notice was sent by recorded delivery and received by the sender. It was never seen by the other joint tenant to whom it was addressed. It was held there was a severance.

Similarly, in *Kinch* v *Bullard*[500] a notice was sent by the wife to her husband, when she was commencing court proceedings. The notice was delivered to the husband's house when he was in hospital following a sudden heart attack. The wife picked up the letter and destroyed it, because she realised that severance was no longer in her interest; if her husband were to die, she would benefit from the right of survivorship. The husband died without ever becoming aware of the notice. It was held that there was a severance, so that the husband's estate was entitled to a half share. The judgment of Neuberger J contains interesting dicta considering two hypothetical questions. The first is, what would be the position if the wife had told her husband, before the date of delivery, that she had changed her mind about severance? The judge thought that the notice would then be ineffective. The second question is, what would be the position if the wife, having received and destroyed the notice, were to die first? Would there then be severance, so that the wife's estate could claim a half share? The judge thought not, because that would amount to fraud on the wife's part. Both answers seem satisfactory. Finally, we should observe one limitation on severance by notice. It is available only when the legal estate is vested in joint tenants; ie, it applies only to land. If the land has been sold, and the joint tenants hold the proceeds of sale, there can be no severance by notice in relation to those proceeds; one of the other methods of severance must be used.[501] This is undoubtedly inconvenient, but it is difficult to see how it can be avoided in view of the wording of section 36(2).[502]

---

[499] [1971] Ch 648.
[500] [1999] 1 WLR 423.
[501] *Nielson-Jones v Fedden* [1975] Ch 222 at 229f.
[502] Compare the different view of Lord Denning MR in *Burgess* v *Rawnsley* [1975] Ch 429 at 440A: "I look upon section 36(2) as declaratory of the law as to severance by notice and not as a new provision confined to real estate. A joint tenancy in personal estate can be severed by notice just as a joint tenancy in real estate." Lord Denning stands alone in this opinion. In *Burgess* v *Rawnsley* Sir John Pennycuick disagreed, and Browne LJ was non-committal.

We must now consider the three modes of severance listed in *Williams* v *Hensman*. The first method is by a disposition of a joint tenant's interest. The disposition must be made during the joint tenant's lifetime; it cannot be effected by a will, since survivorship occurs immediately on the joint tenant's death. Clearly, a disposition of the entire interest of a joint tenant, for example, by a sale or gift, effects severance. A disposition by operation of law, for example on bankruptcy, has the same effect. The cases go further, by holding consistently that a partial disposition amounts to severance; for example, the creation of a mortgage or charge,[503] or the grant of a lease.[504] In the case of a lease, it appears that the severance occurs not only during the term created by the lease, but also amounts to severance of the joint tenancy of the reversionary estate, whether a head lease or the fee simple.[505] A declaration of trust in favour of a third party[506] and a specifically enforceable contract to make a disposition will also amount to severance.[507]

The second mode of severance listed in *Williams* v *Hensman* is by mutual agreement. This mode was considered in detail by the Court of Appeal in *Burgess* v *Rawnsley*.[508] Mr Honick, the claimant's father, and Mrs Rawnsley, the respondent, became friends. They together bought the fee simple in a house, contributing in equal shares to the purchase money. The house was conveyed to them as joint tenants. Mr. Honick lived there, but Mrs. Rawnsley never moved in. Some time later Mrs. Rawnsley orally agreed to sell her interest to Mr. Honick for £750. She then refused to sell to him at that price. When Mr. Honick died, the claimant, her father's personal representative, argued that the joint tenancy had been severed, and therefore that her father's estate was entitled to a half share. Clearly, the oral agreement to sell was not enforceable, and therefore there was no severance within the first *Williams* v *Hensman* category. However, the court held unanimously that the agreement showed an intention by both parties to regard the joint tenancy as ended.

---

[503] *Cedar Holdings Ltd* v *Green* [1981] Ch 129; *First National Securities Ltd* v *Hegerty* [1985] QB 850.
[504] It is clear that the creation of a minor incumbrance, not involving any right to possession, such as a rentcharge or profit, does not sever: Co Litt 185a; *Lord Abergavenny's Case* (1607) 6 Co Rep 78.
[505] The cases are old, or very old, but the proposition in the text is strongly supported by Megarry & Wade, *The Law of Real Property*, 7th ed, p 508. There is a full discussion in Smith, *Plural Ownership*, pp 63 et seq. See also Smith, *Property Law*, 8th ed, p 309. These are difficult issues, well beyond the scope of this book.
[506] *Re Mee* (1971) 23 DLR (3d) 491; *Re Sorenson and Sorenson* (1977) 90 DLR (3d) 26.
[507] *Brown* v *Raine* (1796) 3 Ves 257.
[508] [1975] Ch 429.

The third method of severance listed in *Williams* v *Hensman* is a course of dealing. This is more difficult to define and more difficult to establish by evidence. It is clear from *Burgess v Rawnsley*[509] that this method is distinct from method two. What is required is proof that all the joint tenants in their dealings with one another had treated their interests as severed. Page-Wood V-C cited two cases to demonstrate severance by a course of dealing. The first was *Wilson* v *Bell*[510], where there had been periodic distributions of property between the joint tenants. The second was *Jackson* v *Jackson*[511], where profits of trade had been apportioned between the joint tenants of a business. On the other hand, it was held in a modern case, *McDowell* v *Hirschfield Lipson and Romney*[512], that the conversion of a jointly owned house into two self-contained maisonettes was not a course of dealing sufficient to sever. Many of the modern cases concern negotiations following the breakdown of a marriage, where those negotiations have not resulted in an agreement. In *Burgess* v *Rawnsley*[513] Sir John Pennycuick stated: "I do not doubt myself that where one tenant negotiates with another for some rearrangement of interest, it may be possible to infer from the particular facts a common intention to sever even though the negotiations break down. Whether such an inference can be drawn must I think depend upon the particular facts…One could not ascribe to joint tenants an intention to sever merely because one offers to buy out the other for £X and the other makes a counter-offer of £Y." He also spoke of "negotiations which, although not otherwise resulting in an agreement, indicate a common intention that the joint tenancy should be regarded as severed." In *Nielson-Jones* v *Fedden*[514] there were negotiations following marriage breakdown, and the negotiations were incomplete when the husband died. They had agreed that the house which they owned as joint tenants should be sold and that a smaller house should be bought for the husband out of the proceeds of sale. It was held this was insufficient to sever. The decision seems very doubtful; it is true, as the judge stated, that the overall financial and property agreement was incomplete, but that surely need not affect the clear agreement which they had reached over the fate of the

---

[509] Ibid.
[510] (1843) 5 Ir Eq R 501. See also *Re Denny* (1947) 177 L T 291.
[511] (1804) 9 Ves 591.
[512] [1992] 2 FLR 126.
[513] [1975] Ch 429, at 433.
[514] [1975] Ch 222.

house.[515] However, there was a similar decision in *Gore and Snell* v *Carpenter*[516], where the parties had reached an overall agreement in principle, which included an agreement to sever the joint tenancy. There must be an overwhelming presumption that the parties in these situations will wish to avoid the right of survivorship, and the courts' reluctance to give effect to severance is regrettable.

One final point to consider. What is the position if one joint tenant unlawfully kills another joint tenant? It is an overriding principle of English law that a person who unlawfully kills another person cannot benefit as a result.[517] This is the forfeiture rule, which applies in many different contexts.[518] The rule certainly applies in the case of murder, but also in the case of the most serious kinds of manslaughter. Let us start with the situation where there are two joint tenants, Alan and Brian, and Alan murders Brian. This point arose in the only English case which is fully reported, *Re K, deceased*.[519] It is a tragic story. It concerned a husband and wife who were married in 1974. Throughout the marriage the wife was subjected to violent physical attacks by her husband, but had nevertheless remained loyal to him. They held the matrimonial home as joint tenants. In 1982 there was a violent altercation, in which the wife, trying to protect herself, picked up her husband's loaded shotgun. She threatened her husband with the gun; inadvertently it was fired, and her husband was killed. She was charged with the offence of manslaughter; she had no defence to that charge, she pleaded guilty, and was placed on probation for two years. It was conceded by the parties, and accepted by the judge, that the forfeiture rule applied, and that the effect of the killing was to sever the joint tenancy, so as to deprive the wife of her right of survivorship.[520] An alternative view was to regard the right of survivorship as taking effect, but then for the law to impose a constructive trust on the survivor, so that a

---

[515] In *Burgess* v *Rawnsley* [1975] Ch 429 at 440C Lord Denning MR roundly stated that *Nielson-Jones* v *Fedden* was wrongly decided.
[516] (1990) 60 P & CR 456.
[517] The leading case is *Cleaver* v *Mutual Reserve Fund Life Association* [1892] QB 147.
[518] The court has a discretion to modify the effect of the forfeiture rule where the court considers that it would be just to do so: s 2, Forfeiture Act 1982. See *Re K, deceased* [1985] Ch 85, confirmed on appeal, [1986] Ch 180; n 522, below, and text thereto.
[519] [1985] Ch 85.
[520] The severance analysis was approved by the Court of Appeal in *Dunbar* v *Plant* [1998] Ch 412.

half share would be held by the wife for her husband's estate.[521] However, consider the situation where there are three joint tenants, Alan, Brian and Celia, and Alan kills Brian. Celia has survived Brian, and therefore there is survivorship between them as to one half. What happens to the other half? If there is a severance, a quarter would go to Alan and a quarter to Brian's estate. But that is surely unfair to Celia, because she is deprived, through no act of her own, of her right of survivorship over that half (if she had been the last survivor of the three, she would have taken the entire property). However, there is also the potential to be unfair to Alan, because, as an original joint tenant, he was potentially entitled to at least a one third share. A better solution would be to allow Alan to retain a one third share, but then to impose a constructive trust on him, so that he would hold the remaining one sixth share for Brian's estate.[522]

The conveyancing problem created by a tenancy in common: the problem and the solution

The conveyancing problem which could be created by a tenancy in common can be readily demonstrated. Suppose that Celia by her will gave her house to all her children in equal shares. Suppose that she was survived by four children, c1, c2, c3 and c4, so that they each had a quarter share. Suppose then that c1 died, leaving her quarter share to be divided between her three children, gc1, gc2 and gc3. Each of these grandchildren therefore receive a one twelfth share. Anyone purchasing the house would have been obliged to investigate the title of each of Celia's children and grandchildren, and obtain the consent of each of them, in order to obtain vacant possession of the house. This was widely regarded as the most serious conveyancing problem to be solved by the property reforms of 1925. In short, a tenancy in common could create increasing fragmentation (more tenants in common, and therefore smaller and smaller shares), whereas joint tenancy, because of the right of

---

[521] See per Vinelott J, ibid at 100G, citing a Canadian case, *Schobelt* v *Barber* (1966) 60 DLR 2d 519, and a New Zealand case, *Re Pehar* [1969] NZLR 574. This point, the effect of the killing on the joint tenancy, was not in issue in the appeal, [1986] Ch 180.
[522] A solution along those lines was adopted by an Australian court in *Rasmanis v Jurewitsch* (1970) 70 SR NSW 407; but the outcome there was that Alan and Celia remained joint tenants as to two thirds, and Celia became, in addition, a tenant in common as to one third. Brian's estate got nothing. That result surely cannot be correct.

survivorship, would result in reducing fragmentation. The solution was to impose a trust, so that title to the house would vest in trustees holding on trust for the beneficiaries. The trustees, who would hold the legal estate as joint tenants (thus invoking the right of survivorship should one die), would be able to sell and overreach the rights of the beneficiaries, whose interests would be converted into the appropriate shares of the proceeds of sale paid by the purchaser to the trustees.[523] The following is a description of the statutory machinery designed to achieve this end. Firstly, section 1(6) of the Law of Property Act 1925 provides that "A legal estate is not capable of subsisting or of being created in an undivided share in land..." Section 34(2) of the Act then provides that "Where after the commencement of this Act land is expressed to be conveyed to any persons in undivided shares and those persons are of full age, the conveyance shall... operate as if the land had been expressed to be conveyed to the grantees, or, if there more than four grantees, to the four first named in the conveyance, as joint tenants in trust for the persons interested in the land". The limitation of the number of trustees to four is obviously made to ease the task of a purchaser in investigating the title to the land; it is consistent with the general statutory limitation in the number of trustees to four.[524] Take this example: land is expressed to be conveyed to five persons as tenants in common, and all are of full age[525], and, it may be added, (because it is a general requirement for all trustees) are of full capacity and are willing to act as trustees. The effect is that the legal estate will vest in the first four named as joint tenants holding in trust for the five tenants in common in equity. Any sale or other disposition of the legal estate will be made by those four trustees. If one of them were to die, the right of survivorship would carry the legal estate to the three survivors, but the one fifth share of the deceased as tenant in common will pass to that person's estate.[526] In this example, there is a divergence from the outset between the persons holding the legal estate and the beneficiaries under the trust. That divergence may well grow wider as time goes on. In all cases, the question, at

---

[523] This was originally a trust for sale, as set out in s 35, Law of Property Act 1925. This was never more than a device to introduce the idea of overreaching, but it was such an artificial device that many problems were produced. Happily, s 35 was repealed by the Trusts of Land and Appointment of Trustees Act 1996; there is now a power of sale. See below.
[524] S 34, Trustee Act 1925.
[525] A person under full age cannot hold a legal estate in land: s 1(6), Law of Property Act 1925.
[526] Another trustee could, if desired, be appointed under the statutory power contained in s 36, Trustee Act 1925.

any given time, is: who are the trustees and who are the beneficiaries? The purchaser need only be concerned with the question: who are the trustees? That is because of the power of overreaching. The purchaser needs to be reminded, however, that overreaching can take place only if the proceeds of sale or other capital money are paid to or applied by the direction of all the trustees, being at least two in number.[527]

The imposition of a trust applies also where the beneficiaries are to take as joint tenants. Section 36(1) of the Law of Property 1925 provides: "Where a legal estate...is beneficially limited to or held in trust for any persons as joint tenants, the same shall be held in trust in like manner as if the persons beneficially entitled were tenants in common, but not so as to sever their joint tenancy in equity." The result is illustrated by the following example. Land is transferred to Celia and David as joint tenants. Both are of full age and capacity. The effect of section 34(2) and section 36(1) is that the legal estate will vest in them both as joint tenants, holding in trust for themselves as joint tenants. That sounds very artificial, but it is necessary in order to allow for the power of severance. Suppose that David, during his lifetime, transfers his interest to Emma. That is severance and Emma takes a half share as tenant in common. Moreover, as seen earlier, since there were only two co-owners, the effect is to sever the entire joint tenancy, so that Celia will also now hold a half share as tenant in common. Without a trust, that would revive the pre-1926 conveyancing problem. So, the solution is to impose a trust from the outset. The logic of this scheme is completed by section 36(2) of the Law of Property Act 1925: "No severance of a legal estate, so as to create a tenancy in common in land, shall be permissible, whether by operation of law or otherwise...". Therefore, the result in the above example would be that David would remain as a trustee along with Celia, holding as joint tenants in trust for Celia and Emma as tenants in common in equal shares. Any sale or other disposition of the land would be made by Celia and David.

To summarise, the effect of the Law of Property Act 1925 is to impose a trust in all cases of co-ownership of land. Such a trust is a "trust of land", defined by section 1(1)(a) of the Trusts of Land and Appointment of Trustees Act 1996 (TLATA) as "any trust of property which consists of or includes land". Part 1

---

[527] S 27(2), Law of Property Act 1925. It will be remembered that the two trustee rule is the basis of the distinction between *Williams & Glyn's Bank Ltd* v *Boland* [1981] AC 187 and *City of London Building Society* v *Flegg* [1988] 2 AC 54; see ch 4.

of the Act governs the operation of a trust of land. The following provisions are the most important for present purposes. Section 6(1) provides that "For the purpose of exercising their functions as trustees, the trustees of land have in relation to the land subject to the trust all the powers of an absolute owner." In exercising these powers the trustees shall have regard to the rights of the beneficiaries[528] (one might say, of course!), and must not exercise their powers in contravention of any rule of law or equity (which seems equally self-evident). The powers may be excluded or restricted by the disposition creating the trust, or may be subjected to a requirement to obtain the consent of any person or persons.[529] The trustees owe to the beneficiaries a statutory duty of care in exercising their powers.[530] The trustees, in exercising their powers, must consult the beneficiaries of full age who are beneficially entitled to an interest in possession in the land, and so far as consistent with the general interest of the trust must give effect to the wishes of those beneficiaries, or, in case of dispute, of the majority, according to the value of their combined interests. This duty may be excluded by the disposition creating the trust.[531]

So, we see that the trustees' general powers are hedged about with restrictions and qualifications. The trustees' duties are obviously enforceable by the beneficiaries against the trustees. The trustees will be liable to pay equitable compensation to any beneficiary who has suffered loss, and an injunction may be obtained as appropriate to prevent a threatened breach of duty[532]. However, the question then arises whether a breach of any of these duties, or actions outside any of the qualifications, can affect the title of a purchaser of the land from the trustees. We need to consider section 16 of TLATA, which provides some protection for purchasers. Firstly, it needs to be observed that section 16 does not apply to registered land[533], and that raises questions which are considered below. Section 16(1) provides that a purchaser need not be concerned to see that the trustees have complied with their duty to have

---

[528] S 6(5).
[529] S 8. The court may relieve the trustees of an obligation to obtain a consent: s 14(2)(a).
[530] S 6(9), TLATA; s 1, Trustee Act 2000.
[531] S 11, TLATA. The court may relieve the trustees from the obligation to consult: s 14(2)(a). There are other powers conferred on the trustees, which in the interests of brevity and simplicity are not considered here: the power to partition the land between the beneficiaries (s 7), and matters concerning the right of a beneficiary to occupy the land (ss 12 and 13).
[532] For example, to restrain a threatened sale by one trustee and without consultation with the beneficiaries: *Waller v Waller* [1967] 1 WLR 451.
[533] S 16(7).

regard to the interests of the beneficiaries, or to consult the beneficiaries. Where the trustees convey in contravention of a rule of law or equity, but the purchaser has no actual notice of the contravention, "the contravention does not invalidate the conveyance".[534] Where the trustees' general powers are excluded or restricted, or made subject to a consent or consents, the trustees must take all reasonable steps to bring the limitation to the notice of the purchaser, but the limitation does not invalidate the conveyance if the purchaser has no actual notice of the limitation.[535]

What is the position in registered land bearing in mind that the protective provisions in section 16 do not apply? The fundamental principle is that a purchaser of registered land is entitled to rely on the conclusiveness of the register. The beneficiaries may enter a restriction on the register, for example, to indicate any restriction or qualification of the trustees' powers of disposition, or that those powers are subject to the obtaining of a consent or consents[536]. In the absence of such a restriction, a purchaser who pays the purchase money to two trustees overreaches the beneficial interests, even though the transfer is made in breach of trust.[537] This seems wide enough to protect the purchaser from the consequences of a breach by the trustees of any of the duties imposed on them by TLATA.[538]

Applications to the court

Section 14 of the 1996 Act provides that a trustee or a beneficiary under a trust of land may apply to the court to resolve any dispute relating to the exercise by the trustees of any of their functions, or concerning the nature or extent of a person's interest in the trust property. It would seem that the majority of such disputes concern the question, whether the trust property should be sold. For

---

[534] S 16(2). This is curious wording. No one would have argued that the contravention made the conveyance invalid, so that there would be no transfer of the legal estate. What must be meant is that the contravention does not affect the purchaser's title.
[535] S 16(3). Note the curious wording, and see the comment in the previous footnote.
[536] S 40, Land Registration Act 2002.
[537] S 26, Land Registration Act 2002.
[538] A purchaser who knowingly receives trust property in breach of trust could be personally liable to the beneficiaries; such liability would not upset the purchaser's title. However, the Law Commission's Consultation Paper (No 227), para 5.60, cites *HSBC Bank plc v Dyche* [2009] EWHC 2954 (Ch) for the proposition that, despite s 26, LRA 2002, "overreaching will not take place in registered land where a disposition is a breach of trust".

example, if a married couple are co-owners of the family home, and their relationship breaks down, the result could well be that one of them wishes the house to be sold but the other opposes that idea. The dispute could well be exacerbated if there are young children of the marriage and the person opposing a sale is looking after the children in the family home. On an application under section 14 the court will have to decide whether or not to order sale, immediately or at some point in the future. Section 15 provides that the matters to which the court must have regard, in determining an application under section 14, include:

"(a) the intentions of the person or persons (if any) who created the trust,

(b) the purposes for which the property subject to the trust is held,

(c) the welfare of any minor who occupies or might reasonably be expected to occupy any land subject to the trust as his home[539],

(d) the interests of any secured creditor of any beneficiary."

These factors to some extent replicate the courts' practice in pre-1997 cases. In the pre-1997 era the courts had developed the idea of the continuing purpose; if the property was acquired for a purpose which was continuing, the court would not ordinarily order sale. If, as in the above example, a house had been acquired as a family home and could still provide a home for one of the married partners and children of the marriage, the cases show that the court would not normally order a sale.[540] Conversely, if the purpose had come to an end, sale would ordinarily be ordered.[541] That idea seems to be embodied in factor (b), above, and reinforced by factor (c) where minor children are involved.

Before going further, we need to consider an entirely different jurisdiction which might be invoked in family disputes, and which might conflict with, or produce different solutions from, any which would be reached under sections

---

[539] The children need not be children of the co-owners: *First National Bank plc* v *Achampong* [2004] 1 FCR 18 (grandchildren).

[540] *Re Buchanan-Wollaston's Conveyance* [1939] Ch 738; *Re Evers' Trust* [1980] 1 WLR 1327. In *Bedson* v *Bedson* [1965] 2 QB 666, a married couple acquired premises for two purposes, to live there as their home and to run a drapery business. The wife left, but the husband wished to carry on the business. Sale was refused, but the husband was ordered to pay rent to his wife.

[541] *Jones* v *Challenger* [1961] 1 QB 176; *Rawlings* v *Rawlings* [1964] P 398.

14 and 15 of TLATA. Section 24 of the Matrimonial Causes Act 1973[542] provides that on divorce or judicial separation the court may make an order adjusting the couple's property, including the former matrimonial home. Section 25 sets out a number of factors which the court must take into account, which are far wider than those in section 15 of TLATA. The court is required by section 25(1) "to have regard to all the circumstances of the case, first consideration being given to the welfare while a minor of any child of the family who has not attained the age of eighteen." The courts over the years have made it clear that a high priority, where there are sufficient assets, is to provide homes for husband and wife and dependent children. The court will decide which parent the young children are to reside with, and is likely to order that there will be no sale of the former matrimonial home while it is required to house the children and the parent looking after them. The courts have on several occasions held that the family law jurisdiction is to be preferred to that under TLATA. In *Miller Smith* v *Miller Smith*[543] the Court of Appeal stated that the family law jurisdiction is "in principle far more desirable". The court will therefore, where appropriate, give priority to the family law jurisdiction, for example by adjourning the application under TLATA until the divorce proceedings are concluded. The family law jurisdiction is not available to unmarried heterosexual couples, so that they have to rely on TLATA.

We must now see how sections 14 and 15 have worked out in practice, and to what extent, if any, decisions made under TLATA differ from those made before the Act. One of the first reported decisions under TLATA was *Mortgage Corporation* v *Shaire*[544]. Neuberger J concluded that section 15 had significantly changed the law, and had given the courts greater flexibility as to how they exercised their jurisdiction. Amongst other matters, he thought it significant that after TLATA there was no longer a trust for sale, merely a trust with a power of sale, and therefore now no presumption in favour of sale. He went on to consider to what extent decisions made before TLATA could be of assistance now. His conclusion was as follows: "I think it would be wrong to throw over all the earlier cases without paying them any regard. However,

---

[542] Extended so as to apply to civil partnerships by the Civil Partnership Act 2004 and to same sex marriages by the Marriage (Same Sex Couples) Act 2013.
[543] [2010] 1FLR 1402. See also *Williams* v *Williams* [1976] Ch 278; *Laird* v *Laird* [1999] 1 FLR 791; *Tee* v *Tee & Hamilton* [1999] 2 FLR 613.
[544] [2001] Ch 743.

they have to be treated with caution, in the light of the change in the law, and, in many cases, they are unlikely to be of great, let alone decisive, assistance".[545] Commentators regarded the decision as the dawn of a more liberal era.[546] Subsequent cases have not developed that promise. Gray and Gray call it "A false dawn".[547]

It is instructive to consider decisions made under TLATA in two particular categories. The first category is claims by a secure creditor of a beneficiary. The interest of a secured creditor is expressly stated in section 15 as one of the factors for the court to consider. How is that factor to be weighed against, for example, the interest of a minor child? The question was considered in *Bank of Ireland Home Mortgages Ltd v Bell*.[548] The case concerned a former matrimonial home in which the wife had a 10% share. The house was subject to a charge in favour of the claimant bank, and the outstanding debt amounted to more than £300,000 and was increasing. The husband had left, but Mrs Bell remained in occupation with their son, aged 17. Mrs Bell claimed to be in ill health. The Court of Appeal ordered an immediate sale, ruling that it would be quite unfair to keep the bank out of its money. This was the same approach as the courts had followed before TLATA.[549]

The second category to consider is where one of the beneficiaries is bankrupt. On bankruptcy virtually all the bankrupt's property vests by operation of law in the trustee, holding for the benefit of the creditors. Where the property includes co-owned land, it may be appropriate for the trustee to apply for sale. The leading case before TLATA was *Re Citro (A Bankrupt)*.[550] The case concerned two brothers, Domenico and Carmine, both of whom were bankrupt following the failure of their joint business venture. Their only substantial assets were their shares in their respective family homes. Domenico was separated from his wife, but she continued to live in the house with the three children of the marriage. Carmine lived in his house with his wife and their three children. Nourse LJ, having considered earlier

---

[545] Ibid at para 77. The judge declined to order an immediate sale of the family home, on the application of a chargee, where the beneficiary's signature on the charge had been forged, and there was a possibility that the beneficiary could make the interest payments on the outstanding debt.
[546] That phrase is used by Gray & Gray, *Elements of Land Law*, 5th ed, para 7.5.119.
[547] Op cit, para 7.5.120.
[548] [2001] 2 All ER (Comm) 920; followed in *First National Bank plc v Achampong* [2004] 1 FCR 18; cf *Edwards v Lloyds TSB Bank plc* [2004] EWHC 1745.
[549] See, for example, *Lloyds Bank plc v Byrne & Byrne* [1993] 1 FLR 369.
[550] [1991] Ch 142.

authorities,[551] summarised the law as follows; "Where a spouse who has a beneficial interest in the matrimonial home has become bankrupt under debts which cannot be paid without the realisation of that interest, the voice of the creditors will usually prevail over the voice of the other spouse and a sale of the property ordered within a short period. The voice of the other spouse will only prevail in exceptional circumstances. No distinction is to be made between a case where the property is still being enjoyed as the matrimonial home and one where it is not."[552]

The crucial question, therefore, becomes: what are exceptional circumstance, and were there exceptional circumstance on the facts of *Re Citro*? The majority of the Court of Appeal held that there were no exceptional circumstances in the case before them, even though an immediate sale would lead to housing difficulties and problems with the children's schooling. Nourse LJ said: "Such circumstances, while engendering a natural sympathy in all who hear of them, cannot be described as exceptional. They are the melancholy consequences of debt and improvidence with which every civilised society has been familiar."[553] He went on to say that there was only one reported case where sale had been postponed for any significant length of time, and that was *Re Holliday (A Bankrupt)*.[554] There sale was postponed for five years, but the special feature was that the creditors' money was safe, both principal and accruing interest, and postponement of any sale would not cause great hardship to any of the creditors. Also, the bankruptcy was on the petition of the bankrupt himself; the creditors were not pressing.

Would the decision in *Re Citro* be any different if it arose after TLATA? Section 15(4) of TLATA states that section 15 does not apply if section 335A of the Insolvency Act 1986 applies to the case.

Section 335A provides that, in a bankruptcy case, any application for sale under section 14 of TLATA shall be heard by the bankruptcy court. That court must make such order as it thinks just and reasonable having regard to:

"(a) the interests of the bankrupt's creditors;

---

[551] In particular, *Re Bailey (A Bankrupt)* [1977] 1 WLR 278; *Re Lowrie (A Bankrupt)* [1981] 3 All ER 353; *Re Holliday (A Bankrupt)* [1981] Ch 405.
[552] [1991] Ch 142 at p 157B-D.
[553] Ibid.
[554] [1981] Ch 405.

(b) where the application is made in respect of land which includes a dwelling house which is or has been the home of the bankrupt or the bankrupt's spouse or civil partner or former spouse or former civil partner-

(i) the conduct of the spouse, civil partner, former spouse or former civil partner so far as contributing to the bankruptcy,

(ii) the needs and financial resources of the spouse, civil partner, former spouse or former civil partner, and

(iii) the needs of any children,

(c) all the circumstances of the case other than the needs of the bankrupt."

These criteria are broader and more generous to the bankrupt's family than those in section 15 of TLATA. However, the sting lies in the tail of section 335A. Sub-section (3) provides that, where an application for sale is made more than one year after the commencement of the bankruptcy, "the court shall assume, unless the circumstances of the case are exceptional, that the interests of the bankrupt's creditors outweigh all other considerations." In other words, the broader and more generous criteria apply for only one year. Thereafter, decisions such as *Re Citro*, with its narrow view of exceptional circumstances, will continue to be relevant. There have been a few cases where exceptional circumstances have been accepted. In *Re Lowrie (A Bankrupt)* [555] it was suggested that sale may be postponed for a short time beyond the standard year if that period falls at a particularly difficult time for a child leading up to examinations.[556] Sale may be postponed if the home has been adapted for a disabled child or spouse.[557] Other cases involve severe illness or disability. In *Judd v Brown*[558] indefinite postponement was ordered where there was renal failure and osteoarthritis which limited mobility. In *Re Bremner*[559] a spouse aged 74 was looking after the terminally ill bankrupt, aged 79, who had a life expectancy of six months. Sale was postponed until three months after the bankrupt's death.

---

[555] [1981] 3 All ER 353 at 356.
[556] *Re Lowrie* [1981] 3 All ER 353 at 356.
[557] *Claughton v Charambolous* [1999] 1 FLR 740; *Re Bailey* [1977] 1 WLR 278.
[558] [1998] 2 FLR 360. See also *Re Raval* [1998] 2 FLR 718; *Nichols v Lan* [2007] 1 FLR 744; *Re Haghighat* [2009] 1 FLR 1271.
[559] [1999] 1 FLR 912.

The courts so far have not been particularly receptive to arguments that the restrictions on the court's discretion imposed by the Insolvency Act are in breach of Article 8 of the European Convention on Human Rights (respect for private and family life and the home) or Protocol No 1, Article 1 (peaceful enjoyment of possessions).[560] However, that issue is probably still open.

Sale by a surviving joint tenant; the conveyancing problem and the (partial) solution

Suppose that land is conveyed to Celia and David as legal and beneficial joint tenants. They can sell and overreach their beneficial interests, which are converted into the proceeds of sale. Therefore, the purchaser is protected. If David dies, the trust of land terminates, because it is not possible for one person to hold on trust for herself[561]. Therefore, Celia now holds the property legally and beneficially, and may sell the property without the concurrence of any other person. However, David might have severed the joint tenancy during his lifetime, for example by transferring his interest to his daughter Emma, and if so the trust would continue at his death. On a sale by Celia alone, overreaching would not protect the purchaser. In unregistered land the purchaser would have to rely on the proof of lack of notice, but if Emma was in occupation that would probably be sufficient to give notice to the purchaser.[562] In registered land there would be a similar situation, because Emma would have an overriding interest.[563] For the protection of the purchaser, it became conveyancing practice for Celia to execute a deed appointing another person to act as a trustee with her in order to transfer the land to the purchaser. Overreaching would then operate, whether or not there had been a severance; but where there had in fact been no severance, this was needless complexity and expense. Only Parliament could devise a better solution, and eventually Parliament intervened by passing the Law of Property (Joint Tenants) Act 1964. Section 1 provides that the surviving joint tenant is deemed to be solely and beneficially entitled if the conveyance to the purchaser contains a statement that she is so entitled. That does not apply,

---

[560] See *Jackson v Bell* [2001] Family Law 879; *Barca v Mears* [2005] 2 FLR 1; *Hosking v Michaelides* [2006] BPIR 1192; *Nichols v Lan* [2007] 1 FLR 744; *Ford v Alexander* [2012] BPIR 528. See also n 493, ante.
[561] *Re Cook* [1948] Ch 212.
[562] *Kingsnorth Finance Co Ltd v Tizard* [1986] 1 WLR 783.
[563] *Williams & Glyn's Bank Ltd v Boland* [1981] AC 487. See also ch 4.

however, if a memorandum of severance, signed by at least one of the joint tenants, and recording that the joint tenancy was severed on a specified date, has been endorsed on or annexed to the original conveyance to the joint tenants, or if a bankruptcy order (or a petition for such an order) has been registered under the Land Charges Act 1972[564] before the date of the survivor's conveyance. To enjoy this protection the purchaser must be a purchaser of the legal estate in good faith for valuable consideration. What if the purchaser actually knows that there has been a severance? In *Grindal* v *Hooper*[565] it was held that the purchaser is not protected.

The Act does not apply to registered land.[566] If a severance occurs, a restriction should be entered, or remain, on the register requiring the purchase money to be paid to not fewer than two trustees. However, Parliament overlooked the possibility that the person claiming under a severance could be in actual occupation and therefore have an overriding interest. That was a mistake, but probably forgivable since the landmark decision in *Williams & Glyn's Bank Ltd* v *Boland*[567] lay several years ahead. It meant, however, that in registered land the original problem persisted. An amendment to the Act is long overdue, and it is regrettable that the problem was not dealt with by the Land Registration Act 2002.[568]

---

[564] S 1 of the 1964 Act, as amended by the Law of Property (Miscellaneous Provisions) Act 1994.
[565] (1999) 96/48 LS Gaz 41.
[566] S 3.
[567] [1981] AC 487.
[568] See Cooke [2004] Conv 212; Cooke, *The New Law of Land Registration*, p 55, n 9.

140

Chapter 8

THE FAMILY HOME

There is a long history of litigation concerning rights in the family home (and other family assets), especially since the Second World War. At least two principal factors can be identified as contributing to this flood of litigation: better economic prospects for women, and very rapid inflation in the price of housing. This chapter discusses the major decided cases, and relevant legislative provisions.

Obviously, legal problems are unlikely to arise between people who are living together in a stable relationship, whether marriage, a civil partnership, or cohabitation. However, legal problems are quite likely to arise when the relationship breaks down.

This chapter concentrates on the family home, which is likely, in many cases, to be the principal family asset. It is in that context that most of the major cases have arisen. It must be realised at the outset that it is possible for the family home to be owned by only one of the parties: English law, unlike some civil law systems, does not have any system of community of property in this context. Suppose, therefore, that the home is owned entirely by the husband, and that the wife has no interest in it. If the relationship breaks down, for example, if the husband deserts his wife, leaving her in occupation, the question may arise whether she has a right to stay in occupation. That was exactly the question that arose in *National Provincial Bank Ltd* v *Ainsworth*.[569] Mr Ainsworth was the sole registered proprietor of the house; he deserted his wife, leaving her in occupation with their four children. He then mortgaged the house to the bank, and later he defaulted on repayment of the mortgage loan. These were proceedings for possession of the house brought by the bank against the wife. Before the case reached the House of Lords, there was a line of very controversial Court of Appeal decisions that the deserted wife had a right to stay in occupation, which was effective not only against the husband himself, but also against his successors in title, including the bank. In other words, according to the Court of Appeal, the wife had a proprietary interest in the house (it was called "the deserted wife's equity"). In *Ainsworth*

---

[569] [1965] AC 1175.

a majority of the Court of Appeal followed that line of cases, and held, in registered land terms, that the wife had an overriding interest. However, on the bank's appeal, the House of Lords unanimously overruled that line of cases; it was held that the wife had a personal right against the husband, but did not have a proprietary interest capable of binding the bank, and therefore did not have an overriding interest.[570]

Perhaps the clearest reasoning is contained in the speech of Lord Wilberforce. He first identified the distinction between personal and proprietary rights. He said[571]: "The general question is whether the respondent Mrs Ainsworth as the deserted wife of her husband, the owner of the house, has any interest in or right over it which is capable of binding the bank as a proprietor of a legal interest in the land. This is a general question of real property law. The second question arises out of the fact that the land is registered land. It is, briefly, whether the respondent's interest, or right, is an overriding interest." He then described the features needed to justify holding that a particular right can cross the line to become a proprietary interest. He said[572]: "Before a right or an interest can be admitted into the category of property, or of a right affecting property, it must be definable, identifiable by third parties, capable in its nature of assumption by third parties, and have some degree of permanence or stability." He then applied those descriptors to the right claimed by Mrs Ainsworth as a deserted wife. He said[573]: "The wife's right has none of these qualities. It is characterised by the reverse of them." He also said[574]: "On any division, then, which is to be made between property rights on the one hand, and personal rights on the other hand, however broad or penumbral the separating band between these two kinds of rights may be, there can be little doubt where the rights fall."[575] It is worth examining this line of reasoning, because it has been criticised by some commentators as circular. For example, Gray and Gray state as follows[576]: "The difficulty with

---

[570] Her personal right could be enforced by the wife obtaining an injunction to prevent her husband from entering into any transaction which could interfere with her right of occupation: *Lee v Lee* [1952] 2 QB 489.
[571] [1965] AC 1175 at 1243 A-B.
[572] Ibid at 1247 G.
[573] Ibid at 1247G- 1248G.
[574] Ibid at 1247G.
[575] Lord Wilberforce had earlier shown in his speech that the wife's rights to occupation of the matrimonial home "are at no time definitive, they are provisional and subject to review at any time according as changes take place in the material circumstances and conduct of the parties": ibid at 1247F.
[576] *Elements of Land Law*, 5th ed, para 1.5.29. See also Gray, *Property in Thin Air* [1991] CLJ 252 at 293; Dixon is much more temperate in his discussion of the issue in *Land Law: Issues, Debates, Policy* (ed Tee), 16-18.

this orthodox understanding of proprietary quality is, of course, that it is riddled with circularity: the definition of proprietary becomes entirely self-fulfilling. If naively we ask which entitlements are "proprietary", we are told that they are those rights which are assignable to and enforceable against third parties. When we then ask which rights these might be, we are told that they comprise, of course, the entitlements which are traditionally identified as "proprietary". It is radical and obscurantist nonsense to formulate a test of proprietary quality in this way." That passage completely distorts Lord Wilberforce's reasoning. As can be seen from the passages quoted above from *Ainsworth*, his reasoning is linear, not circular, and is entirely systematic. It deserves to remain authoritative and influential.

However, the limits to Lord Wilberforce's explanation must be recognised. It is intended to be merely an attempt to explain what is meant by the distinction between personal and proprietary rights; it is a minimal, but, in the context, a sufficient definition. The crux of the matter is whether the rights (or the claims) in question bind third parties. How that decision is to be made is merely sketched in by Lord Wilberforce; he does not attempt to state, in any detail, the criteria to be applied in making that decision.[577]

As might be expected, the decision in *Ainsworth* was hugely unpopular in some quarters, for the obvious reason that it had the potential, at least temporarily, to render Mrs Ainsworth and the children homeless. The response of Parliament was to pass, hurriedly, the Matrimonial Homes Act 1967, now, as amended, incorporated into Part IV of the Family Law Act 1996. The Act has been extended to apply to a civil partnership and to a same sex marriage.[578] In the following account, the term "spouse" is to be interpreted as referring also to civil partners and participants in a same sex marriage, and the term "marriage" is to be interpreted as applying also to a civil partnership.

The core provisions of the Act are sections 30 and 31. Section 30 applies where one spouse is entitled to occupy the family home and the other spouse is not so entitled, or is so entitled by virtue only of an equitable interest.[579] Section 30(2) confers on the non-entitled spouse what the Act calls "matrimonial home rights", specifically:

---

[577] See an examination of this wider question in ch 1, "What is Property?".
[578] See the Civil Partnership Act 2004; the Marriage (Same Sex Couples) Act 2013.
[579] It should be noted that, where a spouse has an equitable interest, that interest is quite distinct from the statutory matrimonial home rights.

"(a) if in occupation, a right not to be evicted or excluded from the dwelling-house or any part of it by the other spouse except with the leave of the court...

(b) if not in occupation, a right with the leave of the court...to enter into and occupy the dwelling-house."[580]

Section 31 provides that these matrimonial home rights are a charge on the entitled spouse's estate or interest in the house, and "has the same priority as if it were an equitable interest created at whichever is the latest of the following dates – (a) the date on which the spouse so entitled acquires the estate or interest; (b) the date of the marriage; and (c) 1st January 1968 (the commencement date of the Matrimonial Homes Act 1967)."[581] The charge is a proprietary interest and therefore is capable of binding the entitled spouse's successors in title.[582]

If the entitled spouse has a legal estate, the charge needs to be registered, in the case of unregistered land as a Class F land charge under the Land Charges Act 1972, and in the case of registered land by a notice on the register. The charge does not constitute an overriding interest in registered land, even though the spouse entitled to the charge is in actual occupation of the house.[583] A cohabitant who is not married or in a civil partnership is treated much less favourably. Such a person may apply to the court for an order conferring a right of occupation. Such an order must be for a specified period not exceeding six months, and it may be extended once only for a further period not exceeding six months. Moreover, such an order does not create a charge, a proprietary interest, and therefore can be enforced only against the other cohabitant. So, in the context of cohabitation, we have an echo of *Ainsworth*.

The nature and effect of these statutory matrimonial home rights were considered by Megarry J in *Wroth v Tyler*.[584] It is a cautionary tale. The respondent, Mr Tyler, was the sole registered proprietor of the matrimonial home, where he lived with his wife and adult daughter. He decided that he wanted to move to a cheaper house, and the profit on the move would enable

---
[580] The court is given extensive powers to regulate the matrimonial home rights.
[581] S 31(2) and (3), Family Law Act 1996.
[582] In its original version s 2(3), the Matrimonial Homes Act 1967 provided that the charge, even when registered, would not bind the other spouse's trustee in bankruptcy. That exception no longer applies.
[583] S 31 (10)(b), Family Law Act 1996.
[584] [1974] Ch 30.

him to discharge the mortgage on the original house. His wife and daughter were unenthusiastic about the proposed move. The claimants, Mr and Mrs Wroth, viewed the house several times, and on at least one occasion Mrs Tyler was present and explained the working of various pieces of equipment in the house. On 27th May 1971 contracts were exchanged for the sale with vacant possession of the house by Mr Tyler to Mr and Mrs Wroth for £6,000, completion to take place on or before 31st October. The next day Mrs Tyler, unknown to her husband, registered her matrimonial home rights. Mrs Tyler never gave the purchasers any indication of her reluctance to move. Mr Tyler became aware of his wife's registered charge on 18th June.[585] The transfer was not completed, and proceedings for breach of contract were begun in the Chancery Division of the High Court in January 1972. The case came before Megarry J in November 1972, and was argued for seven days. His decision was that damages should be awarded to the claimants. By the date of completion the market value of the house had risen to £7,500, and by the date of final judgment in January 1973 had risen again to £11,500. On 20th December 1972 the judge assessed damages to be awarded to the claimants at £5,500, but adjourned the case until 11th January 1973 to give Mrs Tyler the opportunity to remove her charge. She refused to do so, and therefore on that date damages were confirmed at £5,500. The judge made a detailed analysis of the statutory provisions. His conclusion was that "The right is in essence a personal and non-assignable statutory right not to be evicted from the matrimonial home during marriage or until the court otherwise orders; and this right constitutes a charge on the estate or interest of the owning spouse which requires protection against third parties by registration. For various reasons, the right may be said to be one which fits into no category known to conveyancers before 1967; the phrase sui generis seems apt, but of little help."[586] The judge pointed out that the rights belong exclusively to the protected spouse, and he was sceptical whether they could be used to protect any other occupier, such as the other spouse, or children, or lodgers. For that reason among others, he declined to grant a decree of specific performance; such an order could result in the Tyler family being split up.

---

[585] It is now the practice of the Land Registry to give immediate notice to the registered proprietor, so this particular feature of *Wroth* v *Tyler* should not recur: see Megarry & Wade, *The Law of Real Property*, 7th ed, para 34-027.
[586] [1974] Ch 30 at 46G. Collectively, the rights might be termed "the status of irremovability".

It seems clear that the ultimate outcome would be a financial disaster for Mr Tyler; a substantial award of damages, together with an order as to costs. Nine days in the High Court do not come cheaply![587] Moreover, one might speculate on the resulting relationships within the Tyler family. A cautionary tale indeed! It might be regarded as a graphic illustration of the law of unintended consequences.[588]

Now let us consider the position where both the parties to a relationship have interests in the family home, in other words, are co-owners. The first question is, how can that situation be brought about? It is obvious that co-ownership can be created by the original conveyance or transfer. However, since any form of beneficial co-ownership of land can exist only behind a trust now regulated by the Trusts of Land and Appointment of Trustees Act 1996,[589] the conveyance or transfer of the legal estate to two or more people necessarily results in those people holding the legal estate as joint tenants and as trustees. The conveyance or transfer will be conclusive as to the beneficial interests only if it contains an express declaration of trust, in favour of the beneficiaries as joint tenants, or as tenants in common in equal or unequal shares. Such a declaration, unless vitiated by fraud or mistake, is conclusive.[590]

In the absence of such an express declaration, the beneficial interests are at large, to be determined ultimately by a decision of the court, if necessary. There has been a cascade of court decisions in the last sixty years or so, and an accompanying mountain of academic commentary and debate. Most of the decisions have been in cases where the legal title to the family home was vested in one person, typically the husband or male cohabitant, and the other person in the relationship has claimed an equitable interest in the home under some form of implied trust.[591] However, some of the more recent decisions have been concerned with cases where the legal title is vested in two or more joint proprietors.

---

[587] The judge envisaged that Mr Tyler would probably be driven into bankruptcy. Ironically, as the law then stood, the trustee in bankruptcy could sell free from Mrs Tyler's rights; see n 551, ante.
[588] It was not argued that Mrs Tyler was estopped by her conduct, in apparently acquiescing in the sale, from claiming that her rights were binding on the purchasers:[1974] Ch 30 at 47F.
[589] See ch 7, "Co-ownership".
[590] *Goodman v Gallant* [1986] Fam 186.
[591] Such a trust may be created informally, without the need for any kind of writing: s 53(2), Law of Property Act 1925.

It needs to be observed that where a marriage or a civil partnership founders, the family law jurisdiction will apply. This gives the court power to redistribute the property for the benefit of the parties and any children of the family.[592] The first priority of the court exercising that power is to provide homes for the separating parties and any children. Any assets surplus to that requirement are likely to be divided equally.[593] Most property disputes involving married partners or civil partners are now likely to be resolved under that jurisdiction. However, that jurisdiction is not effective against third parties, such as a mortgagee or other relatives who may make a claim. Nor, crucially, is it available to heterosexual cohabitants. For that reason, many of the most recent cases concern unmarried cohabitants.

A brief history of these turbulent times will show how difficult the courts have found these issues, and how judicial attitudes have vacillated. The history can be divided into six stages. The earlier cases drew on an old idea of equity, that where property is transferred to one person, but another person has made a significant financial contribution to its acquisition, it is presumed, in the absence of contrary evidence, that the parties intended the contributor to have an interest in the property proportionate to the contribution.[594] That approach generated two questions: what would be regarded as a contribution, and how would the resultant interest be quantified? For example, would a wife's contribution to the household by way of child welfare and household maintenance constitute a contribution, and, if it would, how would the contribution be quantified? Denning LJ, in his first period as a member of the Court of Appeal, grew impatient with that approach. He was influential in persuading the Court of Appeal to adopt a much broader concept of family assets, irrespective of contributions, which the court could distribute as it thought fit, normally to be divided equally. Heavy reliance was placed on section 17 of the Married Women's Property Act 1882 for the proposition that

---

[592] S 24, Matrimonial Causes Act 1973, extended by the Civil Partnership Act 2004 and the Marriage (Same Sex Couples) Act 2013.
[593] *White* v *White* [2001] 1 AC 596.
[594] That idea can be traced back at least to *Dyer* v *Dyer* (1788) 2 Cox Eq Cas 92. An associated idea is that where property is transferred to two people as joint tenants, and one of them has contributed more than the other, equity will presume, in the absence of contrary evidence, that there was a common intention to hold the property as tenants in common in shares proportionate to their respective contributions. See ch 7, "Co-Ownership", n 478 and text thereto and following. At that stage, judges and academics were agreed that equity's approach generated a resulting trust.

the court, in disputes between husband and wife, had a wide discretion to do what was fair and just.[595]

The next stage was the appeal to the House of Lords in *Pettitt v Pettitt*.[596] The husband claimed an interest in the house on the basis that he had done various small scale jobs around the house, mainly of a do it yourself nature. The House of Lords, reversing the Court of Appeal, rejected the claim. The House rejected the whole notion of family assets, and held that section 17 was procedural only; the task of the court is to ascertain the parties' rights according to orthodox property principles, and then to make such order as it thinks appropriate.

Parliament then intervened to enact section 37 of the Matrimonial Proceedings and Property Act 1970. Section 37 provides that a substantial contribution in money or money's worth by a husband or wife to the improvement of real or personal property owned beneficially by either or both of them will entitle the contributor to such share as was agreed or, in default, as may seem in all the circumstances just. Where, for example, the property was originally owned by the parties as beneficial joint tenants, the effect of an improvement falling within section 37 will be to enlarge the interest of the contributor. The result must be a severance of the joint tenancy, making the owners tenants in common in unequal shares.[597]

The next important case was *Gissing v Gissing*,[598] also a decision of the House of Lords reversing the Court of Appeal. The important facts there were that the house was conveyed to the husband, who paid the whole purchase price, partly in cash and partly through a mortgage which he alone repaid. The wife worked outside the home for substantially the whole of the marriage. She had a separate bank account into which her earnings were paid. She spent £220 on the lawn at the house and in buying furniture, and she paid for her own clothes and those of her son. The House held that, since they had kept their property separate, it was impossible to infer any common intention or agreement that the wife should have an interest in the house. Members of the

---

[595] That would seem to be a constructive trust, a trust imposed by the court, overriding, or ignoring, the parties' common intention. See, for example, *Fribance v Fribance (No 2)* [1957] 1 ALL ER 357; *Hine v Hine* [1962] 3 All ER 345.
[596] [1970] AC 777.
[597] For severance of a joint tenancy see ch 7, "Co-ownership".
[598] [1971] AC 886.

House of Lords stated that indirect contributions would be recognised, that is to say, where the parties have ordered their financial affairs in such a way that the payment by one party of some of the joint expenses of the household has enabled the other party to make the direct payments in respect of the house.[599] However, that was not the case on the facts of *Gissing*, where the parties had kept their property entirely separate.

The third stage in this brief history followed the return of Lord Denning to the Court of Appeal as Master of the Rolls in 1962. In a series of cases the Court exercised a wide discretionary jurisdiction, relying on highly selective and unrepresentative quotations from *Pettitt* and *Gissing*.[600] The decisions were, in fact, wholly contrary to the spirit of those House of Lords' cases. A case from this period which has been much approved is *Eves* v *Eves*.[601] In 1968 Janet Eves began to live with Stuart Eves in a house which was owned entirely by him. At that time they were both married, but they intended to marry when they were free to do so. They had a daughter born in 1969. Later that year they found a house which they intended to be their family home. It was bought for £5,600, made up from the proceeds from his former house and a mortgage for £3,200. It was conveyed into the sole name of Stuart Eves. He explained to Janet that if she had been aged 21 he would have put it into their joint names, but that as she was under that age it would have to be in his name alone. She accepted that explanation. Stuart Eves later admitted that his explanation was simply an excuse for not putting the house into their joint names. Their second child was born at the end of 1970. The house was very run down, and Janet did a great deal of work to improve it. Among other things, she broke up concrete in the front garden with a sledge hammer to prepare it for turfing. She also looked after Stuart and the children. In November 1972 they separated; Stuart left Janet in the house with their children. Janet brought this action, claiming that Stuart held the legal estate in the house on trust for himself and Janet in equal shares or such shares as the court might determine. The house was then estimated to be worth £13,000, the equity of redemption having a value of £10,000 or more. The Court of Appeal held that Janet was entitled to a quarter share of the equity of

---

[599] For an example see *Grant v Edwards* [1986] 2 All ER 426.
[600] See, for example, *Falconer* v *Falconer* [1970] 3 All ER 449; *Hazell* v *Hazell* [1972] 1 All ER 923; *Cooke* v *Head* [1972] 2 All ER 38. That line of reasoning was criticised in *Grant* v *Edwards* [1986] 2 All ER 426; see n 606 and text thereto.
[601] [1975] 1 WLR 1338.

redemption. Orthodox reasons for that decision were given by Browne LJ and Brightman J. They said that it could be inferred that there was an arrangement between the parties whereby Janet was to have a beneficial interest in the house in return for her labour in contributing to its repair and improvement, and that the work which she carried out was in pursuance of that arrangement. Those two judges did not agree with the reasoning of Lord Denning MR, who simply held that in all the circumstances, including in particular the excuse that Stuart gave for not putting the house into their joint names, it would be inequitable to allow him to deny her a beneficial share. The law would therefore "impute or impose a constructive trust by which he was to hold [the house] in trust for them both."[602]

The fourth stage followed Lord Denning's retirement from the judiciary in 1982. It is clear that a reaction to his influence set in. The crucial case is *Burns v Burns*.[603] The parties there had lived together for some 17 years. They were unmarried because the male partner was still married to another person. They had two children, born in the early years of their relationship. The house where they lived was conveyed to the man alone; he bought it entirely with his own money and a mortgage which he alone paid. For the first 14 years Valerie Burns stayed at home and looked after the house and the children. She then started to go out to work and over the next three years or so made various contributions to the household expenses. When the relationship broke down she claimed a beneficial interest in the house, but the Court of Appeal, now free from the influence of Lord Denning, applied orthodox principles, and in particular *Gissing*, in rejecting her claim. She had made no financial contribution, and her general contributions to the welfare of the household and the family were, in this context, of no account.

It is worth pausing to note that if Mr and Mrs Burns had been married, she could have applied for a property adjustment order and would almost certainly have been awarded a substantial property or financial settlement; as the law now stands, probably a half share in their combined assets.[604] The correctness of the Court of Appeal's decision cannot be doubted, but the injustice is equally obvious. It is highly regrettable that Parliament has not intervened to remedy the injustice. More on this point later.

---

[602] Ibid at 772*d*.
[603] [1984] Ch 317.
[604] See *White* v *White* [2001] 1 AC 596.

An influential case from this period, on the other side of the line, is *Grant* v *Edwards*.[605] In 1969 the claimant, a married woman with two children, began a relationship with the respondent. That year she gave birth to their son, and they decided to live together. A house was bought and put into the names of the respondent and his brother, who was a purely nominal party with no beneficial interest in the property. The purchase price was £5,576, made up of a cash payment of £1,049 made by the respondent and by two mortgages totalling £4,533. The respondent told the claimant that her name would not go onto the title because it would cause some prejudice in the matrimonial proceedings pending between the claimant and her husband. In 1971 a second child was born. From August 1972 onwards the claimant made very substantial indirect contribution to the mortgage repayments by applying her earnings to the joint household expenses, and by housekeeping, feeding and caring for the children. Without those financial contributions the mortgage repayments could not have been met. The second mortgage was paid off in October 1974. In 1975 there was a fire at the house, and the family moved into council accommodation. The respondent received £4,000 from a fire insurance policy, the bulk of which was spent on repairing the property, which was then let. The rent was used to pay the instalments on the first mortgage. In September 1975 £1,037 left over from the money from the fire insurance policy was paid into a joint account at a building society, which was shared equally between the parties. In 1980 the couple separated. There was then £3,800 outstanding on the first mortgage. The Court of Appeal unanimously held that the claimant was entitled to a half share in the equity. The reasoning was completely orthodox: there was a common intention that they should both have a beneficial interest, followed by the claimant acting to her detriment on the basis of that common intention. There are obvious similarities between the facts of this case and those in *Eves* v *Eves*, and *Eves* was followed and applied. However, two of the judges took the opportunity to criticise the reasoning of Lord Denning in that case.[606]

This fourth stage in the history culminated in the decision of the House of Lords in *Lloyds Bank plc* v *Rosset*.[607] The case is important for the statement of

---
[605] [1986] 2 All ER 426.
[606] Ibid at 432e, per Nourse LJ, at 437c, per Sir Nicholas Browne-Wilkinson V-C. Gray & Gray, *Elements of Land Law*, 5th ed, para 7.3.57, are right to remind us of the dangers of gender stereotyping in cases such as *Eves* v *Eves*.
[607] [1991] 1 AC 107.

the law made by Lord Bridge of Harwich.[608] He identified two alternative means by which the non-legal owner might establish a share in the property, and he said that there was a sharp distinction between the two. The first is where the parties have reached an agreement, arrangement or understanding that the property is to be shared beneficially. Then the person relying on that agreement must show that she has acted to her detriment or significantly altered her position in reliance on that agreement; that will then give rise to a constructive trust. The second means is where there is no such agreement, arrangement or understanding. The court then has to rely on the conduct of the parties both so as to establish a common intention to share the property and as the conduct relied on to establish a constructive trust. Direct contribution to the purchase price, whether at the outset by contribution to the deposit or later by payment of mortgage instalments, will readily found the inference of a common intention and also justify the imposition of a constructive trust. However, Lord Bridge then concluded, "as I read the authorities, it is at least extremely doubtful whether anything less will do."[609] That statement seems to rule out the inference of an indirect contribution, at least in the second of the two categories. Overall the speech of Lord Bridge was subsequently treated as authoritative.

The fifth stage was ushered in by the decision of the Court of Appeal in *Midland Bank Plc v Cooke*.[610] Mr and Mrs Cooke were married in 1971. Their new home was conveyed into the sole name of Mr Cooke for a total price of £8,500. The purchase money was made up of £1,000 provided by Mr Cooke out of his savings, £1,100 from a wedding present given by his parents, and £6,450 advanced on a mortgage made by Mr Cooke alone. From the outset of their marriage both of them remained in work. They kept separate bank accounts. Mrs Cooke did not make any direct payments of the mortgage instalments, but she did pay for other household expenses out of her earnings. She did a considerable amount of work on the house and paid a number of contractors' bills, for redecoration, improvements and repair. She had brief spells of part-time work when their three children were born in 1972, 1974 and 1984. These proceedings were commenced by the bank in 1987, by which time Mr and Mrs Cooke had separated, she remaining in the house with the three

---

[608] Ibid at 132-133.
[609] Ibid at 133A.
[610] [1995] 4 All ER 562.

children. It was common ground that Mrs Cooke was entitled to a share in the house, but in the County Court the judge quantified her share on a mathematical basis. Her only contribution was a half of the wedding present, ie £550, contributing to the purchase price of £8,500. Her share was therefore 6.47%. The Court of Appeal, however, held that Mrs Cooke was entitled to a half share. Waite LJ stated the law as follows: "When the court is proceeding, in cases like the present where the partner without legal title has successfully asserted an equitable interest through direct contribution, to determine (in the absence of express evidence of intention) what proportions the parties must be assumed to have intended for their beneficial ownership, the duty of the judge is to undertake a survey of the whole course of dealing between the parties relevant to their ownership and occupation of the property and their sharing of its burdens and advantages. That scrutiny will not confine itself to the limited range of acts of direct contribution of the sort that are needed to found a beneficial interest in the first place. It will take into consideration all conduct which throws light on the question what shares were intended…The court is not bound to deal with the matter on the strict basis of the trust resulting from the cash contribution to the purchase price, and is free to attribute to the parties an intention to share the beneficial interest in some different proportions."[611] Waite LJ then reviewed the detailed facts, attaching importance, inter alia, to the fact that Mrs Cooke had brought up three children while continuing to work, had used her earnings to pay household bills and also the fact that they were married. He concluded: "One could hardly have a clearer example of a couple who had agreed to share everything equally".

This was new law, seeming to ignore the "sharp distinction" drawn by Lord Bridge in *Rosset*. It produces uncertainty of outcome. It gives rise to the following anomaly. If Mrs Cooke had not been able to found a trust on her direct contribution of half the wedding present, all her other contributions to the welfare of the household would have counted for nothing. She would have been in the same position as Mrs Gissing and Mrs Burns. It might be described as parasitic quantification: once a minimal share is established, it can be increased by evidence of conduct that would not otherwise be relevant at all.

---

[611] Ibid at 574d.

That case was followed, and its effect enlarged, by the Court of Appeal in *Oxley* v *Hiscock*.[612] Mrs Oxley and Mr Hiscock in 1991 together bought a house to provide a home for themselves and Mrs Oxley's children of a former marriage. The purchase price was £127,000. The legal title was put into the sole name of Mr Hiscock. He contributed £60,700, and Mrs Oxley contributed £36,300. The balance of £30,000 was provided by a loan from a building society secured by a charge over the house. They lived together in that house until 2001. By then the building society loan had been repaid. The house was put on the market, and it sold for £232,000. Mrs Oxley bought a new house for herself at a price of £73,000, of which £33,000 was contributed by Mr Hiscock. He bought a new house for himself at a price of £122,000. He paid a further £5,000 to Mrs Oxley, and £3,200 for renovations to her new house.

These proceedings were commenced in the County Court. The judge made detailed findings of fact, and concluded that, in quantifying the beneficial interests, she should follow the approach in *Cooke*. She held that there was a classic pooling of resources, so that both parties intended to share the benefits and burdens of the family home equally. She therefore made an order that Mrs Oxley was entitled to be paid a further sum of £72,056. Mr Hickox appealed. The Court of Appeal calculated that Mrs Oxley's financial contribution amounted to not more than 40%. On the traditional resulting trust analysis, that would have produced a division of the proceeds of sale 40% to Mrs Oxley and 60% to Mr Hiscock.

That was not, however, the way that the matter was approached by the Court of Appeal. Instead, the court, in a very lengthy judgment (some 70 pages) delivered by Chadwick LJ, conducted an elaborate reconsideration of all the major authorities of the last 30 years or so. He drew a careful distinction between the question whether it was legitimate for the court to impose a constructive trust at all ("the primary question") and, if it was so legitimate, the question of quantifying the beneficial interests under the resultant constructive trust ("the secondary question"). He showed that, in both the categories identified by Lord Bridge in *Rosset*, Lord Bridge was considering only the primary question. Chadwick LJ's conclusion was that, in answering the secondary question, "in the absence of evidence that [the parties] gave any thought to the amount of their respective shares, the necessary inference is

---

[612] [2005] Fam 211.

that they must have intended that question would be answered later on the basis of what was then seen to be fair."[613] Applying that test to the facts of the case, and reviewing the whole course of dealing between the parties, the court concluded that to hold in favour of equal shares would be unfair to Mr Hiscock, because it would not give sufficient weight to the fact that he had contributed substantially more to the purchase price than had Mrs Oxley (£60,700: £36,300). The result was therefore, that a fair division, remarkably enough, would be 60% to Mr Hiscock and 40% to Mrs Oxley.

Gray & Gray hailed the decision as "An important breakthrough"[614] in that it relieved the court from searching for a "phantom common intention."[615] Other commentators were markedly less enthusiastic. There was particular criticism that the court could exceed its remit and impose on the parties a result which the court considered was fair and just in the circumstances of the case, rather than the result which the parties could be regarded as having intended. The decision could, on the secondary question, take the courts virtually back to the palm tree justice of the Denning years in the Court of Appeal.

We now come to the sixth and final phase in this history, where the House of Lords in *Stack* v *Dowden*[616] set the law on yet another new course. Mr Stack and Ms Dowden were not married. They started cohabiting in 1983. At first they lived in a house previously conveyed into Ms Dowden's sole name, and of which she was the sole mortgagor. A great deal of work was done on the house, much of it by Mr Stack. That house was sold in 1993 for £90,000, about three times the price for which it was bought. They together bought another house as a family home. The purchase price was £190,000.

This time the house was vested in their joint names as registered proprietors, but without an express declaration of trust.[617] They financed that purchase

---

[613] Ibid at para 69.
[614] *Elements of Land Law*, 4th ed, para 10.138.
[615] Ibid at para 10.139.
[616] [2007] 2 AC 432.
[617] The transfer contained a clause stating that the survivor of the joint tenants could give a good receipt for capital moneys arising on a disposition. The House of Lords held that the clause did not govern the beneficial interests, following the decision of the Court of Appeal in *Huntingford* v *Hobbs* [1993] 1 FLR 736. That point is analogous to that which arises in a mortgage to joint mortgagees, where s 111, Law of Property Act 1925 implies a joint account clause, but that does not affect the beneficial interests: *Re Jackson* (1887) 34 Ch D 732. See also ch 7, "Co-ownership", n 479 and text thereto. Lady Hale pointed out that the Land Registry forms (TR1 for a transfer inter vivos and AS1 for an assent on death) were amended

with the aid of a loan of £65,025 from Barclays Bank, secured by a mortgage of the house and of two endowment insurance policies, one in their joint names and the other in Ms Dowden's sole name. They had four children, born in 1986, 1987, 1989 and 1991. Ms Dowden returned to work after each maternity leave. They separated in 2002. Mr Stack left the house, and Ms Dowden remained there with the children. Mr Stack in 2003 commenced proceedings under section 14 of the Trusts of Land and Appointment of Trustees Act 1996. His principal claim was for a declaration that the parties held the property on trust for themselves as tenants in common in equal shares and for an order for sale. In the County Court the judge held that the house should be sold and that, subject to some minor adjustments, the proceeds of sale, together with the proceeds of the joint endowment policy, should be divided equally. The mortgage interest payments and joint endowment policy premiums, eventually totalling £33,747, were paid by Mr Stack. Ms Dowden appealed. The Court of Appeal, in a judgment delivered by Chadwick LJ which closely followed his approach in *Oxley* v *Hiscock*, allowed her appeal, and ordered that the proceeds of sale should be divided 65% to Ms Dowden, 35% to Mr Stack. The house was sold in 2005, with net proceeds amounting to £764,345. Oddly enough, that division corresponded very closely to their respective contributions to the financing of the house.

Ms Dowden appealed to the House of Lords. The leading speech was delivered by Baroness Hale of Richmond, with the concurrence of Lord Hoffmann, Lord Hope of Craighead and Lord Walker of Gestingthorpe. Lady Hale reformulated the law. She said that the starting point is to determine who holds the legal estate, whether that be vested in one person, as in most of the cases before *Stack* v *Dowden*, or in more than one person, as in *Stack* v *Dowden*. Prima facie, she said, equity follows the law, so that, where there is sole legal ownership, there will be sole beneficialal ownership, and, where there is joint legal ownership, there will be joint beneficial ownership. In both cases, the onus is on the person claiming that the beneficial ownership differs from the legal ownership to prove that the parties had a common intention to make that differentiation. The onus was therefore on Ms Dowden

---

on 1 April 1998 to include a box for the transferees to declare the trusts on which they are to hold the legal estate. If such a declaration were made in every case of joint legal ownership, the problem of implied trusts would disappear; however, the declaration is not mandatory. It might be pointed that such a declaration could be potentially disastrous if the parties' circumstances were to change radically, as for example in *Jones* v *Kernott* [2012] 1 AC 776.

to prove that she and Mr Stack had a common intention that she should have an interest in the house greater than her interest as a joint tenant. Lady Hale provided an indicative list of factors that are to be taken into account in determining that common intention. They cover a wide spectrum: they include, any advice or discussions at the time of the transfer which cast light on their intentions; the reasons why the home was transferred into their joint names; the purposes for which the home was acquired; the nature of the parties' relationship; whether they had children for whom they both had responsibility to provide a home; how the parties arranged their finances, whether separately or jointly or a mixture of both; how they discharged the outgoings on the home and their other household expenses. Her Ladyship added: "The parties' individual characters and personalities may also be a factor in deciding where their true intentions lay. In the cohabitation context, mercenary considerations may be more to the fore than they would be in marriage, but it should not be assumed that they always take pride and place over natural love and affection."[618] Lady Hale accepted the distinction drawn in *Oxley* v *Hiscock* between the primary question, whether it is legitimate for the court to impose a constructive trust, and the secondary question, quantifying the beneficial interests under such a constructive trust. She said that that in all normal cases, the fact that the legal title is put in joint names is a very strong indication that both parties were intended to have an interest, so the primary question is satisfied.[619] She pointed out that, where the legal title to the home is vested in joint names, there is inevitably a trust.[620] However, in the absence of an express declaration of trust, there is room for a constructive trust which will determine who has beneficial interests and in what quantities. It is clear that Her Ladyship required that the search for the parties' common intention applied to both the primary and the secondary question. She was critical of that part of the formulation in *Oxley* v *Hiscock* which, on the secondary question, required the court to find what was fair and just, rather than finding what was the parties' common intention.[621]

---

[618] Ibid at para 69.
[619] For an exceptional case where, despite the property being in joint names, the entire beneficial interest was vested in one party, see *Abbey National Bank plc* v *Stringer* [2006] 2 P & CR DG15 (mother's property transferred into names of herself and her son purely in order to assist him to obtain mortgage loan).
[620] S 36(1), Law of Property Act 1925.
[621] Para 61. See to the same effect Lord Neuberger at para 144. The same criticism must obviously apply also to the approach of Waite LJ in *Midland Bank Plc* v *Cooke* [1995] 4 All ER 562, as described above: n 611 and text thereto.

Having thus formulated the legal principles, Lady Hale then asked whether the facts showed that Mr Stack and Ms Dowden had reached a common intention sufficient to rebut the presumption that equity follows the law. She quickly concluded that the presumption had been rebutted. She placed great reliance on the facts that throughout their relationship they had kept their finances separate and that Ms Dowden had made a significantly greater contribution to the acquisition of the family home. She stated that those circumstance were exceptional,[622] and she upheld the Court of Appeal's award of a 65% share to Ms Dowden.

Lord Neuberger reached the same final conclusion by a radically different route, based on the more traditional resulting trust analysis. Where the legal title stands in joint names, but there are differential contributions, there is a rebuttable presumption that the parties intended to have beneficial interests proportionate to those contributions.[623] The shares so established may subsequently be varied where there is compelling evidence, whether in the form of discussions, statements or actions, from which it may be inferred that the parties intended the alteration. He thought that the making of significant improvements by one party might justify such an inference, as might differential mortgage repayments where the parties have equal means. On the facts of the present case, there was nothing in the parties' subsequent actions to justify a departure from the shares established on the acquisition of the property. Therefore, he concluded, a 35%:65% split was correct.

It would have been very helpful if Lord Neuburger (and indeed the other judges) had commented on the decision in *Midland Bank Plc* v *Cooke*,[624] where, on the acquisition of the home Mrs Cooke's share was less than 7%, but 16 years and three children later had grown to 50%.

In leaving *Stack* v *Dowden*, we should note the contribution made by Lord Walker. Two points are worth making. Firstly, in commenting on Lord Bridge's speech in Rosset, Lord Walker referred to Lord Bridge's great doubt that, in his second category, anything less than direct contributions to the purchase price will suffice. Lord Walker said: "Whether or not Lord Bridge's

---

[622] Para 92.
[623] It should be noted, however, that differential contributions would not necessarily lead to unequal shares, if the court was satisfied that each party had contributed as much as he or she was able to do at the time: see, for example, *Rimmer* v *Rimmer* [1953] 1 QB 63.
[624] [1995] 4 All ER 562, where, on the acquisition of the home, Mrs Cooke's contribution was 6.47%,

observation was justified in 1990, in my opinion the law has moved on, and your Lordships should move it a little more in the same direction."[625] A little later in his opinion,[626] he said that the law should take a wide view of what is capable of counting as a contribution towards the acquisition of a residence, while remaining sceptical of the value of alleged improvements that are really insignificant, or elaborate arguments (suggestive of creative accounting) as to how the family finances were arranged. That is a helpful comment. Secondly, His Lordship said:[627] "In a case about beneficial ownership of a matrimonial or quasi-matrimonial home (whether registered in the names of one or two legal owners) the resulting trust should not in my opinion operate as a legal presumption, although it may (in an updated form which takes account of all significant contributions, direct or indirect, in cash or kind) happen to be reflected in the parties' common intention." That is difficult to accept. It seems to draw a distinction between the underlying law relating to a family home and the law relating to other property, in particular, presumably, commercial property; but that seems to be a variant of the family assets theory promoted much earlier by Lord Denning and decisively rejected in *Pettitt* v *Pettitt*. [628] Moreover, in rejecting the contribution which a resulting trust analysis could make in an appropriate case (where the financial contributions can be more or less precisely identified, and there is nothing in the facts of the case to suggest that a departure from the arithmetical proportions would be justified[629]), he rejects a mode of reasoning which could provide a much quicker, much simpler, and much more certain solution.

Stack v *Dowden* was followed fairly quickly by the decision of the Privy Council in *Abbott* v *Abbott*.[630] The decision involved a fairly straightforward application of the reasoning in *Stack* v *Dowden*, albeit in a one name case. The salient facts are these. The parties married in 1983. In 1984 the husband's mother transferred a plot of land into his name. He set up in medical practice in Antigua. The wife worked in the surgery for a while and then in a travel agency. Their first child was born in 1986, and the wife did not work outside the house again until 1995. Their second child was born in 1987. During 1990

---

[625] [2002] 2 AC 432 at para 26.
[626] Para 34.
[627] Ibid.
[628] [1970] AC 777.
[629] For example, in *Stack* v *Dowden* itself and in *Oxley* v *Hiscock* [2005] Fam 211.
[630] [2008] 1 FLR 1451.

and 1991 their matrimonial home was built on the land previously given by the husband's mother. The construction was financed partly by a bridging loan which was later replaced by a mortgage, and partly by gifts of money from the husband's mother. The bridging loan was paid into their joint account. The mortgage which replaced that loan was made by the husband as the sole owner of the legal estate, but the wife also made herself liable jointly and severally for the repayment of principal and interest on the loan. The loan was also secured by insurance policies on each of their lives. All of the couple's income was paid into their joint account. The wife resumed work in 1995. At first she paid her earnings into the joint account, but she stopped doing so when her husband left the matrimonial home in 1996. They entered into an agreement whereby the husband would pay a monthly sum to the wife, and would also pay the children's school fees, and medical and dental bills. The wife assumed responsibility for paying the mortgage, insurance and property tax on the matrimonial home. They were divorced in 2001. These proceeding were begun in 2002. In the High Court the judge held that the house was held in trust for both parties in equal shares. The Court of Appeal allowed the husband's appeal. The wife appealed to the Privy Council, which restored the trial judge's order. The decision of the Privy Council was delivered by Baroness Hale of Richmond, who, not surprisingly, closely followed her speech in *Stack* v *Dowden*. She stated that "It is now clear that the constructive trust is generally the more appropriate tool of analysis in most matrimonial home cases."[631] Reviewing the whole course of dealing of the parties during the marriage, Her Ladyship attached particular significance to the fact that they had organised their finances entirely jointly, using a joint bank account into which everything was paid and from which everything was paid. It was also significant that the wife had undertaken joint liability for the mortgage repayments.[632] The result was that the wife had proved that a constructive trust should be imposed (the primary question) and that, under that trust, the parties had equal beneficial shares (the secondary question).

The next significant case is *Fowler* v *Barron*.[633] This is a joint names case, and the decision of the Court of Appeal shows that it will be very difficult to rebut the presumption that equity follows the law. The parties had an unmarried

---

[631] Ibid at para 4.
[632] Para 18.
[633] [2008] 2 FLR 831.

relationship for 23 years from 1983 to 2005. At first they lived in a flat owned by Mr Barron. They had a child in 1987. In 1998 they bought a house for £64,950. They made a conscious decision to put the property into their joint names. The transfer did not contain an express declaration of trust. They took out a mortgage in their joint names for £35,000, and the balance of the purchase price was paid by Mr Barron out of the proceeds of sale of his flat. Mr Barron paid the mortgage instalments out of his pension, and also other outgoings such as council tax and utilities' bills. They did not have a joint bank account. They made mutual wills, with each leaving the interest in the property to the other. Miss Fowler worked outside the home for much of the period of their cohabitation. She made some savings out of her earnings but spent the rest of her earnings on herself and the children. Mr Barron normally paid for the weekly shop. They separated in 2005, and these proceedings followed. In the County Court the judge held that the beneficial interest was owned entirely by Mr Barron. The Court of Appeal allowed Miss Fowler's appeal and held that they were entitled in equal shares. Essentially, the reasoning was that, although Miss Fowler had not contributed directly to the financing of the house, she had contributed to the life and wellbeing of the family in financial and other ways, and had made herself jointly liable for the mortgage. The presumption of equal shares flowing from the transfer was therefore not rebutted.

Jones v *Kernott*[634] offered the Supreme Court an opportunity to revisit the decision of its predecessor, the House of Lords, in *Stack* v *Dowden*. Mr Kernott and Ms Jones were not married but lived together from 1983, at first in a mobile home owned by Ms Jones. Their first child was born in 1984. In 1985 she sold her mobile home, and they together bought a house, 39 Badger Hall Avenue, Thundersley, Essex, which was registered in their joint names. The purchase price was £30,000. The deposit of £6,000 was paid from the proceeds of sale of Ms Jones' mobile home, and the balance was raised by an endowment mortgage in their joint names. Mr Kernott paid £100 per week towards the household expenses. Ms Jones paid the mortgage and other household expenses out of their joint resources. In 1986 they jointly took out a loan of £2,000 to build an extension to the house. That probably enhanced the value of the property by about 50%. Their second child was born later that year. They separated in 1993; Mr Kernott moved out, leaving Ms Jones and

---

[634] [2012] 1 AC 776.

the children in the house. Thereafter, Ms Jones remained in the house with the children, she paying all the household expenses. Mr Kernott made no further payments on the mortgage and made very little contribution to the maintenance and support of the children. That situation continued for some fourteen and a half years.

The Badger Hall Avenue house was put on the market in 1995 for £69,995, but it did not sell. Some time later the parties agreed to cash in a joint life insurance policy, and the proceeds were divided between them. This enabled Mr Kernott to put down a deposit on a home of his own. In 1996 he bought 114 Stanley Road, Benfleet, Essex, for about £57,000, with a deposit of £2,800 and a mortgage of £54,150. In 2006 Mr Kernott in correspondence claimed his interest in 39 Badger Hall Avenue. In October 2007 Ms Jones began these proceedings under section 14 of the Trusts of Land and Appointment of Trustees Act 1996. She claimed that she owned the entire beneficial interest in 39 Badger Hall Avenue, or, alternatively, if Mr Kernott had a beneficial interest in 39 Badger Hall Avenue, then she also had a beneficial interest in 114 Stanley Avenue, and that their respective interests should be determined by the court. At the time of the hearing before the judge 39 Badger Hall Avenue was valued at £245,000. The outstanding mortgage debt was £26,664. The endowment policy supporting that mortgage was worth £25,209. 114 Stanley Avenue was valued at £205,000, with an outstanding mortgage debt of £37,968. In the County Court and on appeal to the High Court it was held that the parties' common intention had changed after their separation, as evidenced by the fact that thereafter Ms Jones paid the whole of the mortgage and other household expenses, and that the greater part of the capital gain on the property must have arisen after 1993. By not contributing to that property, Mr Kernott had been able to buy another property on which there was almost as great a capital gain. The parties could not have intended that he should have a significant part of the increased value of 39 Badger Hall Avenue as well as the whole of the capital gain on 114 Stanley Road. The beneficial shares in 39 Badger Hall Avenue were assessed as 90% to Ms Jones and 10% to Mr Kernott. The Court of Appeal allowed Mr Kernott's appeal, holding in favour of equal shares. Ms Jones appealed to the Supreme Court, which unanimously allowed her appeal.

Although the Supreme Court was unanimous in allowing the appeal, there were important differences between Lady Hale and Lord Walker on the one hand and Lord Kerr and Lord Wilson on the other, as to when it is legitimate to impute an intention to the parties, rather than inferring their intention. Lord Collins is somewhere in the middle, since he supports Lady Hale and Lord Walker but considers that "the difference between inference and imputation will hardly ever matter…and that what is one person's inference will be another person's imputation."[635] Lady Hale and Lord Walker would allow only a limited role for imputation. They said: "we accept that the search is primarily to ascertain the parties' actual shared intentions, whether expressed or to be inferred from their conduct. However, there are at least two exceptions. The first, which is not this case, is where the classic resulting trust presumption applies. Indeed, this wold be rare in a domestic context, but might perhaps arise where domestic partners were also business partners[636]…The second, which is also…not this case but will arise much more frequently, is where it is clear that the beneficial interests are to be shared, but it is impossible to divine a common intention as to the proportions in which they are to be shared. In those two situations, the court is driven to impute an intention to the parties which they may never have had."[637] Lords Kerr and Wilson objected to what they thought was the stretching of the notion of inferring a common intention. On the facts of *Jones* v *Kernott*, they thought it more realistic to impute to the parties an intention that Mr Kernott's interest in 39 Badger Hall Avenue should crystallise at the time of their separation.[638] Academic commentators have generally favoured the views of Lords Kerr and Wilson.[639]

The distinction between inferring and imputing a common intention is crucial on the primary question, whether it is legitimate to impose a constructive trust on the legal title. This is especially important in a one name case, where, on the face of it, there is no trust at all. This point is illustrated by *Capehorn v Harris*.[640] There the parties formed a relationship in 1982 and moved in together in 1983. Mr Harris ran a frozen food business in which Mrs Capehorn worked. Their relationship was unstable, with periods when they

---

[635] Ibid at para 65.
[636] An example of this is *Laskar* v *Laskar* [2008] 1 WLR 2695, where mother and daughter bought a flat in their joint names, primarily as an investment. See further n642 and text thereto; n644 and text thereto.
[637] Para 31.
[638] Paras 76 and 89.
[639] Gardner and Davidson (2012) 128 LQR 178; Mee [2012] Conv 167; Doyle and Brown (2012) 26 *Trust Law International* 96.
[640] [2015] EWCA Civ 955.

lived together and periods when they lived apart. Mrs Capehorn kept a separate bank account. In 1991 Mr Harris was declared bankrupt. The frozen food business was continued by Mrs Capehorn, and she employed Mr Harris in the business. In 1993 Mrs Capethorn bought from her mother Sunnyside Farm, which had been her family home. The deposit came from her business, with the aid of a mortgage for which she had sole responsibility. There was no agreement between them in 1993 that Mr Harris should have a beneficial interest in Sunnyside Farm, nor in 2001 or 2002 when they finally separated. In 2002 Mrs Capehorn bought another property, 19 Beaumont Road. This was bought in her sole name, with a mortgage arranged by her and with the loan also secured against Sunnyside Farm. There was no agreement that Mr Harris should have a beneficial interest in 19 Beaumont Road. In 2004 Mr Harris, having been discharged from bankruptcy, set up a new company, LMC Trade Sales Ltd, in which he owned both shares. He lived in Sunnyside Farm and ran the company's business from there. In 2007 the parties reached an agreement whereby Mrs Capehorn agreed to transfer the frozen food business to Mr Harris in return for a payment by him of £750 per week funded out of the business. That sum was paid for some years, but eventually relations deteriorated between them. Mrs Capehorn commenced these proceedings to determine the beneficial interests in three assets, Sunnyside Farm, 19 Beaumont Road and the frozen food business. The judge took a broad brush approach. She said that "Looked at in the round" she "should impute to the parties…an acceptance of the fact that Mr Harris, by reason of his contribution of the business…has acquired a beneficial interest in Sunnyside Farm" amounting to 25%. The judge went on to impute an intention to the parties that Mr Harris should have a 65% interest in the business and that "accordingly he held the two issued shares [in the company] on trust for himself and Mrs Capehorn in shares as to 65% for himself and 35% for Mrs Capehorn. Both parties appealed to the Court of Appeal. The Court held that the judge had misdirected herself in law. The Court distinguished the two questions, whether it legitimate to impose a constructive trust, and, if it is so legitimate, what are the beneficial interest arising under the trust. Sales LJ continued:[641] "There is an important difference between the approach applicable at each stage. At the first stage an actual agreement has to be found to have been made, which may be inferred from conduct in an

---

[641] Para 17.

appropriate case. At the second stage the court is entitled to impute an intention that each person is entitled to the share which the court considers fair having regard to the whole course of dealing between them in relation to the property. A court is not entitled to impute an intention to the parties at the first stage of the analysis." On the facts of the case there was no agreement, express or inferred, between the parties until the agreement of 2007. Accordingly, Mrs Capehorn was held to be the sole legal and beneficial owner of Sunnyside Farm and 19 Beaumont Road, and Mr Harris had no beneficial interest in either of them. Equally, the company was the sole owner of the business and Mrs Capehorn had no beneficial interest in either the business or the company.

The ambit of *Stack* v *Dowden* was considered by the Court of Appeal in *Laskar* v *Laskar*.[642] The facts involved a dispute between mother and daughter. The mother was a secure tenant of a council property, 70 Wood Close, Hatfield, and, as such, was entitled, under the Housing Act 1985, to buy the property at a substantial discount. However, the mother could not afford the whole of the purchase price, and her daughter agreed to provide some of the price. The property was conveyed into their joint names without any declaration of trust, or agreement as to the beneficial interest. They jointly entered into a mortgage with Baclays Bank Plc. Neither of the Laskars ever intended to live in the property. Their plan, which was achieved, was to let the property to various tenants, at rents which would service the mortgage. It was an investment property. Eventually, the relationship between mother and daughter broke down, and they could not agree on the quantification of the beneficial interest. These proceedings followed, starting in June 2004 in the Central London County Court. Judgment was delivered on 7 February 2007, significantly, before the House of Lords' decision in *Stack* v *Dowden*. The judge relied entirely on a resulting trust analysis and concluded, on a mathematical basis, according to what he considered to be the parties' respective financial contributions, that the mother was entitled to 4.28% of the beneficial interest. The mother appealed to the Court of Appeal, after the decision in *Stack* v *Dowden*. The appeal was allowed, despite some doubts expressed by Neuberger LJ; the presumption, in a two names case, that equity follows the law, was applied, but, as in *Stack* v *Dowden* itself, the presumption

---

[642] [2008] 1 WLR 2695.

was rebutted on the facts. The mother was awarded 33% of the beneficial interest.

The only substantive judgment was delivered by Neuberger LJ. His doubt was whether the *Stack v Dowden* presumption applies at all in a case such as this, where the property was acquired primarily as an investment, not as a home. He said[643]: "this was a purchase which, at least primarily, was not in 'the domestic consumer context' but in a commercial context… To my mind it would not be right to apply the reasoning in *Stack v Dowden* to such a case as this, where the parties primarily purchased the property as an investment for rental income and capital appreciation, even where their relationship is a familial one."

That dictum was considered more recently by the Privy Council in *Marr v Collie* (on appeal from the Court of Appeal of The Bahamas).[644] There, the parties established a personal relationship in September 1991, when they were living and working in The Bahamas. The relationship broke down in July 2008, but during its course they acquired various items of property: some parcels of land, a truck, a boat, and some works of art. All these items were acquired in their joint names, but without any declaration, agreement or understanding as to the beneficial interest. When their personal relationship broke down in 2008, they were unable to agree on the ownership of the beneficial interest. In these proceedings the trial judge heard plenty of conflicting evidence from the parties about their respective intentions. He did not find it necessary to make any detailed analysis of the evidence, nor to make detailed findings of fact. His principal conclusion was that the appellant had bought all of the properties as investments, without any financial contribution from the respondent. That approach was presumably based on what he considered to be the applicable law, which was a resulting trust analysis. The judge relied on *Laskar* for the proposition that "it was not right to apply the so-called *Stack v Dowden* presumption in cases where the primary purpose of the property purchased has been as an investment, even if there was a personal relationship between the parties". That meant that the onus was on the respondent to rebut the presumption of a resulting trust by proving that a gift was intended. The judge then stated that the respondent

---

[643] Para 17.
[644] [2017] UKPC 17.

had "fallen far short of rebutting the presumption of a resulting trust." Judgment was therefore given in favour of the appellant. The respondent appealed, and the appeal was allowed in part. The Court of Appeal held that the judge was wrong in placing the onus of proof on the respondent[645]; and further, in relation to several of the properties, there was admissible and credible evidence that the beneficial interest was intended to be held in equal shares.

Mr. Marr appealed to the Privy Council, which held that both of the lower courts had erred. In particular, the Court of Appeal's consideration of the evidence was inadequate in various ways. The Privy Council considered *Laskar* in detail, set against statements by Lady Hale in *Stack* v *Dowden*. Their conclusion was delivered by Lord Kerr on behalf of a panel of five justices including Lady Hale and Lord Neuberger. He stated[646]: "The Board does not consider…that the principle in *Stack* v *Dowden*…applies only in the 'domestic consumer context'. Where a property is bought in the joint names of a cohabiting couple, even if that is as an investment, it does not follow inexorably that the 'resulting trust solution' must provide the inevitable answer as to how the beneficial ownership is to be determined. Lord Neuberger did not intend to draw a strict line of demarcation between, on the one hand, the purchase of a family home and, on the other, the acquisition of a so-called investment property in whatever circumstances that took place. It is entirely conceivable that partners in a relationship would buy, as an investment, property which is conveyed into their joint names with the intention that the beneficial ownership should be shared equally between them, even though they contributed in different shares to the purchase. Where there is evidence to support such a conclusion, it would be both illogical and wrong to impose the resulting trust solution on the subsequent distribution of the property." The final conclusion of the Privy Council was that the lower courts had not properly examined the actual intentions of the parties, and therefore the case should be remitted to those courts for such an examination to take place.

This unifying approach is surely to be welcomed. It would be highly unsatisfactory to have different rules for different categories; the law could be

---

[645] It would seem, therefore, that the judge's interpretation of *Laskar* was mistaken.
[646] At para 49.

led into high technicality and fine distinctions. However, how this decision influences future domestic decisions is difficult to predict with certainty. It is clear that evidence of intention is paramount but this evidential keystone with the detailed finding of facts necessary may lead to prolonged and costly litigation. Although the Court may draw a distinction between purely commercial relationships and commercial arrangements between domestically involved litigants, it remains to be seen how *Marr* will translate into domestic law.

The courts have not found it easy to apply the more holistic approach favoured by Lady Hale in *Stack* v *Dowden* and by Lady Hale and Lord Walker in *Jones* v *Kernott*. It has proved easier to accord primary importance to purely financial considerations, rather than viewing those considerations alongside the much more personal issues of the dynamics of the parties' relationship. Consider *Graham-York v York*.[647] There the claimant had lived with Mr Norton Brian York for 33 years, until his death in 2009. They never married, but from 1982 they lived in a house which was registered in the sole name of the deceased. It was bought for £55,000 with the aid of a mortgage loan of £45,000. That mortgage was replaced in 1990 by a much larger mortgage for £274,295. The deceased had business ventures in property development and letting, as well as interests in the music business; there was a band, which was either led or promoted by him. During the period 1976-1985 the claimant earned fees as a singer with that band, and gave other performances of her own. Her fees were usually either handed to or collected by her partner. Her income was estimated to have contributed about £30,000 to the household. After her partner's death she made a single lump sum payment of £4,000 towards the mortgage debt. During their relationship they had two children, a son born in 1977 and a daughter born in 1978. The son became his father's personal representative and was the respondent in these proceedings. The claimant throughout cooked the family meals, and she and her partner together brought up their daughter (the son was brought up by his grandmother). The judge found that the relationship was dysfunctional; the male partner had a controlling nature and threatening proclivities, including a proclivity for violence. The claimant was described as intelligent but vulnerable. At the commencement of these proceedings the house had an estimated value at

---

[647] [2015] EWCA Civ 72; [2015] HLR 26. The account in the text is loosely based on an excellent case comment by Sarah Greer and Mark Pawlowski, [2015] Conv 512.

between £1.2 million and £1.75 million. The mortgage debt was then about £450,000, to which had to be added costs and expenses due to the building society, so that the equity in the property amounted to around £867,000. The County Court judge inferred from the claimant's financial contributions a common intention that she should have a beneficial interest in the property. As to quantification, the judge said: "In my view a fair reflection of her contributions financial and non-financial over the years would be a 25% beneficial interest in the property". The claimant appealed to the Court of Appeal, which refused to disturb the judge's decision. Almost the whole of the decision delivered by Tomlinson LJ is in terms of the financial contribution made by the claimant, or rather the lack of it. For example, to the argument that considerable weight should be given to the length of their cohabitation, His Lordship responded: "But to be set against that in the present case is the judge's damning finding at paragraph 23 of her judgment that 'even if she [the claimant] were telling the truth about her financial contribution during the 33 years of their cohabitation it does not amount to much'".[648] Reasoning of that sort seems to regard contributions to the household by way of domestic work and child rearing as having little or no value. That seems a far cry from what Lady Hale was advocating in *Stack* v *Dowden*.[649]

It remains only to add a postscript about the law's treatment of unmarried cohabitants. Cohabitation is undoubtedly a social phenomenon of our time. In *Stack* v *Dowden* Lady Hale stated the following: the Census of 2001 "recorded over 10 million married couples in England and Wales, with over 7.5 million dependent children, but it also recorded over two million cohabiting couples, with over one and a quarter million children dependent on them. This was a 67% increase in cohabitation over the previous 10 years and a doubling of such households with dependent children. The Government Actuaries Department predicts that the proportion of couples cohabiting will continue to grow, from the present one in six of all couples to one in four by 2031."[650] The law's response to this phenomenon has been piecemeal, and incoherent. In tax law, for example, sometimes one is better

---

[648] Para 26.
[649] There is also a sharp contrast with *Midland Bank Plc* v *Cooke* [1995] 4 All ER 582, n 610 ante and text thereto; the only material distinction is that in *Cooke* the parties were married, whereas in *Graham-York* they were not.
[650] [2007 2 AC 432 at para 44.

off being married or in a civil partnership (for example, gifts on death between spouses or civil partners are exempt from inheritance tax), sometimes better off being unmarried. Social security law treats a cohabiting couple in the same way as spouses or civil partners. However, financial relief or transfer of property on relationship breakdown is denied to cohabitants; hence, as previously stated, most of the modern cases on the family home arise between cohabitants. For more than twenty years now we have had the absurd anomaly that an unmarried cohabitant is eligible to make a claim against the deceased partner's estate under section 1 of the Inheritance (Provision for Family and Dependants) Act 1975, but cannot make an equivalent claim during the other partner's lifetime. [651] The injustice which can arise is vividly illustrated by *Burns v Burns*,[652] where the parties cohabited for seventeen years and had two children. In 2007 the Law Commission produced a comprehensive report reviewing the law and making proposals for reform: *Cohabitation: The Consequences of Relationship Breakdown*.[653] The Commission propose that cohabitants who have a child together or satisfy a minimum qualifying period to be set by Parliament (perhaps two years) should have access to various kinds of financial and property relief in the Family Courts, analogous to the remedies available to married couples and civil partners. In particular, they should have access to the property adjustment regime, where the claimant can prove that she has made a "qualifying contribution" and that as a result she has suffered an economic disadvantage or the other partner has gained a retained benefit.[654] Regrettably, successive governments have failed to implement these proposals, or any variant of them. Meanwhile, Scots Law has moved ahead by passing the Family Law (Scotland) Act 2006, designed to compensate a partner for any economic disadvantage that she has suffered by cohabiting with the other partner. The provisions of that Act were analysed by the Supreme Court in *Gow v Grant*.[655] The decision contains a notable judgment by Baroness Hale of Richmond.[656] Her Ladyship, with the agreement of Lord Wilson and Lord Carnwath, showed that English law would benefit from a scheme similar to

---

[651] There is a very limited exception in the court's power to transfer a "relevant tenancy" as defined by s 53 and sch 7, Family Law Act 1996.
[652] [1984] Ch 317; see p150, ante.
[653] Cm 7182, Law Com No 307.
[654] Para 4.33.
[655] [2012] UKSC 29.
[656] Paras 44-56.

that now obtaining in Scotland. She referred to research undertaken on the Scottish legislation. She quoted the researchers' comment: "The Act has undoubtedly achieved a lot for Scottish cohabitants and their children". Lady Hale commented: "English and Welsh cohabitants and their children deserve no less".[657] We can hope that legislation will be introduced during the present Parliament; the time for inertia and procrastination has surely passed.

However, that might be too optimistic, because so far inertia has prevailed. The previous Government persisted in a policy of wait and see. However, there have been two encouraging developments. Firstly, in 2015 a Private Member's Bill was presented to Parliament, the Civil Partnership Act (Amendment) Bill 2015. The purpose of the Bill was to enable heterosexual couples to enter into a civil partnership. The Bill received its first reading on 13 January 2017, when the Government made clear that it would not, at that time, support the Bill. Mr Robert Halfon MP, on behalf of the Government, gave two reasons: 1) time was needed to see how the Marriage (Same Sex) Couples Act 2013 has affected civil partnerships; 2) the proposal would require a substantial drafting resource and wide inter-departmental consultation.[658]

Secondly, the Government was challenged in proceedings for judicial review: *Steinfeld and Keidan* v *Secretary of State for Education*.[659] The claimants were a heterosexual couple in a committed long-term relationship. They had deep-rooted and genuine, conscientious, objections to marriage, based on what they considered to be its historically patriarchal nature. They wished to enter into a civil partnership, but their application to the Chelsea Register Office was refused. Their challenge was based on the Human Rights Act 1998, which incorporated the European Convention on Human Rights into English domestic law, with the result that an allegation of breach of a Convention right is justiciable in an English court. The challenge in the *Steinfeld* case was based on Articles 8 and 14 of the Convention. Article 8 confers a right to

---

[657] Para 56.
[658] Both these reasons are spurious. It is difficult to see how the first reason is relevant to the Bill's purpose. The second reason adopts language straight out of the mouth of Sir Humphrey Appleby, the highly obstructive Permanent Secretary and Cabinet Secretary, memorably played by Nigel Hawthorne, in the two television series, "Yes, Minister" and "Yes, Prime Minister". In truth, virtually all the necessary preparatory work was done before the enactment of the Civil Partnership Act 2004 and the Marriage (Same Sex) Couples) Act 2013.
[659] [2017] EWCA Civ 81.

respect for private and family life, and Article 14 provides that the Convention rights shall be enjoyed without discrimination on any ground such as sex, race, colour, language, religion, political or other opinion, etc. The Court of Appeal, reversing the trial judge, unanimously held that there was a potential breach of Article 14 taken with Article 8.[660] However, the majority (Beatson LJ and Briggs LJ, Arden LJ dissenting) held that the Government was pursuing a legitimate aim in waiting to evaluate the various options. The majority declined to set the Government any time limit for decision,[661] a very disappointing conclusion.[662] The result is that further litigation may be required to determine whether the new Government has acted with sufficient urgency.[663] We can but hope that the present Parliament will bring reform[664].

---

[660] The Court relied principally on *Oliari v Italy* (Apps ns 18766/11 and 36030/11, 21 July 2015), a decision of the European Court of Human Rights at Strasbourg. The Court of Appeal held that there was no domestic case law which could override the decision of the Strasbourg court. The Court of Appeal rightly rejected the respondent's argument that there was no discrimination because the claimants could marry; there is still plainly discrimination between heterosexual and same sex couples.

[661] Per Beatson LJ, ibid at para 161: "I consider it clear that the Government will need to make a decision to eliminate the current discriminatory position and to do so within a reasonable timescale".

[662] In other contexts the court has set a precise deadline: see, for example, *R on the Application of ClientEarth v Secretary of State for the Environment, Food and Rural Affairs* [2016] EWHC 2740 (Admin).

[663] With the dissolution of Parliament in May 2017, the Private Member's Bill was lost. The decision in *Steinfeld* will bind the new Secretary of State.

[664] The latest statistics on the registration of civil partnerships show a rise in numbers, despite the availability of same sex marriage: see The Times, 27 September 2017, *Rise of civil unions helps campaign for equal rights*. The Times newspaper also reported on 27 November 2017 that the number of cohabiting couples had risen to 3.3 million in 2017, and that this is the fastest growing family type.